Family
Theories

C.

Understanding Families

Series Editors: Bert N. Adams, *University of Wisconsin*
                    David M. Klein, *University of Notre Dame*

This book series examines a wide range of subjects relevant to studying families. Topics include parenthood, mate selection, marriage, divorce and remarriage, custody issues, culturally and ethnically based family norms, theory and conceptual design, family power dynamics, families and the law, research methods on the family, and family violence.

The series is aimed primarily at scholars working in family studies, sociology, psychology, social work, ethnic studies, gender studies, cultural studies, and related fields as they focus on the family. Volumes will also be useful for graduate and undergraduate courses in sociology of the family, family relations, family and consumer sciences, social work and the family, family psychology, family history, cultural perspectives on the family, and others.

Books appearing in **Understanding Families** are either single- or multiple-authored volumes or concisely edited books of original chapters on focused topics within the broad interdisciplinary field of marriage and family.

The books are reports of significant research, innovations in methodology, treatises on family theory, syntheses of current knowledge in a family subfield, or advanced textbooks. Each volume meets the highest academic standards and makes a substantial contribution to our understanding of marriages and families.

The National Council on Family Relations cosponsors with Sage a book award for students and new professionals. Award-winning manuscripts are published as part of the **Understanding Families** series.

Multiracial Couples: Black and White Voices
Paul C. Rosenblatt, Terri A. Karis, and Richard D. Powell

Understanding Latino Families: Scholarship, Policy, and Practice
Edited by Ruth E. Zambrana

Current Widowhood: Myths & Realities
Helena Znaniecka Lopata

Family Theories: An Introduction
David M. Klein and James M. White

Understanding Differences Between Divorced and Intact Families
Ronald L. Simons and Associates

Adolescents, Work, and Family: An Intergenerational Developmental Analysis
Jeylan T. Mortimer and Michael D. Finch

Family Theories
An Introduction

David M. Klein
James M. White

UNDERSTANDING FAMILIES

SAGE Publications
International Educational and Professional Publisher
Thousand Oaks London New Delhi

For information address:

SAGE Publications, Inc.
2455 Teller Road
Thousand Oaks, California 91320
E-mail: order@sagepub.com

SAGE Publications Ltd.
6 Bonhill Street
London EC2A 4PU
United Kingdom

SAGE Publications India Pvt. Ltd.
M-32 Market
Greater Kailash I
New Delhi 110 048 India

Printed in the United States of America

Library of Congress Cataloging-in-Publication Data

Klein, David M., 1943-
    Family theories: An introduction / authors, David M. Klein and
James M. White.
        p.   cm.   —   (Understanding families; vol. 4)
    Includes bibliographical references and index.
    ISBN 0-8039-5852-8 (c: alk. paper).   —   ISBN 0-8039-5853-6
(p: alk. paper)
    1. Family—Research.   2. Sociology—Methodology.   I. White, James
M., 1946- . II. Title. III. Series.
HQ728.K545   1996
306.85'01—dc20   95-38524

This book is printed on acid-free paper.

96   97   98   99   10   9   8   7   6   5   4   3

Sage Production Editor: Gillian Dickens

For our families and others everywhere

Contents

Preface

For Everyone

In this preface, we want to set the stage for reading this book. We see our intended audience as being diverse. First, our academic colleagues constitute an audience that will be served by the unique approach we have taken. Second, we expect that students, especially advanced undergraduates and graduate students, will acquire this book as part of a university or college course on the family. As a result, we also expect this book to be read by our colleagues in the teaching profession. Our subject will undoubtedly interest many others, such as family practitioners and anyone else interested in explaining family life.

This preface is divided into three parts. The first part is aimed at all the various readers of this volume. The second part is directed at undergraduate and graduate students using the book. Finally, the last part is aimed at our colleagues using the book for instruction in their classes. We do not mean to be exclusionary. On the contrary, we encourage all readers to examine all three parts. Yet we feel that there are some things we need to bring to the attention of students and other things we want to say to those instructors using this book for teaching purposes.

WHICH FRAMEWORKS AND THEORIES?

One question that we expect to arise is, Why did we choose to emphasize a particular set of six theories? As with all academic works, we are building on the shoulders of those who have preceded us, such as Boss, Doherty, LaRossa, Schumm, and Steinmetz (1993); Burr, Hill, Nye, and Reiss (1979); Christensen (1964); Nye and Berardo (1966/ 1981); and Winton (1995). The authors of all of these books organized their treatment of family theories in a way similar to ours. It is interesting to note, however, that the theories covered in these books are never identical. Each of the major surveys has viewed the topography of family theories differently, although not radically so. Indeed, the number of theories surveyed has ranged from 4 to 16. Theories that are notably absent in one survey reappear in another and disappear again in a third; the number included does not simply increase over time.

The way we have selected theories for inclusion in our work is different. Because we want to limit the number of basic ideas for students to learn, we have attempted to cover only what we regard as the major theoretical frameworks. A theoretical framework is identified by its basic theme or metaphor. For example, exchange theories share the basic view of humans as rational economic actors, conflict theories share the view that conflict rather than harmony is the major social process, and family development theories share the metaphors of change and maturation. We deal with the variations within each theory to point out that the landscape is more complex than any set of six theoretical frameworks could accommodate. This approach should keep the number of new concepts and arguments at a manageable level but still allow us to present the richness and diversity of ideas contained in the variations.

Whenever choices like ours are made, questions arise about missing frameworks or theories. For example, some scholars might argue that *functionalism* is not sufficiently addressed in our chapters. We believe that theories often evolve into new forms with new names. In the case of functionalism, the basic form of the functional argument survives within some variants of the ecological framework and some variants of other theories. We do not see functionalism as a family theoretical framework that could stand on its own, even though others in the past have argued otherwise.

In the final analysis, the reader must accept the organizing decisions we have made as one among many possible and defensible ways to divide up the territory. We believe that the theoretical frameworks identified in this volume recommend themselves on the basis of clarity and efficiency of presentation.

ORGANIZATION OF THE BOOK

The first chapter of this book provides a general introduction to the topic of family theory and theory in general. In Chapter 2, we discuss one of the major purposes of theory—explanation—and trace the history of theoretical explanations of the family.

The following six chapters covering theoretical frameworks are organized in the same manner. We now briefly examine the subheadings used to organize these chapters. Each theoretical framework is introduced by a brief fictional account or vignette about some aspect of family life. These accounts serve to focus the reader on the particular form of behavior and interaction that the theoretical framework is intended to explain.

The first subheading the reader encounters in these six chapters is "Intellectual Traditions." This section introduces the reader to a brief and nonexhaustive historical perspective on the ideas in the theoretical framework. This section should be especially valuable for assisting students to integrate this material with material they encounter in other courses in the social sciences and humanities.

The second subheading to be encountered is "Focus and Scope Assumptions." All theories contain basic assumptions, but most important among these are the assumptions that set the boundaries for the theory. Each theoretical framework sets boundaries on explanations and, just as important, focuses on some particular elements or processes in families. Understanding the focus and scope of a theoretical framework assists in understanding the explanatory power of a theory.

The third subheading is "Concepts." Concepts are the building blocks of any theory. In theories, concepts are used to provide meaning and to help classify phenomena. Meanings are provided by formal definitions. Classification is achieved by placing a particular act or event in the broader category of a concept. Concepts also assist explanation when they are used in propositions.

The fourth subheading is "Propositions." In this section, a modest and nonexhaustive list of theoretical propositions gives the reader a simple idea of how explanation might proceed.

The fifth section is "Variations." In this section, a small set of theoretical variations is discussed. These variations are selected to capture the range of differences that the theoretical framework may accommodate.

The sixth subheading is "Empirical Applications." One or two examples are discussed, and the more general theoretical framework or one of its variations is used to explain and interpret an empirical research finding or small set of findings in a topical area. The principal goal here is to demonstrate how the theory interacts with research.

The seventh subheading is "Implications for Intervention." Every theory about families contains some practical implications for therapists, educators, practitioners, and policymakers. Although the critical scientific tests for a theory are based on empirical research, practical implications reveal meanings and shed light on aspects of the theory that otherwise might be overlooked.

The eighth subheading is "Critiques and Discussion." This section covers the major flaws or weaknesses of the framework. Our treatment is aimed at enhancing the student's depth of understanding of the theory rather than to encourage rejection of the theory.

A "Conclusion" section provides a brief synopsis of the major thrusts of the theory and our perspective on the theory. "Food for Thought" and "Suggested Readings" are included in all chapters of the book.

The final chapter of the book presents a typology for analyzing and comparing the six theoretical frameworks. This chapter also takes stock of where we are in the field and offers directions for theory construction we would like to see developed in the future.

For Students

Combined, we have been teaching family theory to undergraduates and graduates for 35 years. We have often been challenged by our students to make theories approachable and to cut through what many students view as scholarly obfuscation. It's difficult to forget some experiences we have encountered, such as the time a student asked why theorists would use an old English word *limn* when the contemporary word *illuminate* would serve very well. The student went on to ask, "If these guys are interested in communicating to others, why would they revert to language that is archaic and remote?" In this case, the instructor could not muster a good response.

Undergraduate and graduate students are not necessarily different from each other in their backgrounds or developed talents. In some years, our best undergraduate student may be more sophisticated than our best graduate student. The one uniform impression we have from our classes is that by the time our students reach the family theory course, they are generally well prepared. We believe the biggest mistake we could make in this book is to write down to our students. This would be a disservice to the students as well as to the theories. What we have chosen is an interesting series of compromises. Of course, we cannot write at a level that is just right for everyone. We have aimed at a level that will stretch the understanding of many undergraduate readers and some graduate students, but most of this stretch will concern the intellectual heritage of the theories. We have made every attempt to keep our discussion of the current theories as clear and approachable as possible. We have, however, nowhere sacrificed plausibility to clarity.

We both recall our own student experiences and have witnessed many cohorts of students sharing similar experiences. Students may read a chapter just before the midterm or final exam. But students may not always read the chapters before their instructor discusses them. For many of you, the ideas, though not inherently difficult, will require both concentration and some absorption time. We think that you should at least begin the course by reading the chapters in advance of lectures and discussions and, if possible, give yourself a few days to think about the ideas.

As an entering graduate student, one of us sat through an hour-long orientation lecture suggesting that the most effective learning was achieved by guided small-group discussions. As polite and somewhat intimidated graduate students, we waited the entire hour for the question period and then asked, "If group discussion is most effective, why did we just get an hour-long lecture?" The lecturer was embarrassed. Even so, we have come to realize that, when covering massive amounts of material, lectures are sometimes the only way. It would be helpful, however, if you could discuss the ideas in this book with other students in your class and some who are not taking the course. Even if you have class time for discussion, do not place all the burden of your learning on those 3 hours a week.

There is an old and probably untrue anecdote about a university teacher who said "sex" whenever student attention waned. Neither of us has yet had to resort to this. We attribute our lack of need for this crutch to the fact that we have a tremendous enthusiasm for theories. There is little doubt that if your instructor is really passionate about the ideas he or she is teaching, this enthusiasm will help to make the subject interesting to students. We hope we have captured some of our enthusiasm in the pages of this book. Moreover, we have confidence that your instructor shares our enthusiasm.

This book is full of robust, subtle, powerful, and magnificent ideas. Whether they are wrong or right, true or false, is immaterial to your enjoyment of the life of ideas. We think the ideas in this book can open a treasure chest of intellectual riches that will enrich your life both now and with the passage of time.

For Instructors

Those who teach courses in family theory come from diverse backgrounds. Some are from academic disciplines such as sociology or psychology. Others are from professions such as nursing, social work, and home economics. And a growing number of instructors have received their training from the newer departments of family and child studies or family science. Both of us are familiar with students from these diverse areas. Between us, we have taught students in family science, sociology, home economics, social work, and nursing. In addition, we have worked on various projects with colleagues from all of these areas. Thus, we have experience with the diversity of readership that this book might receive.

Although we expect a diverse student audience, we also see several common elements that link and unify the interests of this audience.

First, all these students are concerned with families. Second, these students are all taking a course in which the subject matter provides some degree of intellectual challenge. In our experience, students rate research methods and theory as the two most challenging types of courses. We expect many of your students to share this experience of being challenged, regardless of diversity among disciplines and professional programs.

The third common element we see for this diverse readership is that most of the courses in which this book might be used will be required courses for the undergraduate or graduate student's program. As with any required course, you will be challenged to discriminate between the basic and more specialized aspects of the topic that you want your students to learn.

DEPTH AND BREADTH

Because students are likely to bring some degree of anxiety and uncertainty to this often abstract area of family studies, we have attempted to present the theories in the clearest and most succinct manner without sacrificing the necessary depth. The variations within each framework are attempts to show the range of thinking within the framework. Although we do not include all of the variants, we do try to choose those that demonstrate the breadth and range within the theory.

We believe that our coverage of the six major theoretical frameworks is sufficiently generic to allow instructors to include additional readings on variants and applications they deem to be especially important. For example, there are many other versions of feminist theory besides the Marxist-feminism of Shulamith Firestone (1970). Indeed, Firestone (1970) may be one of the more radical versions. We are trying to show the range of the conflict theoretical framework, however, rather than to exhaust the possibilities. A few suggested readings are provided at the end of each chapter. Although some are more appropriate for advanced students, we hope that you can use these or others familiar to you to complement our coverage and to expose your students to other points of view.

It is possible to argue that one or more of the variants we cite do not properly belong to the theoretical framework in which we have placed it. For example, life course analysts might argue that they should not be subsumed under the family development framework but deserve their own framework. Our argument in all such cases is uniform. If a theoretical variant identifies the same key concepts and basic processes as does the theoretical framework, then we feel it should belong as a variant. Returning to our example, life course analysts believe that systematic patterns in the life course are explained by social norms and that individuals develop both ontogenetically and sociogenetically with families. Life course analysts share these assumptions with other family developmentalists.

Another way our approach departs from other authors is the way we see the variants within each of the frameworks. For instance, communication theory is subsumed under the systems theory framework, phenomenology is subsumed under the symbolic interaction framework, feminism is subsumed under the conflict framework, and both demography and sociobiology are subsumed under the ecological framework. Although we have done this with the student in mind, we may eventually discover that such a scheme promotes theoretical unification and cross-fertilization in ways previously unappreciated.

Of course, we have not included everything possible in this introductory survey. We have not included postmodernist thought (or some of its earlier predecessors, such as critical theory and deconstructionism) as a major framework. Several components of this movement, such as deconstructionism and phenomenology, appear as variants of other theoretical frameworks. Throughout this volume, we focus on theories that are either about the family or have received major scholarly application to the family. For example, communication theory was not expressly developed to study families, yet it has become one of the major variants of the general systems framework applied to family communications. We are not able to make a similar claim for postmodernist thought. As interesting as it is, postmodernism has not yet contributed a theory about the family. The same principle can be cited for other omissions.

We occasionally take the liberty of propositionally formalizing theoretical frameworks that have not previously been formally developed. Recasting theoretical arguments is an ongoing process, and you may find that you or your students will benefit from giving additional attention to this.

LIMITATIONS

Although every book has limitations, those of our book will be more sharply felt depending on the level of the course and the students' backgrounds. We have tried to write with the advanced undergraduate in mind. Such a student is likely to have taken courses in history, philosophy, general science, and other social sciences, in addition to family courses. The sections on intellectual traditions in each theoretical framework will call on this general knowledge base and allow the student to locate and integrate these theories within the history of social thought. Because of differences in student backgrounds, we have left it to instructors to fill in whatever gaps in preparation might exist.

Another limitation of this book will emerge when the volume is used with graduate students. It is our experience that graduate students vary greatly in their preparation for graduate-level family theory courses. Naturally, the most advanced of these graduate students might find our book to be of assistance in reviewing what he or she already knows before moving on to more detailed expositions of the theories. For the many graduate students who come to the family area from other disciplines, our book might provide their first introduction to family theory. In the last analysis, we expect that the use of this book in graduate coursework will vary from program to program and student to student.

At the end of each chapter, we have provided a series of entries we call "Food for Thought." We encourage you to use these as given or modified to suit your needs to move students beyond an ability to passively recite the key ideas in the book. Some of these exercises may simply be "thought experiments." You may ask students to write essays on the entries, use them as topics for small group discussion, or explore some combination of work both inside and outside of class.

ORIENTATION

We feel it is especially important that we explain our general orientation to presenting social science theories. Our orientation is different from some other recent surveys of family theories (e.g., Boss et al., 1993). In the past few decades, historians of science such as Kuhn (1970) and scholars concerned with the sociology of science have emphasized the importance of the social context in which theories develop. Both of us have participated in this way of thinking about theories, but we stress that theoretical ideas cannot be adequately judged by such a perspective. For example, it is deceptively easy to dismiss theoretical ideas as coming from a racist, sexist, or other social context. Some philosophers of science have pointed out the sharp division between the "context of discovery" for ideas and the "justification" of ideas. Ideas may be "discovered" in many different ways: deductively, inductively, or haphazardly.

There is no correct way to develop a theory. The justification of a theory involves the rigorous testing of predictions and explanations against our common and shared experiences, regardless of a theory's source or creator. Of course, we do not deny that the nature of theoretical arguments, viewed as textual products, and the attitudes that others have of them are dependent on the social contexts of authors and consumers. All we are saying is that truth or falsity (or even probability and plausibility) does not rest with where or how the ideas originated but rather with what and how the ideas predict and explain.

In science, there is a long and important tradition that hypotheses and theories are to be investigated and judged by evidence rather than how we feel about their authors or their social situations. In the end, most racist and sexist theories are wrong not because they were developed from biased perspectives but because they fail to predict and explain phenomena. After all, every author of every theory has some biases. If the biases of theoreticians were cause for rejecting a theory, all theories would be rejected out of hand.

We find the history and sociology of science endlessly interesting and often they illuminate the ideas in a theory. We supply a modest discussion of intellectual traditions with each theoretical framework for context but not to judge the ideas. We believe that it is our job to provide a clear exposition of the assumptions, concepts, and propositions, thereby allowing students to understand and apply the theories to the evidence provided by their own experience and the data they have gathered from their courses.

David M. Klein
James M. White

Acknowledgments

We would like to express appreciation to the University of British Columbia for granting Dr. White a study leave, during which time he completed the first drafts of Chapters 3 through 9. Dr. Klein completed the first drafts of Chapters 1 and 2, revised Chapter 9, and assisted Dr. White with the final revisions of all other chapters. The order of authorship for this book is alphabetical.

We wish to express our special appreciation to the following colleagues and students for their comments on an earlier version of the manuscript: Dr. Richard Bulcroft, Dr. Wesley R. Burr, Christopher J. Butler, Michelle Y. Janning, and Dr. Gary W. Peterson. We would also like to thank Dr. Bulcroft, and the students in the family theory course at the University of British Columbia, for using an earlier version of the manuscript as a trial text. In addition, we would like to thank Mitch Allen and Jim Nageotte of Sage Publications for their enthusiasm at the beginning and throughout this project, as well as Dr. Bert Adams, the academic series editor on this project, for helping us bring it to completion. Special praise goes to Stephanie T. Hoppe and Gillian Dickens of Sage for their diligence and expertise during the production process.

It may be unusual to do so, but we finally would like to acknowledge each other for the tolerance and understanding necessary to preserve our friendship in spite of putting it to the test on several occasions. Coauthored works tend to be written in one voice, and we have maintained that standard here. We have both learned along the way, however, that we do not entirely agree with each other on all aspects of the subject matter. As a result, there may be some features of this book over which we will continue to disagree in the future. This may have something to do with the controversial nature of theory itself, but we suspect that tension and the sometimes difficult process of coping with it is much more common and important between collaborators than they ordinarily admit in their completed works.

1

What Is a Theory?

Generally speaking, theories are abstract and general ideas that are subject to rules of organization (see Box 1.1). These qualities may be why the study of theory is often difficult for students. All of us are more likely to be interested in concrete experiences, our own or those of others. Theories are not the facts or data of experience, but they are connected to those facts or data.

One complication in linking ideas and data is that the very same data can be organized in different ways. As a result, different theories can be used to make sense of the same set of facts. For example, how are we to interpret the fact of a relatively high divorce rate? One answer might be that the family as an institution is being threatened, perhaps even disappearing. A different answer is that divorce weeds out less viable marriages, thereby preserving the family institution. To evaluate the merits of the two arguments, one must see what other relevant facts are operating and how the entire argument is organized into statements at a more abstract level.

Box 1.1

What Is a Theory?

"A scientific theory might be likened to a complex spatial network: Its terms are represented by the knots, while the threads connecting the latter correspond, in part, to the definitions and, in part, to the fundamental and derivative hypotheses included in the theory. The whole system floats, as it were, above the plane of observation and is anchored to it by rules of interpretation. These might be viewed as strings which are not part of the network but link certain points of the latter with specific places in the plane of observation. By virtue of those interpretive connections, the network can function as a scientific theory: From certain observational data, we may ascend, via an interpretive string, to some point in the theoretical network, thence proceed, via definitions and hypotheses, to other points, from which another interpretive string permits a descent to the plane of observation." (Hempel, 1952, p. 36)

"A theory is nothing—it is not a theory—unless it is an explanation. One may define properties and categories, and one still has no theory. One may state that there are relations between the properties, and one still has no theory. One may state that a change in one property will produce a definite change in another property, and one still has no theory. Not until one has properties, and propositions stating the relations between them, and the propositions form a deductive system—not until one has all three does one have a theory. Most of our arguments about theory would fall to the ground, if we first asked whether we had a theory to argue about." (Homans, 1964, p. 812)

"Deductive theory can be described briefly as an attempt to increase human understanding by providing explanations of why certain things occur. It provides this explanation by having a set of propositions and then deducing that, if these propositions are true, and if certain other conditions are met, certain specific and observable events occur. The more specific events are then 'explained' by the more general propositions that have been used as premises in deducing that the specific events occur. The explanation is only as valid as the propositions and logic that are used in the deduction, but one of the goals of science is to gradually eliminate invalid propositions and increase the number of useful, valid ones." (Burr, 1973, p. 3)

"Theorizing is the process of systematically formulating and organizing ideas to understand a particular phenomenon. A theory is the set of interconnected ideas that emerge from this process." (Doherty, Boss, LaRossa, Schumm, & Steinmetz, 1993, p. 20)

One useful way to understand theoretical arguments is to examine their basic components. We start with the idea that a theory is a systematic collection of concepts and relations. This is consistent with all four of the quotes in Box 1.1. Because there is an endless variety of ways to organize ideas, we will limit ourselves to the requirements for a *scientific* theory. Such theories contain systematically related propositions that are empirically testable (Rudner, 1966). Thus, there are several components that we need to discuss in further detail: (a) concepts, (b) relations between concepts, (c) propositions, (d) relations between propositions, and (e) connections between propositions and the empirical world of observation. Before we look at each of these components, we must distinguish ideas that do not qualify as theories.

Ideas and Data

Science is fundamentally concerned with ideas, data, and the relationship between ideas and data. Theory exists in the realm of ideas. Research takes place in the realm of data. A science advances to the extent that its theories and its studies (i.e., its empirical researches) are productive and mutually reinforcing.

The essence of empirical research is observation. Imagine a husband and wife having a conversation about possibly having a child. The result of this conversation is an agreement one way or the other—to have or not have a child at the present time. To consider the conversation as data (actually as a *datum*, which is singular for data), three conditions must be present. First, the conversation must have occurred, rather than being something that just potentially could occur. Second, the conversation must be observed in some way—that is, the scientist must measure or observe it in a manner that, in principle, could be replicated by another observer. For example, the conversation might be directly witnessed or there might be some record indicating that it occurred. Perhaps the couple have been asked whether or not they have had such a conversation, and they reply that they have.

Third, the record of this conversation is combined with other similar records, which leads to a broader, less idiosyncratic description by the scientist that conversations of this type have a certain frequency or have certain general characteristics. Thus, the data relevant to scientific research are not simply isolated facts or sets of facts. Many conversations take place, but no scientist can become aware of every one of them. An assortment of selected facts are observed and measured, and they are summarized by statements of a more general kind about such facts. The result is empirical knowledge, but that knowledge is not yet connected to theoretical ideas. It is the connection between the empirical knowledge and theoretical ideas that makes scientific knowledge.

For knowledge to be scientific, scientists must explain the empirical facts by ideas or theory. Theories explain these facts by treating particular facts or observations as examples of general principles or processes. For example, there may be certain conditions that encourage couples to conduct conversations about having a child. When the conditions are absent, these conversations do not take place. Or certain factors may affect the nature of the conversation, the likelihood that an agreement is reached, and perhaps even what the actual decision will be.

The linkages between ideas and data can be organized in different ways. If research produces empirical generalizations, the data might lead to the development of a new theory, or the data might be interpreted in terms of an existing theory. When the process goes from data to ideas, we think of it as being *inductive*. Sometimes, a researcher starts with an existing theory, derives expectations about the data (i.e., hypotheses), and then makes observations to see how well the data fit. When the process goes from ideas to data, we think of it as being *deductive*. Theoretical ideas in science are developed both inductively and deductively. In either case, the ideas and the data must fit together in a meaningful way for the theory to be judged adequate.

We caution against too rigid a distinction between ideas and data. Sometimes, ideas can themselves be data. If the husband or wife in our example has ideas about making childbearing decisions, these ideas might be measured and become part of the data. The ideas that spouses have may be beliefs, attitudes, or preferences. These ideas might even be theories—explanations that husbands and wives have about such things as why couples have children at certain times in a marriage. Thus, the ideas held by the people we study are often part of our data. It is also the case that the theories of scientists can be data. If we are interested in why two or more scientific theories about childbearing are popular, we must study scientists and their behaviors. The main reason it is useful to separate ideas and data is that the ideas refer to fairly general concepts and statements about how and why the world *plausibly* works, whereas data refer to observations made about how and why the world *actually* works.

This book is mostly about theoretical ideas. The ideas that concern us are those that supply plausible explanations about families. Many such ideas, however, have been offered over the years by family scientists. We cannot call attention to or restate every single such idea. Instead, we focus on the clusters of ideas, or *frameworks,* that seem to be the most significant and popular now at the end of the 20th century. New theories about the family will be developed in the future. Some will build on one or more of the currently existing theories, but others may have features that cannot now be anticipated.

In the remainder of this chapter, we cover the main ingredients that go into any theory and suggest what makes theories about the family unique. In the next chapter, we explore the idea of explanation in some detail, along with other aspects of theories that depend on a philosophical perspective toward science. The second chapter includes a brief history of the place of theory in family science. The next subsequent six chapters (Chapters 3-8) separately cover six of the principal theoretical frameworks that are important in family science today. Finally, in the concluding chapter, we compare the six major frameworks and look forward to the future of theory in family science.

TERMS AND CONCEPTS

All communication depends on the existence of a shared language. The languages we use have vocabularies and rules of grammar for connecting words into meaningful statements. A vocabulary is like a dictionary. It lists terms and gives denotative and connotative meanings for terms. If we have a vocabulary of defined terms, we have a *conceptual framework.* Some of the concepts may be defined in terms of each other, but the framework is really just a point of departure. As Homans (1964) indicated in Box 1.1, a set of concepts, regardless of how well defined the concepts might be, is not a theory. We cannot have a theory without a conceptual framework, but the framework by itself is not enough.

Some sets of concepts are arranged into categories. For example, when we think about power in families, we may wish to distinguish democratic from authoritarian types of power relations. Perhaps a more refined typology of power relations is useful. Consider one based on two factors, the locus of power and how equally it is distributed. Then, we might have two types of unequal power relations: husband-father dominant and wife-mother dominant. And we might have two types of equalitarian power. One is joint, or *syncratic,* in which decisions are made as a group. The other is segregated, or *autonomic,* in which each member maintains authority over different domains of decisions. *Typologies* based on one or more sets of distinctions between categories of concepts may be very helpful in formulating theories. They can assist us in describing the similarities and differences between families. Such typologies are *not* theories, but because concepts must have shared definitions to be communicated, a conceptual framework does point to a certain consensus among speakers (or writers) that a set of defined terms is useful.

We should not take for granted, however, that agreement about the meaning of concepts always exists. Scientists, whether thinking about abstract theoretical terms or concrete ways of measuring them, sometimes argue about what certain terms mean. Nevertheless, when scientists tend to agree about their concepts, they can be said to share a conceptual framework. At any given time, there tend to be different conceptual frameworks that different groups of scientists think are useful. We will say more about conceptual frameworks when we cover the history of family theory in Chapter 2. For now, the important point is that conceptual frameworks may help organize theories, but they are not by themselves theories.

Another kind of idea that must be distinguished from a theory is a *model.* A model is a *representation* of how something works. Models are usually scaled down or simplified versions of complex relationships between phenomena. In everyday life, we commonly use models of reality to make predictions. For example, if we want to predict what Bill will have for breakfast tomorrow, we might say that he will eat the same cereal he has eaten every other morning or, in more general terms, that people will do in the future what they have done in the past. We may recognize that accurate predictions require much more complicated considerations, but the simple model can be offered as a rough approximation, if we are willing to assume that other factors are extraneous. Models, particularly mathematical models, are very useful in science. Some scientific models are simplified versions of theories. These mathematical models are translations of theoretical processes and relations into a mathematical *representation* and are called *formalizations* of the theory. Such formal representations isolate the major concepts and show how those concepts would be related if all of the extraneous considerations are ignored. To use Hempel's (1952) analogy from Box 1.1, scientific models often are tools that help to connect knots and strings at the abstract level with the plane of observation. Because they are simplified representations, such mathematical models are not theories but only representations. And these representations may be used in more than one theory. At best, we would say that theories can generate many different models and that a particular model might be consistent with several different theories.

Other ideas that are sometimes considered to be theoretical in nature are *school of thought* and *paradigm.* Both of these ideas convey the notion that is also captured by the term *conceptual framework,* namely, that ideas are shared by a community of thinkers and users. A school or a paradigm, however, entails additional features. A school of thought refers to a specific group of scholars who share not only a vocabulary of concepts but also a set of assumptions and procedures for organizing their ideas. Members of such a school, whether or not they work in an actual academic setting, interact on a regular basis and jointly create ideas and practices. They may create theories, they may create methods of research, or they may create other bodies of knowledge. A paradigm is a general set of ideas and procedures for viewing and dealing with a phenomenon. A paradigm is the content of what the social organization of scientists, or the school, shares in common. Although paradigms may originate in a particular school, they often spread and become more widely shared, sometimes throughout an entire field of study.

It is useful to think in terms of schools and paradigms for several reasons. They remind us that theoretical ideas do not just magically appear. Nor are ideas objectively assembled sets of facts. Instead, theories are human creations that depend on interpreting or making sense of experiences. In addition, both terms remind us that theories are often created by sets of scholars working together as a team. Theories are not just the brilliant ideas of individual thinkers who happen to be unusually creative, well informed, or otherwise gifted. Scientists collaborate, negotiate, obtain and wield resources, and sometimes successfully attain high status for themselves and for their ideas.

It can be helpful to think about family theories in terms of the schools of thought that are most responsible for them and in terms of the paradigms implied by them. Sometimes, the current state of the family field is discussed in these terms, even though the existence of particular schools and paradigms has not often been the subject of empirical research. For our purposes here, the important point is that such schools and paradigms are not theories. Some theories may develop within schools, but schools are social organizations of scholars, not the theories that may be produced in schools. Furthermore, paradigms are broader than theories. A paradigm might help produce many different theories, and it ordinarily will lead to the production of many other things as well, such as a basic way of doing research, a set of assumptions that are taken for granted, a puzzle that is commonly posed, or even a textbook.

The concepts of *approach* and *perspective* we regard as more or less synonymous. These two ideas refer to a particular point of view or way of looking at something. Scientific theories typically involve taking an approach or perspective—scientists do not examine every possible aspect of a phenomenon from every possible angle. Theories have a particular focus, and we must know what the focus is to set boundaries of relevance around the theory. When we speak loosely, we may think about the most distinguishing features of a theory as being the approach or perspective that is taken when looking at the world through its "lenses." The virtue of thinking in this way is that it can sharpen the differences between theories. This is especially helpful if two or more theories seem to be similar in other respects, such as the concepts they contain or their general subject matter.

The idea of approaches or perspectives also helps to remind us that two theories may not be exactly opposites or incompatible rivals for our attention. Instead, two theories may complement one another. Each may have a different focus, so each may be a credible formulation given the approach that one takes to the phenomenon. Theories in the family field are often of this sort. Not all the propositions in any single theory are entirely true or entirely false. Sometimes, theories that offer competing hypotheses also provide different and perhaps equally enlightening ways of looking at family life. Although theories contain points of view, however, they also have features beyond this, so we must be on guard to avoid saying that a theory is nothing but an approach. Furthermore, many ideas offer a point of view without constituting a theory. For example, you may take the view that corporal punishment of children by parents is terrible and to be avoided at all cost, but this sentiment does not by itself illuminate your theory about the effects of corporal punishment on children.

Yet another concept we introduce here is *ideology*. Ideologies may be theories of a sort, but they are not scientific theories. Similar to scientific theories, ideologies usually provide an analysis of facts. Scientific theory and ideology are distinguished by the evaluational component that ideologies contain—ideologies enable one to evaluate the "rightness" and "wrongness" of the facts and often to propose a particular course of action to remedy what is wrong. Technically, scientific theories are concerned with producing empirically testable propositions that, if they are valid, supply explanations of, in our case, family processes and behaviors. Ideologies are moralistic in the same sense as religions in that their analysis and evaluation provide a core set of beliefs that cannot be overturned or confirmed by empirical tests, either because the core beliefs are not testable or because proponents will not accept scientific evidence contrary to their beliefs.

Many scientific theories have sprung from ideologies. Much of conflict theory owes a debt to Marxist ideology. The key to borrowing propositions from ideologies for scientific theories is that the propositions must be freed from their evaluational and moralistic component and they must be subject to the same scientific processes of validation as any other theoretical proposition. In other words, such claims must be in principle capable of empirical disproof.

Finally, we introduce a concept that we use throughout this book: *theoretical framework*. What we mean by theoretical framework is that there exists in each scientific field a core of theoretical assumptions and propositions. We do not simply refer to these as theories, because although they are theories, they also are sufficiently general to have given rise to a number of theoretical variants. In this one sense, these

theoretical frameworks are like families, with the core theory providing sufficient richness for the development of offspring.

PARTS OF A THEORY

Every theory consists of identifiable parts. In our examination of
the major family theories in Chapters 3 through 8, we organize our
discussion around the most essential of these component parts. Here,
we want to introduce the general architecture of theories that exist
regardless of the field of study.

Every theory has an *intellectual tradition,* or general way of thinking that has been shared in common by a community of scholars. This
way of thinking evolves over time and therefore has its own history
or biography. Early ideas shape later ideas. The very essence of any
theory, therefore, depends on when we look at it and through the eyes
of which key contributors. Many theoretical ideas in the family field
originate in other fields. General theories about small groups, social
institutions, close relationships, and the like have been offered through
the ages by scholars who identify with many social sciences, humanities, and other disciplines. Promising theories are then sometimes
directly applied to families. Occasionally, a theory is first developed
about families before being applied to other social contexts. We sketch
the intellectual tradition for each theory in later chapters.

At any particular point in time, we could specify the main features
of a theory without referring to its heritage. Being a set of arguments,
a theory does not include old arguments that no longer are made or
ones that do not pertain directly to the subject matter. There is a sense,
however, in which theories are cloaked in flypaper, and the intellectual tradition adheres to the theory like flies to flypaper. Some ideas
in theories may not make much sense unless they are understood in
historical context. Technically, a theory is composed only of the
statements and other elements that currently belong to it, but we treat
a theory's tradition as part of it, mainly to keep at the forefront the
idea that theories often change over time.

A second feature of every theory is a set of *focus and scope
assumptions.* All theories include assumptions about the subject matter
they deal with. As we indicated earlier, every theory represents a
particular point of view, or focus. Often, theories explicitly include

statements about their focus, which help to indicate what phenomena are relevant and irrelevant. Some theories may be quite broad in focus, pertaining to any kind of family relationship, structure, or process. Other theories may be more narrowly focused, perhaps dealing only with parent-child relationships, marital relationships, or some other set of social actors. In addition, theories often include assumptions about their scope of coverage. The scope of a theory is indicated by its applicability in space and time. Some theories may be universally applicable, whereas others are designed to fit particular periods of history or particular cultural or societal conditions.

All assumptions are statements taken for granted as true and foundational to the rest of the theory. Sometimes, these ideas are taken so much for granted that they are implicit rather than being clearly articulated. In such cases, we must offer a guess as to what theorists would assume, based on the texture of the rest of their arguments. The role that assumptions play varies. Sometimes, they are so crucial that the entire theory would crumble if the assumptions were not believed to be true. Sometimes, assumptions merely help to set boundaries of relevance and can be stretched like elastic to see how far the theory can be extended and still make sense. Often, assumptions cannot be directly tested and proven to be true or untrue. One must either accept them or reject them as a matter of principle or by how fruitful they prove in producing explanatory propositions that are testable. Sometimes, however, an assumption may be challenged by a body of accumulating evidence, and this leads to a reformulation of the assumption when the theory is revised.

Of all the ingredients of a theory, the most basic are *concepts*. These are the singular ideas that form a theory's most elemental building blocks. Although some concepts are so "primitive" that meanings can be taken for granted, most theories contain an array of more technical concepts with explicit definitions attached to them. Definitions are provided so that the words being used are not confused with other possible meanings of the same words.

In family theories, the key concepts can refer to whose action is being considered as well as what the action is. Because family life involves relationships between social actors, some concepts describe social interaction, either as a process or as a structure of relationships between people. Some concepts refer to events, others to conditions surrounding the events, and still others to properties of an entire family that persist over a period of time. Because families are made up of persons, the mental and emotional side of human experience may be as important as the directly observable behavior of people. Because families always exist in some kind of environment, some of a theory's concepts may describe how families relate to their environments or even refer to features of the environment itself.

Concepts are essential to theories because they enable us to organize experience. We do not invent a new concept every time we refer to a unique event. For example, we do not need a new term for *marriage* or a new meaning for the event called marriage every time a wedding takes place. Instead, we think of getting married in a more abstract way. We say that all marriages have certain defining properties. If we want to distinguish different kinds of marriages, we establish categories of weddings—we can distinguish elopements from formal weddings, church weddings from civil wedding ceremonies. The categories remain abstractions, however, in that they all refer to specific occasions of a particular type, not to specific instances of weddings.

The more explicit the definition for a concept, the better we can determine when it applies and does not apply. There is a certain arbitrariness to concepts, even those appearing in scientific theories. A concept can mean only what a community of interacting persons agrees that it means. Although scientists sometimes argue about the "proper" meaning of concepts, a theory tends to gain a footing in the scientific community once scholars settle on meanings for the time being.

Many concepts in scientific theories refer to states of affairs with fairly stable properties. For example, we cannot have a coherent theory about the distribution of housework responsibilities if the meaning of *housework* changes every time we use this word. Some of the most useful concepts in theories, however, are variables. A variable is nothing more than a concept that can have two or more manifestations. For example, housework may be performed entirely by one member of a family, or it may be performed by several members in some combination. The idea of "the extent to which housework is performed by multiple family members" is a variable. At one extreme is the performance of all housework by one person, and at the other extreme is the perfectly even distribution of housework among all members. In this example, there may be degrees of distribution between the two extremes. Sometimes, variables have more discrete categories. It may make sense, for example, to distinguish urban families from rural families and to ignore instances that are between these two categories.

Theoretical concepts may vary in two important ways. They may vary between cases, and they may vary over time. Using the housework example, we might be interested in why some families organize housework one way, whereas other families organize it a different way. This involves a comparison between cases. It is sometimes useful to ask why housework arrangements change over time. We might take a long or a short span of time as our focus. A long time perspective might entail changes from one century to another or one generation to another. A short time perspective might entail changes within families before and after a particular event or as families move from one circumstance to another during their existence as a group. Theories are usually concerned with not only what is going on but also why concepts vary in certain ways—the concern is with what makes families differ from one another and what makes them change. Concepts, often expressed as variables, are useful for suggesting not only what is happening but also why. Some concepts are used to understand other concepts.

To relate concepts to each other, we need statements asserting how the concepts are related. Such statements are called *propositions*. A proposition is the assertion that Concept X is related to Concept Y in a particular way or by a particular relation. Propositions are the declarative statements or claims about how the world of abstract concepts fit together.

Theoretical propositions can be expressed in a large variety of ways. Often, they take the form, "If X, then Y." This could mean that X is a necessary, sufficient, or both necessary and sufficient condition for Y. The Y may be logically implied by the X. This would certainly be the case if Y is a more particular subset, or type, of X. Alternatively, the "If, then" statement may simply mean that X and Y occur in an invariant sequence. First comes X, then comes Y. Sometimes, X refers to a particular magnitude, and Y also refers to a particular magnitude. Thus, whenever X has a certain value, Y has a corresponding value. When X has a different value, Y has a corresponding different value.

Thus, the values for X and Y can be said to *covary*. It is also possible to argue that Y is caused by X. This may mean that X is the primary cause or just one of many influential prior conditions.

Knowing the concepts in a proposition and what they mean is crucial. Equally important is knowing the nature of the relationship between concepts. If concepts are the building blocks of a theory, relationships between concepts are the binding mortar. As we have just suggested, these relationships may refer to logical connections, sequential connections, covariational connections, or causal connections. Theories may rely exclusively on just one of the four types of connections, but more often they rely on two or more of these types.

As all four of the quotes in Box 1.1 imply, theories contain *sets* of propositions (Hempel, 1952, uses the word *hypotheses* to refer to propositions). Although it is conceivable that a theory might involve one, and only one, proposition, this rarely if ever occurs as a practical matter. Instead, theories employ multiple propositions—three or more concepts are related in specific ways. Furthermore, because the propositions are relatively abstract, there must be some way to link them to the world of observable experience, the world of data.

Burr (1973), Hempel (1952), and Homans (1964) (see Box 1.1) all suggest that the propositions must form a deductive system—there must be a logical connection between the propositions and between at least some propositions and the world of experience. The way we make the connection with experience is the subject matter of *research methodology*. Because this book is about family theories, we have little to say about methods for conducting family research, but it should be apparent that theories may have strong implications for the ways we conduct research. It is of some importance to consider how using a particular theory places restrictions on the kinds of data that will be relevant and on the kinds of measurements and other strategies for obtaining evidence in favor of or against the theory.

Doherty et al. (1993) emphasize that we ordinarily want to understand a phenomenon and then organize our ideas to understand it. This does not mean that we always first make observations and then develop a theory. It also does not mean that there is some alternative to arranging propositions in a deductive way. Ideas and data are continually in a state of interaction. We can start with ideas or we can start with data, but the basic ingredients of a theory do not depend on where we start.

Given an intellectual tradition, plus a set of assumptions, concepts, and propositions, a host of theories can be identified. The theories can differ from each other in the specific configurations of traditions, assumptions, concepts, and propositions associated with them. But it is important to distinguish the forest from the trees. Indeed, if we look only at theoretical "trees," we would find literally hundreds, if not thousands, of theories about families. Every rendering of a theory by a scholar or team of scholars is in some ways different from every other rendering.

To simplify the picture and to concentrate on the theoretical "forest," we use two devices in this book. One device is to cluster the primary theories into one of six categories, or theoretical frameworks, as indicated in the titles of Chapters 3 through 8. Other authors describing the range of family theories have used different bases for distinguishing them, sometimes resulting in a different number of theories or different names for them. We return to this matter in the final chapter. Our other device is the argument that the major theories have several variations. Within a particular tradition, groups of scholars have tended to emphasize certain ideas over others. It is as if each theory has a trunk, and as it develops over time, certain branches emerge. Because restricting ourselves to six theoretical frameworks may prove an overly simplistic way to view the forest, we highlight the various branches on each theoretical tree. The variations tend to emerge over time and take on distinctive features of their own, just as do branches of a tree. We emphasize the "living" branches—the variations that seem to us to be current at the present time. Certain branches, indeed whole trees, may die for lack of nutrients, and the same is true of theories. We have little to say about these once-important theories and variations, although it is worth remembering that both trees and ideas can undergo a dormant state only to be revived later.

We have emphasized that scientific theories, to be useful, must connect to the world of experience. All of the quotes in Box 1.1 call attention to this aspect of theories. Hempel (1952) calls it the "plane of observation." Burr (1973) says that we are interested in explaining "specific observable events," and Doherty et al. (1993) say that we are trying to understand "particular phenomena." Even Homans (1964), who does not explicitly refer to such an idea, nevertheless agrees with this view; he merely does not want to confuse specific or concrete phenomena with theories about them. Thus, we may say that scientific theories have empirical applications.

The number of empirical applications that a given theory has may, of course, change over time. When a theory is first formulated, few if any such applications may be obvious. If the theory is to survive and flourish, however, its range of empirical application is likely to grow. All of the theories we examine in this book have a fairly wide range of empirical application. If they did not, we would not be emphasizing them.

For illustration purposes, we select a small number of such applications for closer examination. Deciding that a set of empirical observations is in fact an application of a particular theory may not always be easy. We might hope that it is simply a matter of deductive logic. Sometimes, however, the application is more heuristic. A theory may not lead us to have definite expectations about what an observation should be like in a very precise way. Usually, however, we should be able to argue that a different theory would lead us to expect different results from our observations. Therefore, rather than insisting that a set of propositions has a definite set of empirical applications before it can be considered a theory in the first place, we need a more relaxed standard of judgment. The more precisely specified and the larger in number, the more empirical applications provide credence to a theory.

Another type of application for theories is to assist practitioners, therapists, and interventionists addressing the host of social problems facing families and individuals. We discuss the relationship between theory and practice further in Chapter 2. Here, we note only that applications of a theory provide credence for the theory and use of a theory in addressing social problems is one such important application.

It would be wonderful—and certainly a boost to simplicity—if scientific theories were free of faults. No theory, however, at least none in the family field, has ever attained the status of perfection. As theories are developed and given empirical applications, flaws tend to be exposed, leading scholars to modify and refine the theories. The outcome may be improvement, but this is incremental and tentative, awaiting the next criticism, repair, and so on as the cycle continues.

If one or more flaws turn out to be devastating to a theory, the theory may be abandoned or at least neglected for a time.

The weaknesses that a particular theory has are not so much parts of the theory as qualities that are judged to interfere with its construction or performance. Criticisms or debates about a theory become part of the theory's intellectual tradition as these concerns become known in the scientific community. We cover the main criticisms for each of the six theories in this book. As with all criticisms, the point is not to reach some conclusion that one theory is better than another in any kind of ultimate and irrevocable sense. Rather, by becoming aware of current shortcomings, we are alerted to aspects that warrant further attention as the process of theory construction unfolds in the future.

We have introduced the major features all theories share, and these will be at the center of our treatment of family theories in this book. It is important to remember that theories are complex objects of thought. We can highlight only some of the principal components involved in each case. We do not attempt to cover all facets of any intellectual tradition or all assumptions, all concepts, all propositions, all variations, all applications, or all criticisms associated with any family theory. Our coverage represents only an introductory sketch. We offer a variety of references and suggested readings along the way to encourage you to delve more thoroughly into the details of each theory.

FUNCTIONS OF THEORY

Scientific theories serve many purposes. Here, we emphasize how they contribute to understanding. It is widely recognized, however, that knowledge for its own sake is not the only worthwhile goal in life. We all want to do something with our knowledge. Having knowledge about families may help individuals lead more productive or rewarding family lives. This would, of course, be a more attainable goal if all members of all families shared the same knowledge. For those in one of the helping professions, theories about the family may provide knowledge to improve their services as therapists, program evaluators, or social policy advisers. For those who are political activists, agitators for modest or revolutionary causes or the reduction of major social problems, or even staunch defenders of the world as it is or once was, theoretical knowledge about families can be put to fruitful use. Many of these applied or practical functions are considered in Chapter 2. Without meaning to diminish the importance of any of these practical uses of theories, we concentrate here on the ways in which theories contribute to the immediate goals of science.

1. *Accumulation.* Theories assist in the accumulation and organization of research findings. Much of the pursuit of knowledge involves the collection and analysis of empirical facts, filtered through the lenses of researchers. A body of empirical knowledge, however, is just a pile of findings. Theories tell us how to select and arrange research findings into meaningful groupings. If no existing theory is available for this purpose, new theories can be constructed from findings through a process of tentative generalization.

2. *Precision.* Theories articulate ideas in more carefully specified ways than is allowed by everyday language. Thinking theoretically forces one to clarify what concepts and relations really mean and what they include and exclude. Communication is facilitated by this precision, so long as the communicators are trained in the language of science.

3. *Guidance.* Theories direct researchers to develop and test hypotheses (i.e., empirical statements about what the data are expected to look like). Because theoretical ideas entail abstract, plausible, and tentative arguments, they must be checked against the empirical evidence for confidence in them to grow. Theories point to new kinds of relevant evidence for which findings do not currently exist. It is relatively easy to find or create evidence in support of a theory that one likes, however. Theories, therefore, also promote a critical spirit of inquiry. Efforts are made to refute theories, not just to support them. If a field contains two or more theories that yield incompatible hypotheses, it may be possible to design a study or a series of studies that help to decide which theory is better in the respects investigated.

4. *Connectedness.* Theories demonstrate how ideas are connected to each other and to other theories. Theories are systematic sets of ideas. The parts of a theory fit together in a coherent way. Knowing

what the parts are and how they fit together helps to distinguish one theory from other theories. This also helps us to see what two or more theories share in common or how they could be connected or combined by bringing together elements of each.

5. *Interpretation.* Theories help to make sense of how the phenomena they cover operate. There are at least two aspects of sensibleness in interpretation. One is essentially descriptive: A theory should enable a good description of the subject matter with which it is concerned. This does not necessarily mean that the theory must fit our intuitive judgments of the way things work. In fact, a theory may challenge many intuitions or commonsense views of the world. Rather, to enable us to describe a subject, a theory provides a plausible picture of structures or processes that we can accept as reasonable, given the assumptions in the theory. The other feature of interpretation is that theories evoke or promote "stories" about the way things work. If we can visualize concrete or even general scenarios of how things work, the theory is providing an interpretation.

6. *Prediction.* Theories point to what will or can happen in the future. If a theory helps us understand what has happened in the past or is happening now, that is desirable, of course. To continue to be useful, however, a theory must contain propositions equally applicable to future events and experiences. This does not mean that any theory accurately foretells the future, only that it should not be irrelevant to the future. If we know what a theory predicts, this can contribute to the guidance function mentioned above. If a theory predicts something that is subject to human intervention and alteration, future actions may invalidate the theory. Normally, however, a theory is expected to hold up in the future to the extent that its predictions are confirmed. Even if predictions are not confirmed, the theory may be basically correct, and only the conditions under which it works may require revision.

7. *Explanation.* Theories provide answers to "why" and "how" questions. As the quotes in Box 1.1 from Burr (1973) and Homans (1964) suggest, explanation is often considered to be the single most important function of a theory. Because explanation is so central to

the functioning of theories and because it has a variety of different meanings, we address this topic in more detail in Chapter 2. For now, we make the point that without theories we cannot determine why and how things happen the way they do. In our everyday lives, we may be satisfied by saying that one specific event, say a divorce between two friends, happened because of one or more other events that took place before the divorce. Such reasoning captures some of what goes into a scientific explanation, but it overlooks the most important aspect. Scientific theories explain by relying on deductive arguments. Specific events and the connections between them must be derived from more general statements for us to say that the events and the connections between them have been explained.

It is crucial to remember that although functions or goals like those we have listed represent ideals, this is no guarantee that a particular theory will fulfill such ideals. In fact, we can use the seven listed functions as standards against which to measure the performance of a theory at any stage of its development. A theory may perform well in some respects but less well in others. Determining such facts helps us decide where our energies need to be directed to improve the theories that we have or invent better ones.

Family Theory

Ideas about human families can come from many sources, including scientific disciplines concerned with the study of entities that are not families, as well as personal experiences with our own families. No potential source should be dismissed, although we should be aware that those sources selected likely will affect key features of the theory that emerges. Most of the family theories that exist today draw on ideas from "external" sources. Family theories are not insulated sets of ideas, and family theorists do not merely talk to each other about family ideas.

For a theory to be about families, there must be at least one *family concept* in the theory. We cannot decide what a family concept is, however, unless we first decide what a family is. Let us, therefore, begin by thinking of a family as a social group. We need to identify the distinguishing features of this group. Below are some of the major ways that families differ from such groups as associations of coworkers and networks of close friends.

1. Families last for a considerably longer period of time than do most other social groups.

Of course, some relationships in families are not enduring. Marriages can be broken by divorce or death fairly soon after they are formed. Yet, we normally think of our own families as lasting throughout our lifetimes. We actually are born into a family that already exists. Our parents remain parents even after we become adults. We add members to the family when we marry and become parents. Our siblings remain siblings throughout our lifetimes. Although it is possible for coworkers and close friends to maintain relationships for very long periods of time, families are the only groups that virtually require lifetime membership, even though some members are added and subtracted along the way. Belonging to a family is involuntary in the sense that we do not choose which parents are going to give birth to us. Other groups tend to be much more voluntary, in that we have some choice about joining them in the first place.

2. Families are intergenerational.

Through the act of giving birth, families include people who are related as parents and children. If elders live long enough, we have ties to grandparents, and maybe even to great-grandparents and great-great-grandparents. At some point, we ordinarily have living members of both older and younger generations, and we may eventually become grandparents or great-grandparents ourselves. Other kinds of groups may include people with fairly large age differences, but families are the only groups that virtually guarantee this.

The fact that the human infant at birth is a virtually helpless creature and cannot approach self-sufficiency for almost 20 years means that the intergenerational bond is particularly crucial to human survival. Every child needs some sort of caretaker and caregiver, whether it is a biological parent, an adoptive or foster parent, or somebody else who takes the responsibility for providing nurturance during the early

years of life. It is no accident that our image of family includes an
intergenerational component.

*3. Families contain both biological and affinal (e.g., legal, common
law) relationships between members.*

It is the biological act of birth that creates the fundamental family
tie. This act also means that we share at least some inherited characteristics or proclivities with family members that are directly or
indirectly related to us by birth. At least until humans perfect the
cloning of adults, and perhaps even then, the process of becoming a
person will be based to some degree on biology. Families are in the
business of producing and sustaining persons and personhood. Even
though work groups or friendship groups may sometimes contain biologically related members, such groups tend to have other purposes.

There is also a social side to this process of creating persons. No
society leaves the biological act of birth or the rearing of children to
chance. Personhood is achieved through a process of socialization.
That socialization is subject to secular and religious rules about how
the process should be carried out. Pursuant to these rules, family
members have rights and obligations, which tend to be codified in both
laws and informal agreements.

Aside from adoption, which is widely legitimated by laws although
not always widely practiced, the major legal provision about families
concerns marriage. We may not think of a marriage in itself as
constituting a family, but we recognize marital relationships as part of
families. Some families are *conjugal,* in that they contain one or more
marriages. It might even be argued that if humans didn't have families
they wouldn't need marriages, although families may often function
well without marriage. In any case, marriage itself involves rights and
obligations under the law, and it also creates family ties in law. Some
of our family members join and leave the group either because of our
own marriages and divorces or because of the marriages and divorces
of other family members.

Other kinds of groups are subject to regulation by laws (e.g.,
contracts) and informal agreements, of course. Such regulations may
exclude as well as include people in work and friendship groups, and
they govern proper conduct within such groups. What such groups do

not have, however, are relationships anything quite like, for example, cousins or aunts and nephews, which arise because our mother's sister is married.

4. *The biological (and affinal) aspect of families links them to a larger kinship organization.*

It follows from what we already have said that families are not just small groups of closely related individuals who live together or interact on a frequent basis. Families extend outward to include anybody sufficiently related to us by blood, marriage, or adoption. This kinship group may have the identifiable boundaries of a *clan,* or it may be loosely organized and diffuse. Everybody stops counting distant relatives as family members at some point along the periphery. Nevertheless, the ties of kinship create the potential for lineages and collateral (i.e., within generation) family relationships that can become quite extensive. Through kinship, families are tied to history, tradition, and multiple generations of group members. In some societies, these kinship groups are major features of the social, cultural, political, and economic landscape. Work and friendship groups tend to be much more temporally and spatially encapsulated.

To answer the question in Box 1.2, we likely will find ourselves asking other questions. Do we visualize the people listed in each example as all being part of one family, or do they belong to two or more different families? Are the listed persons the only ones in the family or could there also be others (i.e., is this a whole family or just part of one)? Should we think of these persons as members of an "actual" family, or are they a family in either a symbolic sense or in the way they function in their relationships? Are we thinking of how common or uncommon a grouping is in a particular society, either in frequency or in what is expected as normal, natural, and acceptable by law or custom? And are both affinal and consanguineal relationships identified as family relationships?

We could discuss additional arguments about the distinctive features of families as groups. For example, we could draw attention to certain qualities of social interaction that are commonly found in families but not elsewhere. One of these is that family members supposedly care about one another as whole persons (cf. Beutler, Burr,

---

Box 1.2

Which of These Is a Family?

A husband and wife and their offspring.
A single woman and her three young children.
A 52-year-old woman and her adoptive mother.
A man, his daughter, and the daughter's son.
An 84-year-old widow and her dog, Fido.
A man and all of his ancestors back to Adam and Eve.
The 1979 World Champion Pittsburgh Pirates (theme song: "We Are Family").
Three adult sisters living together.
Two lesbians in an intimate relationship and their children from a previous marriage of one woman and a previous relationship of the other woman with a male friend.
Two children, their divorced parents, the current spouses of their divorced parents, and the children from previous marriages of their stepparents.
A child, his stepfather, and the stepfather's wife subsequent to his divorce from the child's mother.
Two adult male cousins living together.
A 77-year-old man and his lifelong best friend.
A childless husband and wife who live 1,000 miles apart.
A widow and her former husband's grandfather's sister's granddaughter.
A divorced man, his girlfriend, and her child.
Both sets of parents of a deceased married couple.
A married couple, one son and his wife, and the latter couple's children, all living together.
Six adults and their 12 young children, all living together in a communal fashion.

Bahr, & Herrin, 1989). Whatever criteria are considered, however, the distinctiveness of family groups tends to be only a matter of degree. Nonfamily groups, such as networks of friends or coworkers, usually have some family properties but fewer of these properties or in less obvious amounts.

It also is worth noting that we can conceptualize the family not only as a concrete group or social organization but also as a social institution. As an institution, family includes all of the beliefs and practices of and about all of the families in a particular society or geopolitical context. It also includes the ways in which different families are connected to each other and to other social institutions. For example, in most modern and well-developed societies, families tend to have a private character, each one walled or fenced off from other families and from public view much of the time. There also are expected and experienced linkages between families and schools, families and the workplace, families and governments, families and the mass media, and so on. Because members of families often share economic resources and collaborate in both productive labor and the consumption of resources, it is also useful to consider families as being involved in a society's system of social stratification. Thus, some families have more wealth, power, and status than do other families.

With an idea of the meaning of family, we can begin to envision what counts as a family concept. Some of these concepts describe the composition, or size and configuration, of family membership. Some describe the structures and processes of interaction that take place between family members. Some describe the ways that families relate to their environments. Some will describe the whole family as a group, the family as an institution, or the nature of the ties between two or more members within the family group.

A theory that is much more general than one about the family may have relevance for a theory about the family. All that is needed is some way to tell whether or not families are different from the other groups or institutions covered by the theory. For example, if we want to argue that the size of any group affects the way it organizes itself to accomplish a collective task, then we can consider several things about families. Are families ever large enough to be covered by the more general theory? Are there certain limits to the ways that families organize themselves so that families cannot experience the effects that are found in other groups? We may be able to apply general theories about societies, cultures, or groups to families, but we always have to ask if families are miniature societies or cultures or if they are unlike other groups in crucial ways. We should not just take for granted that families are identical to other kinds of social arrangements.

Similarly, we should not just assume that any statement or concept about an individual person applies directly to a family. Persons can think and feel and take action, but what does it mean to say that a family or a parent-child dyad or a married couple thinks, feels, and acts? One of the continuing hazards of conceptualizing and theorizing about social groups such as families is the tendency to *anthropomorphize* them. Especially in societies whose members have strong tendencies to think individualistically in terms of personal freedom and independence, we may be overly eager to mix *levels of analysis*. It can be easy to forget that concepts about social groups and social institutions must apply to relationships between people. Because human families contain persons, we cannot totally ignore personalities or other psychological concepts. We need, however, to be continually alert to avoid the mistake of thinking of a family as a "super person." Families may sometimes have sufficient homogeneity among their members to say that a family is "old" or "gregarious" or "proud" or "angry," but these can be nothing but metaphorical phrases, for they tell us nothing about the relationships essential to the group itself.

Individual persons are relevant to understanding families in one very important respect. Much of what we know about families is based on what individual persons tell us about them. It is often difficult to learn about any one family from the viewpoint of a couple of members, let alone all of the members. If you were to ask one of us to describe how our family works, and then you asked the same thing of that person's spouse, you might get somewhat different answers. This is partly because husbands and wives can have different perceptions of the very same family. It also is partly because different family members can have different families! For example, my kinship group may not entirely overlap with my spouse's kinship group. My grandparents may be in my family and my spouse's grandparents may be in her family, but our two sets of grandparents may not be in each other's family, at least not if you ask them!

Because families can be described in a wide array of concepts and variables and contain multiple members with potentially many attributes, it is unreasonable to expect any theory about families to encompass everything of potential importance. Some family theories deal with particular subunits. Some deal with certain features of social relationships and ignore others. Indeed, family theories may be founded on different distinguishing features of families—some theories may apply to families as groups, but not families as institutions, or vice versa. Or some may focus on the structural or functional aspects of families, whereas others focus on patterns of everyday interaction in families. Family theories may pertain to different time horizons and to different cultural contexts. In a way, the meaning of family is a "moving target," and we must look at how the idea is used within a particular theory.

Some family theories are macroscopic, in that they deal with (a) linkages between families and other groups or institutions, (b) comparisons between families in different cultures or societies, (c) fairly broad periods of history, or (d) some combination of these. Theories are maximally macroscopic when they can be claimed to be universally applicable in space and time. Other family theories are microscopic, in that they deal with (a) an individual family member, (b) personal relationships within families, (c) a single culture or society, (d) episodes of short duration, or (e) some combination of these.

The theories we cover in this book tend to have or at least include claims of broad relevance, although we will discover that they differ considerably in how macro- or microscopic they tend to be. It will be useful to identify what the limits of relevance are as you study each of the theories. We share our own impressions in Chapter 9.

Because there must be at least one family concept (or variable) in a theory to call it a family theory, the first thing we need to do is look for and find such a concept or concepts. Then, a simple but crucial test can be performed. We ask, in what part of the theory are the family concept(s)? Are they part of the explanation, or are they part of what is being explained? Of course, sometimes the answer will be that they are in both places. One family concept or set of family concepts can be used to explain another family concept or set of family concepts. Many family theories will not be like this, however. Some family theories are *theories about families* in the sense that we want to explain something about families. In these cases, the explanation could be anything nonfamilial. An explanation of family violence in terms of broad social norms about violence or in terms of economic conditions in a society are two simple examples of this approach. The other possibility is what might be called *familial theories*. In this case, the theory uses family concepts to explain something nonfamilial. Arguing that a decline in family values is responsible for a society's crime and drug problems or that parental divorce affects the behavior or mental and emotional state of a child is a simple example of this alternative approach.

What is most interesting about the familial type of theory, regardless of what is being explained, is that it may place a little or even all of the burden of explanation on family concepts. If the theory includes the argument that familial factors are just some of the relevant factors, then it is only partially a family theory. We would judge such a theory as being a family theory only as a matter of degree. This may make our decision about whether or not we are dealing with a family theory at all rather difficult and subjective. Nevertheless, many theories are very much like this, and we need a way of dealing with them. On the other hand, if we encounter a theory in which the entire explanation is based on familial concepts, we might be either impressed or skeptical. The current state of family theory in the field is such that views differ as to whether we should be impressed or skeptical. We return to this issue later. You should begin to shape your own opinion as you are reading this book.

A Final Note: Theory,
Theories, Theorists, and Theorizing

It will be helpful if you keep in mind the distinction between theory as a singular and collective noun. Technically, every separate formulation or rendering of a theory is a different theory. The versions may be very similar or very different. Together, however, they are a collection of theories. Sometimes, you will encounter the term *family theory* in a more abstract sense. Here, the singular is used when something plural is meant. Family theory in the abstract refers to everything that is or pertains to all the real theories that exist or potentially could exist.

For a theory to count in any practical sense, a theorist must communicate it. Therefore, we tend to say that a theory is what someone has written down on paper or what people tell you when asked or when they volunteer to speak. Because theories have this communicative aspect, it is important to remember who is communicating. People have and communicate ideas. Although scientists may evaluate the validity, or truth value, of a single theoretical proposition, theories are nonetheless the product of the theorists and researchers who create and use them. We scientists often make it seem as if theories have a life of their own apart from what anybody thinks of them. We must remind ourselves that this is not really the case. The nature of a set of ideas depends on who creates and uses them.

Theorists theorize. It is important to know not only what theorists end up producing but how they think. Because this, too, is not available for direct observation, theorists must tell us or show us how they think. As you move through this book, you can learn a little about how theories are constructed and begin to test your own creative theorizing skills.

Finally, although only individual theorists have ideas, nobody can think or communicate in a social vacuum. Traditions of a theory depend on what others before us have theorized. They also depend on what others are doing at the moment, for we often create theories together, in collaborative teams or "schools." We also can change our theories, because when we communicate our ideas, the audience communicates back to us sooner or later. Thus, theorizing is a dynamic process.

Food for Thought

1. Now that you have read this chapter, reread the four quotes in Box 1.1 at the beginning of the chapter. They should now make more sense. Do these quotes represent divergent views of scientific theories or one perspective expressed in four different ways?

2. Think of any relatively simple knowledge claim. For example, "The sky is blue" is such a simple claim. Once you know what the speaker means by *sky* and *blue,* you are in the position to establish the truth or falsity of the claim. Does the truth or falsity of a knowledge claim depend on who makes the claim (e.g., authority), on the background of the person (e.g., education level, scientist, racist), or only on the empirical validity of the claim?

3. "Prostitution" is not a family concept. Discuss why it is not. How might "prostitution" be used as part of a "theory about the family" and also a "familial theory"?

4. An example of a knowledge claim is, "Families are more likely to have members with large age differences than are other social groups." Does the truth or falsity of this knowledge claim depend on who makes the

claim (e.g., authority), on the background of the person (e.g., education level, scientist, racist), or only on the empirical validity of the claim?

Suggested Readings

Beutler, I., Burr, W., Bahr, K., & Herrin, D. (1989). The family realm: Understanding its uniqueness. *Journal of Marriage and the Family, 51*, 805-816.

This is a bold attempt to identify the distinguishing characteristics of families. The commentaries by scholars that follow on pp. 816-829 indicate the controversy surrounding the proposals of Beutler and his colleagues.

Burr, W. (1973). *Theory construction and the sociology of the family.* New York: John Wiley.

This book, despite its age, remains an excellent introduction to theory construction and philosophy of science. The first chapter is outstanding.

2

Explanation, Philosophy, and the History of Theory in Family Studies

Explanation Explained: Setting Up an Example

Felicia is worried about her son, Andy. He is not doing well in school. He also seems to be running around with a bad crowd of friends. Felicia is concerned that he is going to get busted for possessing drugs or that he will come home someday saying he has gotten some girl pregnant. School and police authorities have indicated to Felicia that they also have these concerns about Andy. To make matters worse, Felicia is worried about herself. Her boss at the mall is always harassing her, her coworkers are not very friendly toward her, and Felicia is anxious about being overweight and unattractive to men. Her ex-husband is a "deadbeat dad." He is not providing the legally required financial support to Andy. He hardly acknowledges that Andy is his son. Felicia worries about losing her job and making ends meet. She is frequently depressed, and she is beginning to think that she is a terrible mother. Andy's problems are the result of her own problems, she thinks. She yells at Andy a lot, and he curses back and shows Felicia no respect. She has no idea what to do and is increasingly upset about how miserable everything is for both Andy and herself. Every day is just one hassle after another.

We present a partial and hypothetical example here, but it serves to set the stage for thinking about scientific explanation and how it works. Let us begin by identifying some general concepts that could apply to many Felicias and Andys.

One useful idea may be *parental stress*. Indeed, family scholars have consistently researched and studied this area (e.g., Boss, 1987, 1988; Menaghan, 1983). In the context of our example, parental stress can refer to all of the concerns that people like Felicia have about their jobs, friends, personal inadequacies, and so on. Another relevant idea is *child competence*. This refers to how well people like Andy are doing in school, in their peer relations, and so on. The third useful idea for our example is *parental support*. This can refer to the way parents treat their children. A supporting parent is one who encourages, praises, displays love and warmth, and so on toward her or his children.

We need somewhat abstract definitions that are also thorough and precise enough to distinguish these three concepts from each other and from other ideas that are superficially similar to them. Once we have three adequately defined concepts, we can create propositions linking them. We begin our demonstration using a simplified "If X, then Y" format.

Proposition 1. If not parental stress, then parental support.

Proposition 2. If parental support, then child competence.

Notice that we could have stated Proposition 1 differently. It might read, "If parental stress, then not parental support" or "If parental stress is absent, then there is the presence of parental support." What we need is some way to show that the two ideas, stress and support, go together in opposing ways.

Looking at our two propositions may suggest a third:

Proposition 3. If not parental stress, then child competence.

This statement seems implied by the first two. If both Propositions 1 and 2 are true, then Proposition 3 would be true.

We could approach the task of relating our concepts in a number of different ways. One alternative way is to preserve the same basic reasoning but to think of all three concepts as variables that have degrees of presence or absence. There may be more or less stress, more or less support, and more or less competence. We also might argue that the variables are causally related. In this case, we would restate Propositions 1 and 2 as follows:

Proposition 1. The amount of parental stress negatively influences the amount of parental support.

Proposition 2. The amount of parent support positively influences the amount of child competence.

Suppose we want to emphasize that parental support is a necessary intervening or mediating condition—that is, no amount of parental stress has an effect on a child's competence unless parental support is working as a linkage between the two. If we approach the matter this way, we probably would be unwilling to argue for another proposition that parallels Proposition 3. We would not say that "the amount of parental stress influences the amount of child competence." Restricting linkages between variables in this way is often desirable. When concepts are connected as continuous variables, we often expect the connection to be probabilistic rather than deterministic. When two probabilistic statements are so connected, it is often unreasonable to expect the variables that are unique to each (e.g., stress and competence) to also be probabilistically connected (Costner & Leik, 1964).

To continue with our example, let us suppose that we wish to link our propositions to the "plane of empirical observation" (Hempel, 1952). We want to be able to test the propositions to see how true they are for a large number of Felicias and Andys, as well as for people who are quite unlike Felicia and Andy. To do this, we would create *operational definitions* for our three concepts, or variables. For example, we may say that parental stress is to be measured according to scores on a survey instrument that parents complete. Similarly, we could say that parental support is to be measured by an instrument designed to code what parents do when they are directly observed interacting with a child. Finally, we could say that child competence is measured by such things as school records, teacher and peer ratings, and so on.

There may be many appropriate ways to measure our concepts, but whichever ones are proposed or used, we would end up with some hypotheses that could be checked against real data. One such hypothesis might be the operational version of Proposition 2: We would hypothesize that the score on our observational measure of parental support is positively related to the score on our assessment tool for child competence.

There may be many questions about how adequate the measuring devices are, but it is clear that to have a chance to support the hypotheses, we must be able to study a range of circumstances, or *variation*. We must find parents experiencing low as well as high stress, supportive as well as unsupportive parents, and competent as well as incompetent children. Another crucial concern that must be addressed is whether or not we are dealing with family concepts. Unless we can identify at least one of these, there is no chance for us to claim that we are working toward a family theory. The best claim for having a family concept in our example concerns parental support. This concept, or variable, is what links one family member to another. It begins to describe the interpersonal relationship between two family members. Neither stress nor competence have this feature. Just because stress has "parental" attached to it and competence has "child" attached to it does not make either a family concept. The notion of parental stress would only be a family variable if it referred to a type of stress uniquely associated with the parental role. Indeed, both ideas may simply refer to the behavior of persons in a variety of situations. The idea of stress is a psychological notion; it does not describe a family because it does not necessarily imply that a family is stressed. Similarly, competence in our example refers to the competence of a person rather than the competence of a social group. Therefore, we can say that our propositions are relevant to families but only because the concept of support serves as a bridge to other concepts that refer to the behaviors and psychological states of individuals who are members of families.

Locating an Explanation

Given the concepts and propositions we have at hand in our example, where do we turn to find an explanation? There are many possibilities.

TRANSITIVITY

Recall that we derived Proposition 3 from the juxtaposition of Propositions 1 and 2. Therefore, we might say that Proposition 3 is explained by the combination of Propositions 1 and 2. Certain statements are true by virtue of the fact (or supposition) that other statements are true. Proposition 3 is true because we think that statements can be *transitive*. This is one way to make deductions. Its most general form is: "If X, then Y; if Y, then Z; therefore, if X, then Z." In deduction, if the premises are true (Propositions 1 and 2), then the conclusion (Proposition 3) must be logically true. In science, however, we must further demonstrate that what is logically true is also empirically the case.

EXPLAINING DATA

We already have indicated that scientists want to explain patterns in empirical data. Our example suggests how we might do this. If the data we collect about our three concepts fit the empirical hypotheses we have made, and if the hypotheses incorporate good measures of our more abstract concepts, then we can say that the data are deductively explained by our theoretical propositions. The world (our data) works the way our logical theory says it should, so we have explained how the world works.

LINEAR CAUSATION

If we focus on our alternative formulations of Propositions 1 and 2, we have another way to find an explanation. In this case, we would argue that variation in child competence is explained by variation in parental support, which is in turn explained by variation in parental stress. Now, almost any kind of empirical study we conduct is likely to suggest that such explanations are partial at best. There are many reasons, but the primary one is often the fact that consequences do not have simple causes. We might need many more variables beside parental stress and parental support to fully explain child competence. Some of the additional variables needed might be familial, but some might not be. We might not be satisfied until we know what makes some parents more stressed than others. In any case, because the example attends to a very few factors and ignores a host of others, we might say that our propositions represent a partial causal "model" but not a fully specified causal theory.

NONLINEAR SEQUENCES

Still another way to reason about families is to say that we have come up with a set of time-ordered, or sequenced, events and experiences. Many processes, such as those found in child and family development, seem to "jump" in distinct steps or reach a threshold and then the process changes directions. These processes are interactive and curvilinear rather than simply linear and additive. Take the example of the curvilinear relationship between physical punishment of children and child compliance (Steinmetz, 1979). It seems that low and high levels of physical punishment fail to affect compliance but that middle levels of punishment are effective. An example of an interaction effect is toilet training. High levels of toilet training by parents are only effective when the child has matured sufficiently to gain voluntary control of the relevant muscles. Physical maturation and training must both be present for the desired outcome to be attained.

FUNCTIONAL EXPLANATION

Functional explanations imply that something exists because of its consequences. There are two major forms of functional arguments, *structure-functional* arguments and *purpose-intention* arguments. Structure-functional explanations are quite common in the social and biological sciences. For example, we might explain the existence of a structure such as the opposable thumb by the function (grasping) it performs for the organism. This adaptation (structure-function) allows the organism better chances for survival. This argument relies on the goal (or telos) of the organism or system to "explain" the adaptation.

The purpose-intention form of functional argument relies on the purpose of the actor being explained by the consequence of an action. For example, we might explain parental support by child competence—that is, the "intention" or "purpose" of parents in being supportive is to foster competence in their children. There are some difficulties in thinking this way, however. To speak of purposes means that there is some human agent who is trying to accomplish something. We might argue that parents "want" competent children, but then we are left wondering why there are parents like Felicia who appear to be unsuccessful. What prevents people—or social groups or even societies as a whole—from achieving what they want? Is it "stress," and if so, why? Can we be confident that all people have the same purposes in mind when they do something? Furthermore, it is unreasonable to argue that the future causes the present, so we should avoid saying that Andy's incompetence tomorrow makes Felicia supportive or unsupportive today. Much more sensible would be the inclusion of some variable that directly represents the goals or objectives that social actors have. Then, we can argue that today's goals influence today's or tomorrow's behavior.

Another troublesome aspect of purpose or intention explanations is that they usually imply that if X has a consequence, X will be affected in the future. For example, if parental support really produces competent children, then parents will become increasingly supportive. This line of reasoning might be effective if X has one common level or score. It might be sensible to ask why almost everybody gets married sooner or later and then look for the purpose or function of marriage to provide an explanation. Thinking this way might be helpful if we imagine that most parents are supportive most of the time. Such thinking, however, will not help us understand Felicias and Andys, for they appear to be exceptions.

We have considered five approaches that might be useful, under the proper circumstances, to help us find explanations: transitivity, deductions from theories to data, linear causation, nonlinear sequences, and functional reasoning. In real attempts to build theories both in and outside the family arena, combinations of these five approaches may be used. For example, we might organize our theory into a set of causal assertions, develop hypotheses, and either generate new data or inspect existing data. Then, depending on how well the data fit, we might say that we have causally explained the outcome variable in our theory and at the same time deductively explained the empirical generalizations that fit or approximate our hypotheses.

There is still one more aspect of explanation, however, that is not captured by any of the above views. We still lack a coherent interpretation, an intellectually satisfying *story* about why our three key concepts fit together the way they do. There are many ways to move toward this interpretation, and we illustrate just one here.

Why is it that parental stress is related to a lack of support for the child, and why is the lack of support related to child competence? One story we might construct relies on the definitions of some of our terms. Stress can be defined as the psychological feeling resulting when a person's resources are inadequate for the demands he or she faces (Goode, 1960). If a parent such as Felicia is already overloaded and does not have resources to meet demands placed on her, then we can see that parental support is simply another one of these demands. Therefore, it is unlikely that Felicia will be able to meet this demand. Children respond well and tend to comply with parental goals when parents use positive evaluations and support (e.g., Steinmetz, 1979). In the absence of parental support, however, it is unlikely that Andy will behave competently in school and social situations. We could even entertain the speculation in our story that although children prefer positive attention, any attention is better than none, and Andy will behave in a manner that elicits some sort of attention from his distressed mother.

The three concepts we have chosen have certain properties. Family Member A (e.g., the mother, Felicia) has some personally relevant characteristic or state of affairs. Member A then does something to or with Family Member B (e.g., the child, Andy). Finally, Member B has some personally relevant characteristic or state of affairs. Perhaps this kind of scenario is typical. It could be pointing to the general way, regardless of content, in which family members relate to each other as persons through the vehicle of social interaction. We could say that our simple case represents the fundamental idea that "the family is a unity of interacting personalities" (Burgess, 1926). We can therefore interpret our little three-concept scheme as an instance of a much more widely applicable process. We might even want to consider whether or not this is how all individual persons become connected to each other in durable social groups or even in rather casual encounters.

The search for a plausible interpretation can go in any of several directions. The next six chapters are devoted to exploring these alternatives in some detail. The fundamental point now, however, is that we can have a set of concepts, well defined, neatly linked, and adequately measured, and we can have some ways to help us explain what is happening. Without connecting these ideas to more fundamental ideas at a more abstract and general level, however, the interpretation may be very incomplete. We can have "miniature" theories that focus on such things as "parental stress," "parental support," and "child competence," but these should be embedded within more encompassing images of how the world is organized so that we can interpret our minitheories and better understand their uses and limitations.

Theory, Practice, and Intervention

Later in this chapter, we discuss the history and development of family science and family studies. Despite the fact that family sciences developed from many different fields, much of the early theorizing was aimed at addressing perceived social problems such as divorce and child neglect. Currently, many scholars and practitioners continue to address social problems such as teen pregnancy and healthy sexual practices. More important, these scholars and practitioners may believe that theory should be relevant to not just studying these subjects but also alleviating the problems.

It is relatively noncontroversial to say that theories may assist us in producing a knowledge base in regard to social problems. There is more controversy as to the degree to which theories should espouse evaluations of the subject matter studied. It is one thing to say that theories produce knowledge relevant to what some perceive as a social problem and quite a different thing to say that the theory implies that certain behaviors are bad or undesirable. In the first sense, theories are charged with the production of knowledge. Individual scientists may want to study teen pregnancy because they think it is a problem, but they would not claim that the theory they use makes such claims. On the other hand, there is an increasing number of scholars who seem to argue that theories have an evaluative component just like religions.

We would argue that science is charged with the "description" and "explanation" of phenomenon and that religion and other moral interventionists are charged with claims about what is right and wrong. Indeed, claims that are moral, such as "Teen pregnancies are bad," cannot be evaluated by science. On the other hand, science enables us to assess the probability of later marital disruptions for those who had a teen pregnancy. Whether the pregnancy is desirable, moral, or bad is a question for ethicists or theologians. So the argument is not that science is value-free but that science is not morally evaluative. Any scholar who decides to study something does so in part as an expression of values. Yet, in science, the claims emanating from research and theory are to be claims that can be judged by their logical and empirical adequacy rather than their moral rightness. Indeed, scholars of the family realize the pitfalls of moralisms, which are often culture bound and time bound. After all, premarital teen pregnancies in some cultures, such as Micronesia, were considered necessary for females to prove their fertility and make them attractive mates in the marriage market.

The applicability of a theory and the knowledge base it produces to assist practitioners in addressing social problems and producing therapeutic interventions are major testimonies to the empirical grounding and richness of the theory. Indeed, a theory that proves useful for practitioners is one in which the concepts have empirical referents and the propositions are clear. To this extent, the serviceability of a theory for practical applications is an important aspect of the theory. But theoretical claims such as defining what a good person is or what is right or correct behavior are moral, not scientific theories.

It is important to distinguish between theories of intervention and the application of family theories for the purposes of intervention. Theories of intervention deal with basic concepts and propositions about how to effectively produce a desirable change, whether the change is desired by the intervening agent, by the families and members being changed, or by both. Such a theory might include ideas about the behavior of the agent and the conditions under which the agent's behavior is expected to have an effect. In such theories, what the agent does may be treated as one or more antecedent variables, and the outcome variables would include various family phenomena. For a fully adequate theory of intervention, it might be necessary to understand the causes of intervention as well. Usually, however, the principal image is of an outside agent doing something to change families. A theory of intervention, therefore, is considered to be a good one if it clearly and accurately describes and explains the way an intervention works to produce an intended effect.

In contrast with theories of intervention, it is possible to design interventions by working directly from theories about family life. If these theories are designed to explain family phenomena, or even if they posit familial causes of other phenomena, this knowledge can point to variables that if manipulated can produce desired effects. Notice that, if used alone, family theories applied to interventions do not necessarily indicate anything about who the agent is or how the agent acts. This type of application also is limited in the sense that it must be possible to change the important causal forces in the theory, but some family theories contain variables that would be difficult if not impossible to change.

We can illustrate the difference between the two primary uses of theory for intervention by considering "family violence." Suppose there is a theory suggesting that the cohesiveness of families positively influences the likelihood of physical aggression among family members. The most violent families may be those with "enmeshed" relationships. If it seems reasonable to intervene to reduce family violence, we could search for ways to reduce family cohesion, thus directly applying the theory. If we wished instead to apply a theory of intervention, we would need to see what kinds of agents using what kinds of methods are able to reduce family violence. It is possible, of course, for the theory of intervention to operate on the causes of violence (e.g., cohesion) rather than directly on the undesirable family behavior itself. This would be an example of combining a theory of intervention with a theory about the family.

In this book, we emphasize the direct application of family theories to intervention. For each of the theories covered in subsequent chapters, we consider the implications for intervening to change families. We have, however, little to say about theories of intervention. How best to intervene can be a complex matter, and there are several specialized professional literatures in this area.

Another important consideration concerns various types of intervention. At least four generic types have been commonly emphasized:

therapy, education, social policy, and social movements. In the case
of therapy, some problem with family functioning is identified. One
or more members go to a therapist, whose job it is to help the family
change. The therapist, who may belong to one of several professions,
will use a theory of intervention to at least attempt to help the family.
Whether or not the family members understand or agree about their
problem, therapeutic intervention is designed to reduce or eliminate
the problem, and the treatment will be effective if the theory of intervention used by the therapist is adequate. Notice that there ordinarily is
a voluntary decision on the part of a family or individual members to
seek help for a problem that is not being solved by the family on its
own. Notice also that the treatment tends to be applied to one family
at a time. The field of marriage and family therapy has grown considerably in recent decades, and some interventions are applied to
several families at once in a group setting, but therapists tend to employ
interventions case by case.

Education, however one wishes to define it, also constitutes an
intervention. Elementary school teachers, college professors, and
many other professionals provide abundant information to families
and their members. Another active area in the family field is family
life education. Although more people can be reached with educational
programs than with therapeutic ones, the direct recipients of education are often individual members of families. Education does not
emphasize changing families so much as providing information that
families can use to help themselves. There is less of a problem focus in
education than in therapy, for education is a lifelong effort and people
can always learn more, even to enrich an already glorious family life.
Although family members surely educate each other in many matters
and in many ways, we tend to think of education as an intervention
by an external agent in transaction with one or more members of
several families.

Social policy includes both general principles or goals and programs
of action to meet those goals. Whether local, regional, national, or
international in scope, governments create and enforce laws and
regulations that affect families. In addition, corporations can establish
policies that either help or harm families. Although it even makes sense
to consider the policies that each family makes for itself, most social
policies and service programs target fairly large categories of families

or members of families. Any time a policy or a program driven by a policy changes, an intervention has occurred. Some social policies are designed for purposes other than to help families but nevertheless have an impact on them. For example, clean water legislation may be directed at the public at large, but it can improve the health of people in families and thus indirectly enable families to function better.

The fourth type of intervention we consider is social movements. These generally involve the organization of many people from different families who share a common concern. However well organized and resourceful a social movement might be, the goal is to influence others to change their behaviors and perhaps their attitudes about all families or certain kinds of families. Although the techniques may be therapeutic in part, they are more often some combination of education and political action. Protest marches, lobbying campaigns, and even terrorism are among the tactics that participants in social movements may use. This type of intervention is unique, for it reminds us that families may organize to intervene in the ongoing affairs of "outsiders." Whether or not a particular family or its members are active in a social movement, however, "bystander" families are likely to be affected either by the process or by the result of the effort. One reason that social movements generate countermovements is that groups with different interests become polarized on opposite sides of an issue. We are not trying to suggest that every social movement is focused on families, either as participants or as the issue of concern, but clearly such movements can affect families even when not intended to. For example, the Gay Rights movement's cry for the marital and family status that heterosexual couples may enjoy affects the form of families in the future.

When we examine family theories later in this book, it will be important to ask which kind of intervention or combination seems to be most congenial to each theory. In some cases, the answer may be that the theory has few implications for intervention. In other cases, the answer may be that a theory discourages any kind of intervention. Many theories may seem to simply ignore this issue. Particularly when a theory is created to understand how and why families work, there is unlikely to be much attention given to how one might or should change anything. For example, I may be able to offer a reasonable explanation of divorce, but I may have no interest in trying to alter the divorce rate.

Those who are interested in understanding and in explanation are often different from those who want to change families or to help them in some way. Therefore, theorizing and intervention are often seen as separate realms, with different groups of interested professionals. This division can be overemphasized, however. For example, clinicians or educators cannot hope to be effective without theories to guide their practice and their understanding of the people they help or instruct. Furthermore, every description or explanation of how families—or anything else—work must contain at least implicit notions or seeds of ideas about what could be changed if someone wanted to pursue change. The main reason some interventionists question the value of theory is that they think it is somehow divorced from the reality of the world. But a good theory has precisely the opposite feature. It often has been said, and we agree, that there is nothing more useful than a good theory. And good theories must be more than wishful thinking. They also must be based on empirical evidence. For their part, theorists often are skeptical of practitioners or others who could be called interventionists because the theorists know that change of any kind cannot be pursued unless the change is valued. Theorists are not uniformly against change, but they may have no particular interest at the moment in changing anything. Theorists tend to separate what is and what ought to be, even if they may act like a theorist some of the time and like an interventionist at other times. In North America and many other parts of the world, family theorists and researchers are usually also educators, so they must learn to combine their theorist role with at least some type of intervention.

The Relevance of Philosophy

The term *philosophy* can refer to both the values and way of thinking of a person and, as well, the academic discipline. Both meanings are important in understanding the emergence and growth of family studies, but for the moment, we focus on the importance and relevance of academic philosophy, especially academic philosophy of science, for family theories.

The methods of philosophy are logic and other forms of discursive reasoning. Philosophers do not use the empirical methods of science to establish the credibility of their ideas. Some philosophers, known as philosophers of science, examine the principles by which scientists work through reconstructing the logic of scientific processes. Whereas sociologists of science systematically study the behaviors and thoughts of scientists and the social organization of the sciences, philosophers of science explore what science should be like in terms of abstract ideas. There are several ways in which this philosophical study is important.

The Historical Legacy. The discipline of philosophy is historically prior to the scientific disciplines. The ancient Greek philosophers, among others, had many creative ideas about human affairs and the workings of the natural world. It was out of the Enlightenment philosophy of the 18th and 19th centuries that the modern sciences in the Western world were born. During this period, it was common for individual scholars to be both philosopher and scientist at the same time or to easily shift back and forth between the two. It has only been during the 19th and 20th centuries that the various scientific disciplines have branched into special fields to which a person could devote an entire career.

The historical legacy of philosophy as a precedent to the sciences has meant that philosophy, as a formal discipline, has influenced all sciences. Many of the influences have been indirect. The so-called physical sciences, such as physics and chemistry, emerged first. Between 1850 and 1900, the philosophical principles embedded in these earlier sciences spilled over to the natural sciences, such as botany and zoology, and the social sciences, such as psychology and sociology. During the 20th century, as family science emerged as a subspecialty within several of the social sciences, the philosophical underpinnings continued to operate. Now, near the end of the 20th century, we are able to think of family science as a distinct field with a multi- or interdisciplinary character or even as a unique discipline in its own right. We have attempted to capture the flavor of the indirect path from philosophy to family science in our choice of quotes in Box 1.1: Hempel is a philosopher, Homans is a sociologist, and the others are family scientists with various disciplinary backgrounds.

Philosophical Authority. Scientists often rely on philosophers as authorities. Of course, the discipline of philosophy has not been stagnant in recent centuries or even recent decades. New ideas are constantly being proposed and debated. A particular philosophy of science may be popular at a given moment, but later it is challenged and some other philosophy may take its place at or near the top of the heap. Scientists, including family scientists, frequently turn to the literature produced by philosophers to see what the current issues are. When scientists need to justify the basic principles guiding their search for answers to important questions, they sometimes seek guidance from philosophers of science or from other kinds of philosophers.

Family scientists as well as other social scientists often turn to philosophers as authoritative voices when they are dealing with theoretical issues. This practice is amply demonstrated by such works in the family field as Burr (1973), Sprey (1990), and Thomas and Wilcox (1987). This selective reliance on philosophical authority reminds us that theory in any field is bound up with philosophy. Even if family theories do not begin as deliberate confrontations with fundamental philosophical questions, they inevitably imply philosophical assumptions.

Personal Philosophies. Whatever impact the ideas and words of professional philosophers may have on practicing family theorists, each such theorist also has a philosophy of her or his own. This philosophy is a set of background principles and assumptions, quite removed from empirical proof or disproof, that guides our thinking. Some of these philosophical ideas form the basic tenets or assumptions about reality that we must make to produce a theory with a certain form or content or by a certain method.

PHILOSOPHIES OF SCIENCE

It is now often asserted that there are different, if not rival, philosophies of science. This is apparent in professional philosophy itself and—more important for this book—among family scientists as well. The philosophies we adopt influence the way we conduct our scientific practice, including the theories we create and our attitudes toward the theories of others. We sketch below a few of the central philosophical views that may help to distinguish family theorists and other family scholars from one another. Key elements of three philosophies of science appear in Box 2.1. We have called these "positivistic," "interpretive," and "critical" philosophies of science (e.g., Neuman, 1994). We do not claim that these are the only three alternatives in family science—indeed, we discuss other alternatives, such as feminism and postmodernism, in subsequent chapters. At this juncture, we present Box 2.1 to illustrate the nature of philosophical assertions. To further illuminate the issues involved, we focus below on truth claims and values.

A group of philosophers working in Vienna in the early part of the 20th century argued that knowledge claims are either true or false and that the job of scientists is to verify the true claims. Another philosopher, Sir Karl Popper, disputed this view. Popper (1959) argued that knowledge claims could be shown to be false, but that there is no way to prove them to be true. Popper's position has become influential among not only philosophers but also practicing social scientists. Whether or not family scholars have read Popper, his ideas have indirectly influenced family theorizing, helping to usher in what is sometimes called a postpositive era in the philosophy of family science (Thomas & Wilcox, 1987).

A central difference between positivism and other philosophies of science is their perspective on values. It should be obvious that no human behavior is valueless in some absolute sense. Indeed, all of the philosophical arguments we are considering are themselves evaluative. To say that science should be without values is to value valuelessness. To value something is simply to hold and to express a conception of a desirable state of affairs.

One of the key reasons that science emerged historically as a way of thinking and working somewhat different from the arts, religion, and politics was concern about the distortions in knowledge—along with considerable human suffering—that seems to result when reasonableness, fairness, and facts are devalued. Science is not without faults, just as no individual human being or social organization is faultless, but value neutrality is very similar in at least some ways to value tolerance or respect for value diversity. But this is a matter of degree, and the value-relevant and value-laden positions push further the

Box 2.1

Three Philosophies of Science, Applied to Family Studies

POSITIVISTIC View of Knowledge. There are objective truths, processes, or realities to be discovered about families.

Values: Family science can and should be value neutral if not value free.

Criteria for Evaluating Family Theories: Good theories should be rationally constructed (e.g., internally consistent, simple, coherent, clear, explicit, general, abstract). Good theories also should be empirically relevant (e.g., testable, fit well with data).

Goals: Explanation and prediction.

Scholarly Style: Analytical, causal, deductive or inductive, deterministic or probabilistic, factual, logical, materialistic, mathematical, mechanistic, observant, planful, precise, quantitative, structural, etc.

INTERPRETIVE View of Knowledge. Truth is subjective, and all knowledge about families is created by interpreting actors engaged in conversations with one another.

Values: Family science is value relevant, and family scientists should become aware of and open about their own values.

Criteria for Evaluating Family Theories: Good theories should have literary qualities (e.g., elegance, imagination, narrative power). Good theories also should be based on data grounded in the experiences of family members.

Goal: Understanding.

Scholarly Style: Artistic, evocative, existential, hermeneutic, humanistic, intuitive, metaphorical, phenomenological, postmodern, processual, self-reflective, sensitive, speculative, spontaneous, symbolic, etc.

CRITICAL View of Knowledge. Truth is imposed by those with the power to shape knowledge.

Values: Family theories are value laden. All values should be exposed and challenged to create opportunities for change.

Criteria for Evaluating Family Theories: Good theories contextualize phenomena and allow for pluralism. Good theories also are emancipatory, prescribe changes, display the theorist's ethical stance, and fit well with the theorist's personal experiences.

Goals: Emancipation or empowerment of oppressed people and social groups.

Scholarly Style: Constructivistic, dialectical, feminist, liberal or radical, macroscopic, pluralistic, postmodern, processual, relativistic, etc.

ideals of tolerance and diversity, sometimes to the extreme point of complete relativism.

Writing several decades ago about science as a vocation, the sociologist Max Weber made some interesting comments:

> Today one usually speaks of science as "free of presuppositions." Is there such a thing? . . . All scientific work presupposes that the rules of logic and method are valid. . . . Science further presupposes that what is yielded by scientific work is important in the sense that it is "worth being known." In this, obviously, are contained all our problems. For this presupposition cannot be proved by scientific means. It can only be interpreted with reference to its ultimate meaning, which we must reject or accept according to our ultimate position toward life. (quoted in Gerth & Mills, 1946, p. 143)

More recently, Christensen (1964, chap. 24) provided an analysis of the value issue in family science. His assessment was quite Weberian. Christensen advocated neither the rejection nor espousal of nonscientific values by theorists and other scientists. Rather, he advocated the identification and separation of nonscientific values from scientific values. This may continue to be the most common view among family scientists, but it is not the only view. According to the "critical" philosophy in Box 2.1, for example, scientific "facts" are inseparable from the values that scientists have about their subject matter.

To summarize, philosophical ideas establish principles that help frame the ways that family theories and other aspects of scholarship are created and used. Philosophical ideas are themselves foundations for scholarship, but they cannot be scientifically proven true or false. Professional philosophy has had mostly indirect effects on family theories. What matters most is to understand the working philosophies of practicing family scientists (Klein & Jurich, 1993).

A Brief History of Theory in Family Studies

Each theory in family science has its own historical legacy, as we discuss further in subsequent chapters. Our focus here is on major themes and examples of how family theory has been important to scholarship throughout history. We refer to several useful accounts of this history and recommend them for greater depth of coverage.

Adams and Steinmetz (1993) have recently surveyed contributions of the "classics," which encompass ideas up to the 20th century. Early philosophers were often interested in prescribing ways of living according to their own values. Adams and Steinmetz call attention to this infusion of ideology, and they note that it sometimes was accompanied by efforts to describe families in more dispassionate ways. Only scattered references to family life per se are contained in the classical works, with little resemblance to the kind of scientific explanation we have now come to expect of scholarship.

Much of the early work centered on attempts to find the origins of marriage as an institution and to trace its evolution as societies moved toward a more modern form (Adams & Steinmetz, 1993, pp. 76-78). Some scholars searched for the ultimate purposes of marriage or the family. Some saw progress or at least the adaptation of family life to changing social circumstances. Some lamented the declining importance of the family, especially as industrialization and urbanization gripped the Western world in the 19th century. Adams and Steinmetz (1993, p. 86) conclude that the closest these philosophers came to a real theory was a model of parental socialization that resulted in positive outcomes for children and the meeting of needs for both generations when parents became elderly. For the most part, however, and whether obvious or subtle, ideology in the classics, Adams and Steinmetz (1993) found, "is seldom totally absent, although its presence makes a theory neither right nor wrong" (p. 93).

Howard (1981) has examined the history of U.S. family sociology from 1865 to 1940. He also notes the early emphasis on evolutionary thinking, as well as the interest of "moral reformers" in doing something about the problems families seemed to be facing because of the industrial revolution. Howard considers the period between 1890 and 1920 a progressive era. Even as moral reformers and charity workers expanded their initiatives, the idea that families could adapt to changing environments became popular. An emphasis on the psychosocial interior of family life took hold, and educational programs to foster the socialization of children seemed promising. If families were sometimes struggling and disorganized, it was because they were caught between two conflicting value systems, one emphasizing traditional images of the family and the other based on the requirements of the modern democratic and capitalistic state.

The years 1920 to 1940 constitute the latest period Howard describes in detail. In these years, the key theme in family scholarship shifted from ecology to interaction among family members, with the goal of personal adjustment. In 1924, the American Sociological Society (now the American Sociological Association) established its Family Section, and at about the same time, Ernest Groves developed the first systematic college course in family life education at Boston University. Howard also notes as a countertheme during this period a renewed emphasis on the institutional level of analysis, with studies of families in a community context and attention to cultural diversity on a broader scale. In a chapter published with Howard's book, van Leeuwen (1981) notes that European family scholars remain more interested in the institutional, or macroscopic and historical, levels. On both continents, however, "the norm developed that family scholars should refrain from moral and political evaluations" as they increasingly relied on empirical data collected through field work" (van Leeuwen, 1981, p. 133).

Reflecting on much of the same body of work mentioned above, Christensen (1964, chap. 1) concluded that systematic theory building in the family field did not begin until about 1950. Concepts and rough orientations were taking shape in the first half of the century, along with a growing industry of empirical research, but without formalized explanations meeting the requirements of propositional theory. Although not highlighted in any of these historical accounts, an upswing in scholarly interest about families within many academic disciplines appeared before 1950, with contributions by sociologists, anthropologists, psychologists, home economists, and social workers, among others. Yet Christensen's designation of 1950 as a turning point seems to be basically correct. An inspection of the *International Bibliography of Research in Marriage and the Family, 1900-1964* (Aldous & Hill, 1967) shows that of almost 4,000 entries before 1950, only 7 contain "theory" or a cognate term in their titles. Of the 12,000 entries for the 1950-1964 period, 93 entries contain such terms. By comparison, for the 2-year period from 1991 to 1993, 264 of 7,600 entries in a subsequent inventory (Touliatos, 1994) pertain to family theory. Interestingly, the largest proportion of theoretical works prior to and during the 1950s dealt with courtship and mate selection—this was the first topic to receive systematic and cumulative theoretical treatment.

Aside from the increasing attention to family theory in the scholarship of the field since 1950, the last half of the century can be subdivided into three stages, each with its own set of themes:

Conceptual Frameworks: 1950-1966. The single most prominent theme in family theorizing during the 1950s and early 1960s was an emphasis on identifying conceptual frameworks (see the discussion of conceptual and theoretical frameworks in Chapter 1). This emphasis is evidenced by a series of works devoted to the topic (Christensen, 1964; Hill, 1951; Hill & Hansen, 1960; Nye & Berardo, 1966/1981). The number and character of the particular frameworks varied, but the basic idea remained the same. As research on family life accumulated, most analysts attempted to give explanations for their findings. The explanations often were narrowly focused, and it was difficult to see how various studies fit together. The attempt to identify frameworks was a search for underlying principles that might help in the construction of general theories for the field. It was not claimed that such theories already existed, nor was it often assumed that a single integrated theory would be practical. Rather, the idea was that by comparing the currently fragmented works with respect to the concepts and assumptions they used, scholars might be able to work toward the building of family theories in a more coordinated way.

Christensen (1964) captured the spirit of this period well in the closing remarks of his introductory essay to the *Handbook of Marriage and the Family:*

> As has been said several times, there is urgent need for better theory. Critics of family research have described it as being amateurish, trivial, scattered, often sterile, and sometimes moralistic. . . . There is still need for correcting what Goode (1959, p. 186) spoke of as a "hornet's nest of conceptual and terminological problems." There is still need to isolate and then integrate, insofar as seems feasible, the theoretical frameworks which can guide the discipline. And there is still need to find and then specify the relationships among empirical generalizations in order to constitute true theory. (pp. 29-30)

Formal Theory Construction: 1967-1979. A change in tone characterized the next several years of work on family theory. Following Hill's (1966) address on receiving the first Burgess Award for a career of scholarly achievement in the family field, attention turned toward methods of deductively and inductively creating theories, using a clearly delineated propositional format. Many examples of this type of work emerged. Nye and his colleagues presented a propositional theory of family stability (Nye, White, & Frideres, 1969), followed by a propositional theory of age at marriage (Bartz & Nye, 1970). Goode and his colleagues published a massive volume listing hundreds of propositions relevant to scores of family topics (Goode, Hopkins, & McClure, 1971).

The most important works of this period, however, were those spearheaded by Burr (Burr, 1973; Burr, Hill, et al., 1979, Vols. 1 & 2). In his 1973 volume, Burr applied the principles of deductive, propositional theory-building provided by philosophers and sociologists to 11 different topical areas of research. In the first volume of Burr, Hill, et al. (1979), Burr and his colleagues applied the same procedure to twice as many areas, involving experts in those areas as chapter authors. In Volume 2, Burr, Hill, et al. (1979) focused on five general theories that were not substantively limited. The editors noted that the second volume was not comprehensive in its coverage of general theories, and they acknowledged difficulties in linking the two volumes. Inductively integrating materials from the first volume proved difficult because of the lack of semantic equivalence across domains, the complexity of models in the first volume, and the lack of a way to bridge macrolevel and microlevel propositions (Burr, Hill, et al., 1979, Vol. 2, pp. xii-xiv).

Organizational developments within the National Council of Family Relations (NCFR) also were important during this period. In his Burgess address, Hill (1966) had called for the creation of a Theory Section to parallel the existing Research Section. Although his initiative was defeated, by the late 1960s NCFR had created the joint Research and Theory Section that continues today. Hill did not relent in his effort to give visibility to theorizing as a major professional activity, however. With the help of others, he created the Workshop on Theory Construction, which began with meetings at the NCFR annual conference site just prior to the regular NCFR conference. The workshop served as a training ground for both students and more advanced family scholars, allowing them to nurture and demonstrate their talents in theory building. In 1975, the name of the workshop was expanded to Theory Construction and Research Methodology. This workshop also survives today. In its first 24 years, over 560 papers were presented, and over 730 different participants appeared on its programs. It is interesting that both the section and the workshop evolved to combine theoretical and research interests. This symbolizes the extent to which family scholars see the two enterprises as fundamentally connected.

Pluralism: 1980 to the Present. It is always difficult to gain perspective on developments in a field when they are still swirling and the next major turning point is unforeseen. Lacking the distance afforded by time to reflect backward, we tend to see the present as chaotic or transitional. Of course, this perception also may mean that our tendency to periodize the past is an oversimplification, and all moments of intellectual history (and even family history) are fuzzier and more complex than they appear in retrospect. Nevertheless, the publication of the two edited volumes by Burr and colleagues (Burr, Hill, et al., 1979) seems to represent the high-water mark, if not the culmination, of the theory construction movement.

The pluralism of the past several years has several possible interpretations. It can be seen as a continuation of the quantitative growth of contributions by scholarly participants in family theory and research. It can also be taken to be a furthering of fragmented and specialized interests. Or it can be viewed as a new respect and tolerance for diverse philosophies, theories and theory-building methods, and research strategies.

Doherty et al. (1993) provide a cogent summary of nine main trends, although they give these developments somewhat more recent origins than we would. We excerpt their list from a more detailed discussion:

1. The impact of feminist and ethnic minority theories and perspectives
2. The realization that family forms have changed dramatically
3. The trend toward greater professional (multidisciplinary) inclusiveness
4. The trend toward more theoretical and methodological diversity

5. The trend toward more concern with language and meaning
6. The movement toward more constructivist and contextual approaches
7. An increased concern with ethics, values, and religion
8. A breakdown of the dichotomy between the private and public spheres of family life and between family social science and family interventions
9. Greater recognition by family scholars of the contextual limits of family theory and research knowledge (pp. 15-17)

To be sure, Doherty et al. see challenges posed by, and potential problems with, these emergent developments, but their basic posture is laudatory and optimistic. But any idealistic hope on the part of some leaders in the field that we would eventually converge around one grand theoretical scheme to explain everything about families has now been completely dashed and discarded. What we see is the continuing proliferation of theories, the eclectic combination of elements from different theories, and variations and transformations within existing theories. It is as common now, if not more common than ever before, for theorizing to be narrowly focused on particular topics and issues. Countless minitheories, middle-range theories, and models of mostly causal processes, all closely linked to Hempel's (1952) "plane of observation," characterize the literature, particularly in professional journals and in the proceedings of conferences and workshops.

The other main trend in recent years has been a vigorous questioning of the philosophical foundations in the field (cf. Osmond, 1987; Thomas & Wilcox, 1987). The result has been a turn toward interpretive and critical philosophies (see Box 2.1) and away from at least some elements of the positivistic philosophy. It is important to remember, however, that the entire scholarly community does not move in unison in any one direction or another. Some theorists attempt to blend and integrate, whereas others find one philosophy or even one theory compelling and the others inadequate. The current scene is a curious and shifting mixture of consensus and conflict over theories and theory-building methods.

In light of the current situation, a precaution is in order as we now prepare to explore in some detail a half dozen of the currently important theoretical frameworks in the family sciences. Our own map of the alternatives is not the only possible one, nor is it necessarily complete and otherwise adequate. In 1950, only the symbolic inter-

actional perspective, among the theories we cover, would likely have
been widely recognized. Until the mid-1960s, three other perspectives
that we do not cover as distinctive were commonly identified (structure-
functional, institutional, and situational). By this time, the developmental perspective had gained recognition, but several others were
either widely rejected or absorbed into other points of view. When
Nye and Berardo (1966/1981) attempted to comprehensively cover
conceptual frameworks at the end of this period, they even added six
more, each roughly representing an academic discipline (i.e., anthropology, psychoanalysis, social psychology, economics, legal studies,
and Western Christian studies). When Broderick (1971) reviewed the
theoretical developments of the 1960s, he saw several new possibilities. Of these, the exchange and systems perspectives have continued
to thrive, and they are represented in our following chapters. By the
end of the 1970s, a similar review by Holman and Burr (1980) added
conflict, behavioral, ecological, and phenomenological perspectives as
being of at least secondary importance. Of these, we give major
attention only to the conflict and ecological perspectives. When Nye
and Berardo (1966/1981) reissued their 1966 book, they added exchange, systems, and conflict theories in their introduction, as well as
"social individualism" and "transactional analysis," neither of which
seem to have progressed thereafter. Finally, the most recent comprehensive treatment includes more than a dozen chapters on distinct
theoretical perspectives (Boss et al., 1993).

In a recent study (Klein, 1994) of over 100 family scholars, the
participants were asked to rate 11 alternative theories as to how
favorably disposed they were toward them. Of those we emphasize in
this book, their ranking, in descending order was: symbolic interactional, developmental and systems (tied for second place), exchange,
conflict, and ecological. In general, however, the participants indicated dislike for very few, and most were favorably disposed toward
several. Furthermore, the scholars nominated dozens of others that
they liked, although the nominations seldom coincided. We conclude
from this pattern of findings that no single scheme focused on only a
small number of general theoretical perspectives would be universally
accepted.

A fruitful typology of theories is only partially in the eye of the
beholder. Some threads seem to be common to the various alternative

classifications, and some reflect historical changes in the field regarding the popularity and promise of the alternatives. Nevertheless, each mapping of the territory is at least somewhat dependent on the purposes and viewpoint of the author. In our case, we aim for relative simplicity to meet the needs of readers. We capitalize on the existing complexity mainly by covering some of the varying and more recent emphases within the broader traditions. After exploring the alternatives, we return in Chapter 9 to the problem of fitting the theories into a coherent overall picture.

Food for Thought

1. Imagine that you have just read a family theory that discusses *dysfunctional families* and *unhealthy families*. Would these terms suggest a scientific theory or a moral theory?

2. Discuss with your colleagues what the difference is between "a theory about families" and "a theory about family therapy."

3. Do you think the propositions we have used in regard to family support and child competence might assist practitioners? Reexamine those propositions and see if they make claims about the most desirable or correct outcome.

4. In the television show *Star Trek: The Next Generation,* the crew of the starship *Enterprise* is bound by the "prime directive," which requires them not to interfere in the development of other worlds and cultures, despite the fact that crew members sometimes have much greater knowledge. Why do you think the "prime directive" makes sense? How is this similar to the distinction between those who study families and those who want to intervene in family affairs to "help" people?

5. A scholar argues that "Children are worse off than they were 50 years ago." Briefly formulate two plausible explanations, one that is based on causal logic and one that is based on deductive, but noncausal, logic.

Suggested Readings

Adams, B., & Steinmetz, S. (1993). Family theory and methods in the classics. In P. Boss, W. Doherty, R. LaRossa, W. Schumm, & S. Steinmetz (Eds.), *Sourcebook of family theories and methods: A contextual approach* (pp. 71-94). New York: Plenum.
   This is an excellent historical overview of the development and evolution of family theory.

Thomas, D. L., & Wilcox, J. E. (1987). The rise of family theory: A historical and critical analysis. In M. B. Sussman & S. K. Steinmetz (Eds.), *Handbook of marriage and the family* (pp. 81-102). New York: Plenum.

This provides a solid historical picture from the perspective that the field is moving to a less "positivistic" approach.

3

The Exchange Framework

Kevin and Sarah have been dating seriously for about 6 months. Both agree that they have a close relationship with a lot of warmth and support. After going to a romantic movie, Kevin and Sarah go back to Kevin's apartment and are in the middle of some pretty serious petting when Sarah says, "Kevin, if we are going to do it, I want you to use a condom. I have one in my purse." Kevin says, "Gosh, honey, are you serious? Don't you trust me? I mean, it's not as though I have AIDS or something." Sarah seems to be caught off guard and pauses for a moment before responding. "Kevin, I know how you feel about me, and I trust you, but a condom makes good sense because it is easy for anyone to pick up a sexually transmitted disease. Some of these diseases are hard to detect and even harder to cure, especially for women. I don't want to end up not being able to have children when I am ready to as a result of carelessness." Kevin quickly blurts, "But these things are so plastic. You know, Sarah, a guy doesn't feel anything if he wears one of those!" Sarah's voice carries a tinge of anger or bitterness. "Kevin, I wanted to make love with you, but now I feel you are just after your own pleasure and don't really care about the possible consequences for me. I am the one who gets pregnant, I am the one who has to get an abortion or carry the baby for 9 months, and in the end I am now the one who has to ask for a commonsense preventive measure that would protect both of us." Kevin's tone now becomes disappointed but still angry. "Come on, and I will take you home."

This sketch of Kevin and Sarah's interaction provides us with an illustration of two people pursuing their self-interests. Kevin's self-interest is to maximize his sexual pleasure. Sarah's self-interest is to avoid the costs associated with unprotected sex. From this standpoint, often called *utilitarianism*, both Kevin and Sarah are acting rationally, but they are operating on different values. The essence of utilitarianism is that individuals rationally weigh the rewards and costs associated with behavioral choices. They choose those activities that maximize their rewards.

Utilitarianism is a philosophical perspective that has heavily influenced exchange theories in the social sciences. The central focus of exchange theory is on motivation. Human beings are viewed as motivated out of self-interest. What does it mean to say that utilitarianism focuses on motivation? Motivation is what induces a person to act. The focus, therefore, is on the person and what propels that person to action. Theories inspired by utilitarian thinking are based on the assumption of individual self-interest. This in turn means that we as social scientists can understand a person's actions by understanding the individual's interests or values. These interests allow the individual to account for both costs and rewards and make choices that maximize the actor's "utility" or profit. The basic notion, then, is that rational actors choose a course of action that produces the greatest benefit.

Exchange theorists usually explain the existence and endurance of social groups such as the family by their appeal to the self-interest of individual members. Individuals come together in groups so as to maximize their rewards. Of course, membership in social groups may also necessitate compromise and even costs to the individual member. If the costs of group membership exceed the rewards of group membership, then membership in the group is no longer a rational choice. Thus, the family group is usually conceptualized as a source of rewards for the individual members.

Intellectual Traditions

Utilitarian thinking refers to several varieties of theory. Some examples of utilitarian thinking are the ethical utilitarianism of the Epicureans and later Jeremy Bentham and John Stuart Mill, psychological hedonism, and the ideal utilitarianism of G. E. Moore. A complete picture of all the variants of utilitarian thinking would require volumes rather than pages. We direct our attention to the forms of utilitarian thinking found in the social sciences, particularly in the area of family studies.

Among the varieties of philosophical utilitarian thinking are "voluntaristic," or "interest," theories of value. In these variants, great emphasis is placed on the unfettered choice of individuals. One of the originators of this perspective, Adam Smith, held an economic view of humankind based on the belief that people act rationally to maximize benefits, or "utility." When choice was externally controlled or determined, however, actors could not make rational choices. This view was the basis for laissez-faire economics and, in addition, much of the utilitarian theory in the social sciences today.

In current social science, utilitarian thinking is quite obvious in microeconomic theory of the family (Becker, 1981), social psychology (Emerson, 1976; Homans, 1961; Nye, 1979), organizational sociology (Blau, 1964), and rational choice theory (Coleman, 1990; Hechter, 1987). There are major differences of emphasis between these authors, especially in how they unite individual motivation to macroscopic processes of reciprocity and social change. The focus of all these theories is on the rational utilitarianism of the individual, however.

Many of these theories have been termed *exchange* theories. This has led to some confusion with a group of theories that are structural and not at all focused on individual motivation. For example, the French anthropologists Claude Lévi-Strauss (1969) and Marcel Mauss (1954) are often called exchange theorists, but their focus is on the institutional norm of reciprocity and the social functions of exchanges in terms of group solidarity and the formation of group alliances. Other theorists, such as John Scanzoni (1970) and Randall Collins (1975), have a conflict-resource orientation; they only marginally fit in our characterization of utilitarianism due to their additional emphasis on macroscopic structures. In the study of the family, utilitarian thinking is generally referred to as exchange theory, and we follow this convention.

In the contemporary study of the family, Ivan Nye (1978, 1979, 1980) has been a foremost proponent of exchange theory. Nye's (1979) formal propositional statement of exchange theory relied heavily on the social-psychological approach of his predecessors from psychology, Thibaut and Kelley (1959). Although Nye's (1979) version of utilitarianism does include the norm of reciprocity and group-level exchanges, these macrosocial concepts are not well integrated with the social-psychological utilitarianism that is his principal focus. Nye (1979) entitles his chapter "Choice, Exchange, and the Family," thus emphasizing the voluntarist assumption guiding his version of utilitarianism. To date, Nye's (1979) statement of utilitarianism applied to the family is the most thorough and ambitious. Although there have been more recent summaries of exchange theory (Sabatelli & Shehan, 1993), our characterization of the core of the theory takes into account the thoroughness and completeness of Nye's (1979) vision.

Focus and Scope Assumptions

The individual is real. The assumption that the individual is real is technically referred to as methodological individualism. This assumption implies that group phenomena, social structure, and the normative culture are constructed by the actions of individuals. Thus, if we understand the actions of individuals, we will also understand these macrosocial phenomena. In regard to the family, this is an important and perhaps tenuous assumption. In exchange theory, the family is viewed as a collection of individuals. But we are all aware that mate selection, parenting, and many other family matters are regulated by both formal norms (laws) and informal ones. Regarding mate selection, for example, laws in some jurisdictions forbid certain "degrees of consanguinity," such as marriage with one's dead sister's husband (e.g., Manitoba and British Columbia). Clearly, these laws are unjustified by contemporary scientific understanding in genetics. How can these laws be understood solely as the result of the self-interest of individual actors and their self-interested behavior? This is the task set by the assumption of methodological individualism. James S. Coleman (1990), in the first chapter of his book *Foundations of Social Theory*, tackles this question from a utilitarian, or exchange, perspective. We recommend his discussion as supplying one of the best direct confrontations with the challenges of methodological individualism for the study of social groups and institutions.

Prediction and understanding come about by understanding the individual actor's motivation. Many theorists who assume methodological individualism do not attempt to understand individuals' actions through motivation. Those who hold utilitarian and micro-exchange perspectives usually do, however. Although these theorists acknowledge that individuals are always constrained in their choices, within these constraints any choice can be understood as based on the actor's motivation rather than exogenous forces or constraints. In this sense, exchange theory is a voluntaristic theory in the same way in which Adam Smith's theory was voluntaristic. This insight led Nye (1979) to state that the basic theory is about choice (p. 4). Because families are a relatively long-lasting social group, the voluntaristic assumption leads exchange theorists to assume that families are rewarding to individual members. The fact that children do not voluntarily choose their parents may provide some difficulties for the theory.

Actors are motivated by self-interest. Even with the assumption that the actor's motivation explains behavior, a theorist could still assume that motivation is multidimensional or not conscious (as in the concept of subconscious) or founded on inherent drives such as those Freud proposed. But micro-utilitarian exchange theories usually include the assumption that individuals are unilaterally motivated by self-interest—individuals seek things and relationships they regard as beneficial for themselves. The notion of self-interest raises some interesting questions regarding what we commonly know as altruism. Even some variants of ethical utilitarianism have been based on the assumption that we should act to accrue the greatest good for the greatest number. But for family exchange theorists such as Nye (1979), collective interests and altruism are derived and explained by the self-interests of individuals. So although self-interest is not necessarily the hallmark of all forms of utilitarian thinking, it is a basic assumption in regard to exchange and choice theory.

Actors are rational. It is easy to agree with the assumption that actors are rational. All of us like to think that we are rational human beings. But how often do we stop and think about what it means to be rational? This is a more complex assumption than we initially might have thought.

To be rational is to have the ability to calculate the ratio of costs to rewards. This is an analytic ability. One crucial dimension of rationality is that it is the same for all actors. Any two rational actors in identical situations with identical values and identical information would necessarily reach the same result in their calculations and thus pursue the same behavior. This assumption of rational actors is as important for microeconomics as it is for choice and exchange theory because it allows the interchangeability of actors and the concept of general rational actors captured in notions like "the consumer."

The idea of rational actors evolved from the rationalist philosophies of the Age of Enlightenment. Many students will recall that the Enlightenment was characterized by a newfound confidence in the ability of humans to reason. What was meant by reason was deduction or analytic thought. Such analytic thinking was believed to be independent of experience or sense data. Indeed, many philosophers, such as the French philosopher René Descartes, believed human rationality provided unequivocal knowledge that was true (QED). Indeed, the view of humans as rational actors originating in the work of Enlightenment philosophers such as John Locke provides much of the rationale for our current legal system. For example, juvenile offenders are treated differently from adults because they are believed to have not yet fully developed the ability to calculate rewards and costs. The rational assumption also provided the basis for much of the economic theory of Adam Smith.

It is easy to confuse rationalism with other words that share the same root but have a very different meaning. For instance, *rational* is *not* interchangeable with *rationalization*. A rationalization is an attempt to provide an apparently rational justification for one's behavior after the behavior occurred—it is not proof of a choice but rather a fabrication after the fact. Later, we further discuss the *ex post facto* nature of rationalization, which critics of exchange theory raise as an objection.

Concepts

Reward and Cost. A reward is anything that is perceived as beneficial to an actor's interests. A simple way to conceptualize cost is as the inverse of reward. Although costs may be negative rewards—things perceived as not beneficial to an actor's self-interest—we should be careful to also include as implicit costs cases in which rewards are missed or forgone. It would be naive to assume that the concepts of costs and rewards are unique to utilitarian theories. Certainly, Watsonian and later Skinnerian psychology emphasizes rewards and punishments. Although the basic notions are similar, the theories differ because the assumption of rationality is largely absent from these psychological theories. Indeed, behaviorists deny that conceptual processes need to be included in explanations of human behavior and posit that only behavioral patterns of stimulus and response need be examined. This view is at odds with the emphasis in exchange theory on rationality.

Microeconomics is focused on economic rewards and costs. Exchange and choice theorists view rewards and costs as being formulated from a much broader array of values than used in economic theory. For example, Nye (1979), Blau (1964), and Foa and Foa (1980) each list six sources of rewards and costs—though each list is different. We consider these general sources of costs and rewards in greater depth below.

When we examine the basic concept of rewards more deeply we find definitions referring to things or relationships that bring pleasures, satisfactions, and gratifications. Such definitions come uncomfortably close to a naive hedonistic calculus weighing pleasure and pain. Such a hedonistic view falls apart rapidly when the complexities of decisions are examined. For example, one may climb a mountain because it is gratifying, but it also involves risk and hardship. Indeed, it is doubtful that mountain climbers would find the task as gratifying if it did not contain the risk and hardship. Many of our most gratifying experiences are in part gratifying because not everyone is willing to undertake the hardship or risk.

Profit, or Maximizing Utility. The notions of reward and cost do not alone explain behavior. If one attempts to explain that an actor

behaves in a certain way because it is rewarding, the resulting "explanation" is overly simplistic and fails to account for the many elements
that were rationally calculated by the actor. Indeed, reward and cost
alone supply us with little other than a form of behaviorism.

It is the concept of profit, or utility, that allows the theory to avoid
such criticisms. Profit is defined as the ratio of rewards to costs for
any decision. Actors rationally calculate this ratio for all possible choices
in a situation and then choose the action they calculate will bring the
greatest rewards or least costs. Thus, the mountain climber weighs the
rewards of climbing a mountain, such as the social approval of other
climbers and the aesthetic enjoyment of the climb, against costs such
as the risk of being killed or injured in a rockfall or avalanche. From
this example, you can see that it is the notion of rational calculation
of profit that makes exchange theory more than naive hedonism.

*Comparison Level (CL) and Comparison Level for Alternatives
(CL+).* In complex situations, the evaluation of profit available to an
actor may be divided into two comparison levels. The first is the
comparison (CL) of what others in your position have and how well
you are doing relative to them. The second comparison (CL+) is how
well you are doing relative to others outside of your position but in
positions that supply an alternative or choice. For example, if instructors at your university were given a 3% raise in salaries, they might
ask how well they are doing relative to instructors at other universities
(CL). The second comparison they might make is how well they are
doing relative to others in private enterprise and government with
equivalent education and training (CL+).

The role of comparisons in the evaluation of choices has mainly
been emphasized by Thibaut and Kelley (1959) and Nye (1979). This
perceptual orientation is especially useful for family researchers wanting to explain phenomena such as timing of children or the decision
to divorce. The decision to divorce provides a good illustration of the
two comparison levels. For example, a husband may compare (CL) his
profit ratio for his marriage with what he perceives other husbands he
knows are receiving in their marriages. The second level of comparison (CL+) would be to compare his profit as a husband with the
profit he perceives in other possible, unmarried positions, such as
divorced and remarried husbands. According to the theory, if he were

to calculate greater profit for an alternative position, he is more likely to choose a divorce.

For family researchers, evaluation levels represent one of the more attractive components of the theory because they allow us to understand changes of marital and family status. Comparison levels can be used to understand a choice such as divorce, and they can also be used to understand the degree of satisfaction or gratification an actor associates with an outcome. Sabatelli and Shehan (1993) propose that the notion of comparison level could help us understand why young couples with children experience lower marital satisfaction than couples in other stages of family life (e.g., Rollins & Feldman, 1970). Sabatelli and Shehan (1993) point out that couples with young children are in a period of family life that follows a stage (early marriage) marked by high satisfaction and thus constituting a high comparison level. Demands and expectations associated with child rearing take time and energy away from fulfilling the high marital expectations in the way they were satisfied prior to children. Hence, the comparison of present rewards with what one has previously received is linked to greater dissatisfaction with marriage.

Rationality. We have previously discussed rationality as a basic assumption necessary for the calculation of the ratio of rewards to costs. If you think about things and relationships that you find rewarding in your life, however, you will probably notice that the value of these rewards changes with time and situation. In addition, you would surely note that not all rewards are equally weighted. For example, you might be thirsty and want a drink, but not all liquids that would quench our thirst are equally valuable (as any cola commercial attests). Furthermore, the value of a reward may decrease as you gain more of it (marginal utility); a dollar to a rich person has less value than a dollar to a poor person. To deal with the changing value of rewards and costs, it is necessary to add the idea of the importance, salience, or weight of alternatives. To understand any actor's choice as rational, we need to know what the person considers rewarding and costly and, in addition, we have to know the relative weights (or salience) for each of the rewards and each of the costs.

A simple example might clarify this idea. Imagine that your family is trying to decide on a destination for a summer vacation. You have narrowed the choices down to backpacking in the backcountry near Jackson Hole, Wyoming, or visiting the campgrounds along the Oregon coast. To reach this stage, each family member has to compare the possible alternatives, such as taking individual vacations rather than a joint vacation. This is similar to the second comparison level, or what Thibaut and Kelley (1959) called the comparison level for alternatives. Is it a reward or cost to go on a family vacation? Do you enjoy being together or is it more valuable to spend some time away from family members? After there is agreement that a family vacation is more valuable, the next step is to decide on the destination. Do you value hiking in the mountains or walking miles of uncluttered beaches? Do you want the adventure of backpacking or the more placid contentment of watching the Pacific Ocean? Are there activities for all family members in both spots? Each value, such as adventure and diversity of opportunities for other family members, is weighted by the importance or salience of this for you. Finally, you make a choice based on the maximization of profit for you. Of course, your family as a whole might choose the other alternative.

This example raises a critical question. How could a researcher ever examine the complex decisions of family members in one family, let alone a large sample of families? Certainly, the theory appears too cumbersome for a detailed accounting of rewards, costs, and relative weights for each individual, for every decision in each and every family. Exchange theory can be used in such investigations, however, by making two assumptions. One assumption we have already discussed: Because actors are rational, they are interchangeable. This assumption means that given the same rewards, costs, and weights, any actor would make the same choice as any other. The second assumption is one we have not discussed in any detail. It is the assumption that for large numbers of actors we can assess the rewards, costs, and weights as those that would be held by a modal, or average, actor. In other words, we assume that for most people in a social group or social system, rewards, costs, and weights are relatively uniform. There may be variation in how people look at rewards and costs, but there is great overall uniformity and little systematic variation.

Exchanges and Equity. The rational weighing of costs and rewards in an unconstrained environment in reality seldom happens. Usually, we live in a social system characterized by social interdependencies; some of the rewards we may desire are dependent on the cooperation of others, or we may need to trade with others something we have of lower value in exchange for something of higher value. This is an economic view of society. In most instances, maximizing profit entails exchanges with others. Social relationships that last over some period of time do so in part because they offer profits. A rational person is willing to incur some losses to maintain such profitable relationships. Marriage may be one such relationship, in which inequities at one point in time are tolerated because of the expectation of future rewards from the relationship. Certainly in families, vacations are planned not so as to optimize the profit for any individual but rather to fairly and equitably distribute rewards to all.

In a few exchange perspectives (Scanzoni, 1972; Sexton & Perlman, 1989), the principle of equity is viewed as being central to the maintenance of social relationships and groups. After all, siblings play together because of a set of negotiated and agreed-on exchanges perceived by them to be a fair exchange. Families decide on a vacation spot based not on any one individual's profit but on an equitable distribution of rewards for all members. Husbands and wives can be viewed as in a fair exchange situation, and when the situation becomes unfair or imbalanced, we expect divorce or separation. As we shall see later, marriages are seldom exactly equitable at any point in time, and some people may be so committed to marriage that inequity is not an issue. Indeed, if equity generally operated in marriage, we would not have so much literature on division of household labor in the family (e.g., Pina & Bengtson, 1993).

Generalizable Sources of Reward. The concept of a set of general rewards and costs for actors in a specific social system is absolutely necessary if exchange theory is to be applied to groups and large numbers of people and families. Of course, some of the most interesting research questions are not about one family or person but about why people in general behave in a certain way. For instance, we may want to know why married couples delay childbearing or why people wait until their late 20s to get married. Examining why one person, say, Martha Jones, delayed marriage would not give us the answer we seek. For example, Martha was hospitalized with a major disease from her 20th birthday until she was 30 years old. We doubt that this explains why most people delay marriage. The answer to our question would usually come from representative survey research using large numbers of respondents. If we attempt to explain our respondents' choices by maximization of profit, then the question arises as to how we can compute the ratio for all of these actors in our sample.

The notion of general sources of costs and rewards enables us to compute a general accounting of saliencies, costs, and rewards and establish a general choice that would be most profitable for actors in a social system. Indeed, the relative stability of general costs and rewards in a social system allows actors to make rational decisions. Various theorists have proposed different general sources of rewards and costs. Homans (1961) originally emphasized social approval as the most general source of rewards and costs. Other theorists have felt a need for the inclusion of other sources. Blau (1964) proposed the social rewards and costs of personal attraction, social acceptance, social approval, instrumental services, respect, and power. Foa and Foa (1980) proposed love, status, services, goods, information, and money. Nye (1979) proposed social approval, autonomy, predictability/ambiguity, security, agreement, and equality of resources. Nye makes the claim that many of these sources are culture free and may be used anywhere in the world, but he fails to tell us which ones have such universal generalizability. None of the exchange theorists have spent their energies addressing general salience weights for these general costs and rewards, but in specific applications they usually make an argument as to why one set of rewards or costs is more salient than another. Because salience may change dramatically with situation, the question is perhaps best left open at the general theoretical level.

Because most social exchange theorists identify social approval as a reward or cost, we can use that source for a general example. Let's return to the question, "Why do people delay marriage?" and see what kind of answer we can formulate according to exchange theory, using the broad category of social approval for rewards and costs. We must first postulate the profit linked to marriage. In North America, most people marry at least once. According to exchange theory, a rational actor would marry to maximize profit. We must all agree that marriage is socially approved more than alternative forms of relationships such as cohabitation, singlehood, and so on. Our parents, religious institutions, and political institutions view marriage as the appropriate relationship between coresident heterosexual adults.

It is not hard to make the argument that one of the major reasons we marry is social approval. Why are young people delaying marriage? Very simply, marriage roles and responsibilities (especially pregnancy and child care) interfere with the social approval attached to other early life course expectations such as finishing education and getting started in a career. Today, as opposed to only 20 years ago, these educational and work expectations apply to both males and females as sources of social approval. Thus, young men and women delay marriage so that they may first achieve these other socially approved statuses. After all, most of us had parents, teachers, and clergy who advised us to finish our education and get a job before getting married. Although there are many gaps in our explanation, it nonetheless serves to illustrate the way in which general sources of reward might be used to explain social patterns such as delay of marriage.

Propositions

Exchange theorists explain individual and family phenomena by identifying general propositions that seem to cover the particular phenomenon of interest. This is, of course, the procedure for all deductive theories. In the case of exchange theory, the number of general propositions required for any explanation are very few. According to theory, social phenomena can be explained with very little conceptual and propositional baggage. When a theory leads to successful explanations with very little baggage, we call it *parsimonious*. This simplicity is seen as an asset in comparing competing theories. Let's examine the propositions called for in exchange theory.

Actors in a situation will choose whichever behavior maximizes profit.

The simplest and most powerful proposition in exchange theory is simply that an actor will choose that course of action that offers the greatest rewards relative to costs. One implication of this proposition is that actors may not necessarily choose options that provide the greatest rewards if the costs are high relative to costs associated with other choices. A less rewarding option may be selected because the costs are less dear. This fact should caution us that unlike the case in behaviorism, in exchange theory profit rather than reward determines behavioral choices.

Actors in a situation where there are no rewards seek to minimize costs (Principle of Least Costs).

Some of you might ask, What if there are only potential costs in a situation and no rewards? The theory actually incorporates this concern but in an implicit rather than explicit way. Implicit in exchange theory is the concept of reward and cost being interchangeable due to the notion of calculation of profit. If profit is the ratio of rewards divided by costs, then clearly a fraction results when costs exceed rewards. Because division is the same operation as subtraction (the dividend is how many times you can subtract the denominator from the numerator), we can see that costs are mathematically equivalent to negative rewards. Indeed, a cost is a negative reward. Implicitly then, the proposition regarding maximization of profit becomes the minimization of costs. This rule, or proposition, about minimization of costs can then be applied to the special case in which there are zero rewards but different costs associated with choices.

One of the more vexing problems for exchange theory has been the computation of long-term costs and rewards versus short-term costs and rewards. We give up many immediate rewards to achieve long-term rewards. For example, those who believe that a university education has the purpose of getting a good job might sacrifice 4 years of income while they are in a university, and many other immediate rewards, for what they perceive as higher rewards after they graduate. In a marriage, one spouse might pass up the satisfaction of making an angry response to an affront from the other spouse for the marriage to last over the longer term.

Compared with school groups and work groups, families are relatively lengthy in duration. The analysis of long-term rewards and costs is essential to understanding the behavior of its members. We can extrapolate two general propositions in this regard from Nye (1979, p. 6):

When immediate profits are equal, then actors choose according to which alternative provides the most profit in the long term.

and

When long-term profits are equal, then one chooses the alternative that provides the most profit in the short term.

These two propositions allow us to gain some perspective on the calculation of profit by interjecting time as a complicating variable. We still have to add the relative salience to the actor of immediate rather than deferred gratification. And of course, these propositions tend to provide guidelines for analysis rather than predictions, as it is doubtful that we would often encounter situations in which profits are equal.

The propositions in this section suggest that exchange theory is deterministic. If we knew all of the values and salience weights composing an actor's calculations, we could accurately predict the actor's choice and behavior in any given situation. The only obstacle to such accurate predictions would be errors in our measurements, which might lead us to speak in probabilities rather than necessities. Nonetheless, this is a causal perspective in which the actor's perceptions, values, and calculation of profit compose the causal variables and the actor's choice and behavior are the effect variables. As a result of this strongly deterministic view, exchange theorists might, for example, argue that those actors who choose to get married calculate that marriage is more rewarding than remaining single.

Variations

We have been following Nye's (1979) version of exchange theory, but it is important to note the diversity within exchange theories. We classify the many variants on the basis of whether they are microsocial or macrosocial. You may recall that a microsocial theory includes the assumption that the individual is the active unit of analysis, whereas in macrosocial theories the active unit of analysis is the social group or institution. Although all theorists would like to think that they have successfully bridged the chasm between micro- and macroperspectives, there are in reality few theories for which one can make such a claim. Individual exchange theories usually involve simply adding up all the individual motivations and calling that group motivation or developing a "great man" theory whereby one actor is responsible for social change and therefore only one motive need be analyzed (Homans, 1967). Macroexchange theories examine the exchanges between groups and the resulting social solidarity and alliance formation. Individuals are largely lost in the larger social group and in most ways unidentifiable and unrecoverable as part of an explanation.

MICROEXCHANGE THEORIES

In our characterization of exchange theory, we have followed the microsocial perspective associated with Nye (1979), Levinger (1982), Lewis and Spanier (1979), Sabatelli (1988), and Thibaut and Kelley (1959). There are other variants of this microsocial perspective, but these are not family theories. For example, Coleman (1990) and Hechter (1987) have both authored variations on a type of utilitarianism referred to as *rational choice theory*. Both of these authors take the individual as the basic unit of analysis and attempt to construct macrosocial applications through a notion that some rewards can only be achieved by groups and social organization. Although neither of these rational choice theories has been directly applied to the family, they were influenced by an earlier work by the Nobel-prize-winning economist Gary Becker (1981), whose work *A Treatise on the Family,* presented a rational actor economic theory of the family. Becker (1981) and his followers have met with considerable criticism that their approach is both too focused on economic profit and too individualistic. We will have more to say about these criticisms of exchange theories in the next section.

Another example of a microexchange variant is the theoretical work of Emerson (1976), dealing with the relative balance, or ratio, of rewards in social relationships. His unit of analysis is the relationship rather than the individual. His microsocial approach might be suitable to the study of the family, but there has as yet not been any research applications of his work directed specifically at studying families.

One of the more important variants of exchange theory used to study family relationships is *equity theory*. Although equity theory is directly derived from exchange theory propositions, it contains the additional proposition that fair exchanges are more profitable to relationships than are unfair exchanges. If A and B are in an unfair relationship, then the social norm of reciprocity is not maintained and the relationship is likely to be discontinued by one of its members. Thus, whenever a relationship provides profitable outcomes, it is essential for the maintenance of the relationship that exchanges be equitable. One can immediately see how equity might be applied to exchanges between marital partners and in family relations. Indeed, family scholars have used equity theory to study such longer-term family relationships (e.g., Scanzoni, 1972; Sexton & Perlman, 1989). It is interesting to note that several investigators of equity in marriage (e.g., Pina & Bengtson, 1993; Sexton & Perlman, 1989) have concluded that, at best, equity appears to have restricted explanatory value for marital relations.

MACROEXCHANGE THEORIES

As we said in our introductory remarks to this chapter, we are mainly concerned with presenting the microsocial exchange perspective, as that is the perspective generally applied to the study of the family. We do not want to leave the impression, however, that macrosocial exchange theorists have totally ignored the study of the family. You may have noted that our previous discussions of micro-exchange theories focus mainly on the individual's choices and decision making. Certainly such decision making can be applied to decisions such as the selection of a mate or the choice between divorce and staying married. Macroexchange theories tend to be focused more on the group or organization, however.

The transition from a microexchange to a macroexchange perspective is achieved by the addition of several concepts to those we have already reviewed. First, most macroexchange theorists identify two types of exchanges: *restricted* exchanges and *generalized* exchanges. Restricted exchanges take place at one point in time and involve little trust. For example, when you buy something in a store you hand money to the salesperson who then gives you the item you have selected.

Generalized exchanges take place over a longer period of time and therefore require more trust. An example of a generalized exchange is lending money to a friend or relative and trusting that repayment will be made at some future date. The trust required in generalized exchanges is buttressed by the *norm of reciprocity* found in equity theory. That individuals find the relationships in a family group profitable is in part due to the fact that the family group maintains profitable exchanges with other social organizations such as schools, churches, and the economy. The essence of macroexchange perspectives is the view that these group and organizational exchanges are more central than individual decision making.

In *structural exchange theories,* the individual's choices are viewed as being determined by the macroexchanges between group and organizations. Note that this is just the opposite of the view in microexchange theories such as rational choice theory that the individual's decisions determine the group's exchanges. Perhaps the best example of macroexchange thinking applied to the family is provided by the work of the French structuralist Claude Lévi-Strauss. Lévi-Strauss (1969) developed a theory that the fabric of societies is constructed by norms that require generalized social exchanges between groups. At the heart of these generalized exchanges are the exchanges between kin groups and clans. Prescriptive mating norms require the formation of alliances between groups through the exchange of mates. For example, in a moiety, or two-clan system, if you are a member of the Bear clan and want to form a political, social, and economic alliance with the Eagle clan, you could create a mating rule such as, "Bear women must marry Eagle men." The strongest expression of this alliance rule would be totemic incest, for example, forbidding an Eagle man to marry an Eagle woman. Lévi-Strauss's (1969) work has been criticized as not being applicable to voluntary mate selection systems such as our own, but his work has led to some interesting applications, such as Harrison White's (1963) book examining mathematical models of kinship. In general, the more macrosocial utilitarian theories have not been applied to the family as a unit of analysis but rather to larger kinship groups such as clans. As a result, North American family scholars have tended to favor the more microsocial variants of utilitarian thinking.

Empirical Applications

One way to understand a theory is to apply it to some examples. In this section, we apply exchange theory to two areas of research in the study of the family: divorce and sexual relations.

DIVORCE

Over the past half century, divorce in North America has increased dramatically. The past two decades have seen a slowing and stabilizing of divorce rates, but the risk of divorce is sometimes estimated to be as high as one divorce out of every two marriages. Divorce means difficult and painful adjustments for children as well as the husband and wife in a family. It is not surprising, then, that the explanation of why partners separate and divorce continues to occupy the attention of a significant number of family scholars.

Among the many possible explanations of divorce, exchange theory appears to offer one of the more promising roads to understanding. Briefly, according to exchange theory, each spouse analyzes the marriage by using the two comparison levels. First, a spouse compares profits relative to other marriages. If he or she feels deprived relative to other marriages, then the marital satisfaction of that spouse would be low, creating a motive for choosing separation and divorce. As Lewis and Spanier (1979) have aptly pointed out, however, many unhappy spouses remain married due to other constraints. Exchange theorists view these other constraints as "costs" associated with divorce. In the second comparison level, the spouse calculates the rewards and costs (profit) associated with possibilities other than marriage, for example, being single and divorced. Among the possible costs to this alternative would be child support, alimony, peer disapproval, the church's disapproval, kinship group disapproval, sexual deprivation, loss of interaction with one's children, role loss, and so on. Some of the possible rewards might be finding a more compatible partner, freeing family members from a confrontational and conflict-ridden home life, and freeing oneself from family responsibilities. The computation of the perceived alternatives to marriage depends on a diversity of variables, such as the gender ratio of the community in which one lives and the ages of one's children.

One of the major stumbling blocks for successfully applying this exchange theory explanation to divorce is that the rewards and costs in the two comparison levels seem to change over the life span of the individual. This is evident in the paradoxical finding pointed out by White and Booth (1991) that the great bulk of divorces (30%-40%) occur in the first 5 years of marriage—at the very point in the life span that is associated with the highest marital satisfaction. Furthermore, as marital satisfaction declines over the life course, so does the risk of divorce. It seems a paradox that we should find the greatest number of divorces when marriages are the happiest!

White and Booth (1991) explain this paradox by proposing that as marriages proceed through the life course of the spouses, the importance of marital happiness tends to decline—longer-duration marriages have relatively high costs for dissolution (called "barriers" following Lewis & Spanier, 1979). White and Booth (1991) propose that longer marriages with high costs for dissolution require very high levels of marital unhappiness to propel spouses to divorce, whereas early marriages with few costs to divorce require greater levels of marital happiness to keep them together. Thus, the paradox is explained by the life course changes in salience and the ratio of rewards and costs. Lewis and Spanier's (1979) model of marital stability has been challenged by a competing exchange model offered by Thomas and Kleber (1981), who propose that regardless of marital quality, marital stability will be high when there are few alternatives and high barriers to dissolution. White and Booth (1991) feel that in addition to solving the paradox between high divorce rates and marital satisfaction, their data resolve the debate in favor of Lewis and Spanier's (1979) model. We believe grounds remain for further research on these competing models.

GENDER DIFFERENCES
IN SEXUAL BEHAVIOR

Our second application of exchange theory is drawn from propositions presented by Nye (1979) regarding sexual behavior, although we focus not on the formal propositions but on what the explanation would look like. But first, what is it that we want to explain about gender differences in sexual behavior? In most, if not all, cultures, sex seems more actively sought after by males than females. Although there may exist a biological answer to why this is the case (see Chapter 8), most authors assume that the biological drive is very malleable in how it is satisfied. Furthermore, many of the behaviors that could be associated with a higher sex drive in one gender, such as prostitution, are usually labeled social rather than biological problems.

Nye (1979) argues that males are more likely to exchange rewards (especially money or marriage) for sexual access. Because exchange theory is essentially a motivational theory, Nye posits that sex is more profitable for males than it is for females. Nye is not assuming a more vital sex drive for males than females. Such an assumption would place the entire explanation on the shoulders of the biological importance, or salience, of sex for males over females. As a social scientist, Nye seems to assume that the biological drive for the two genders is equal and he therefore searches for a social explanation.

First, Nye argues that in all cultures women take the major responsibility for the children they bear. Unwanted pregnancy is thus more costly to females than it is to males. Even in the most modern societies, paternity is still difficult and expensive to prove. Contraceptives can be used to prevent the potential outcome of unwanted pregnancy, but contraception also is usually left to the female. These are real and potentially high costs to intercourse. A second differential is that men for the most part report better outcomes from sex than do females. Males are more likely to achieve orgasm than are females, and females are more likely to experience frustration from sexual relations.

The result of these differential costs and rewards is that relative to females, males, in general, find that sex offers greater rewards and fewer costs. As a result, men must either have sexual relations with those who find it as rewarding as they do (homosexuality) or they must increase the rewards for females. Nye says that the usual ways in which these rewards are increased for females is for males to offer either money or the probability of marriage. Other rewards, such as status and security, might be more salient at various points in the life course.

Nye's application of exchange has great scope and breadth. For example, it could explain female adornment as a sexual attractor that functions to increase the value of the exchange. Because married persons have already struck a bargain, we would expect much less difference between men and women in postmarital sexual relations. This prediction is consistent with the fact that a difference of less than 10% exists between male and female extramarital affairs (Blumstein & Schwartz, 1983). Furthermore, we can make some general predictions, such as that when the costs of contraception (inconvenience and medical complications) are equally distributed among both genders and sexual knowledge is shared among both genders so that both genders enjoy the same level of outcome, then we would expect less sexual bargaining with marriage and money. Keep in mind that Nye's (1979) theory remains to be tested and must be shown to provide a better explanation than competing theories, but this example does illustrate exchange theory's potential breadth of explanation.

Implications for Intervention

Exchange theory has numerous implications for family policy, treatment, and intervention. We can only sketch a few of these to give the flavor of the richness of this theory for application to family issues.

One of the most influential applications of the theory is in the area of intervention and prevention in marital and parent-child interactions. This application has largely been constructed on the view that parent-child and husband-wife relations represent *behavioral exchanges*. Gerald Patterson and his associates at the Oregon Research Institute pioneered this approach (Patterson & Reid, 1970). Currently, many scholars and practitioners use the behavioral exchange approach. For example, Bagarozzi (1993) suggests that in designing behavioral contracts with spouses, therapists should focus on increasing positive or rewarding behaviors and decreasing negative behavioral exchanges. Clearly, such an intervention would increase the profitability of the marital relationship. Markman and his colleagues have developed a prevention program (PREP) for enhancing marriages and decreasing divorce based on the notion that distressed couples seem to enter a reciprocal exchange of negative behaviors (e.g., Renick, Blumberg, & Markman, 1992). Although these authors view their program as empirically based rather than founded on exchange theory, the basic interpretive notion of behavioral exchanges remains true to the exchange perspective.

Another area of application for the theory is in the area of family policy. Haveman and Wolfe (1994), following Becker (1981), take a human capital, or rational choice, approach to child welfare and education policy. They view parents, schools, and government as making "investments" in the human capital of our children. To the extent that we invest unwisely or in a miserly fashion, we reap the failures of succeeding generations and social problems such as crime and economic dependence. Haveman and Wolfe (1994) review the relative costs of geographic moves, parental separation, and several other variables on the eventual success of children. These costs are seen as our inability to invest wisely in the human capital of tomorrow's generation and society. Haveman and Wolfe's *Succeeding Generations* is one of the clearest applications of economic exchange principles to the interpretation of family data and the framing of family policy.

Critiques and Discussion

Our focus in this section is on the criticisms commonly directed at microexchange theories. We recognize that each of the criticisms discussed is more applicable to some microsocial variants than others. Our central target must be the general notions we have presented above and principally derived from Nye (1979). One caveat should be mentioned: No social theory solves all the problems we raise in our critiques. Our criticism is not aimed at convincing the theorist or the student that one theory is better than another. Rather, these critiques are intended to illuminate the choices we make in adopting a theoretical stance and point out the areas that are in need of more creative thinking by the next generation of scholars.

As we mentioned at the beginning, microsocial exchange theories are usually based on *methodological individualism,* the assumption that the individual is the appropriate unit to study to gain an understanding of the family. As far as we know, there has never been a definition of the family as simply an aggregation of individuals. Yet, when we take the individual's ratio of rewards and costs as the basis of our theory about families, we are assuming that the aggregation of individual members is the family. Theoretically, this would make the family no different from any other collection of actors. Yet the family has characteristics that seem unlike other social groups. For most of us, our families are lifelong social groups that we enter by birth and leave by death. Our families have roles that are unlike work group roles, such as filial obligations toward the parents. And our families have biological and social relations (blood and marriage) that are unlike those in any other social group. Thus, to assume that individual actors are interchangeable and that families as social groups can be explained by the motivation of individuals seems problematic.

Explaining social order poses a problem for all the forms of utilitarianism. If we view explanation as emanating from individual motivation, then it is usually difficult to demonstrate how we developed social norms and social institutions. Although most microsocial theorists include a discussion of the norm of reciprocity (you should help those that help you), it is much less clear how this norm is derived from individual self-interest. In addition, in analyzing costs and rewards, theorists readily accept the "given" nature of social norms and institutions without indicating how these are explained by the theory. For instance, in weighing the rewards and costs of not wearing clothing on a hot summer day, you automatically take into account formal norms (laws) and informal norms. Most of you recognize that no matter how rewarding you might find going without clothing, there are strong formal and informal norms that constrain your behavior. The major answer utilitarians have given this question regarding social order is known as the *social contract*. There are many variants of this idea, but basically it involves the assumption that individuals band together and form a social order so as to have security of person and property. This social contract implies that some individual freedom is relinquished so that order may be maintained. But this view, although admitting the importance and power of social institutions, largely begs the question of how these social institutions evolve and change. Clearly, most of you have no recollection of relinquishing some of your freedoms in exchange for order. Rather, you were socialized by institutions to be on time, to behave in certain ways, and to expect formal and informal sanctions if you transgressed the social order.

Another problematic area for microsocial exchange theory is altruistic behavior. Many times we see (and praise) behaviors that seem to be characterized by the individual giving up rewards and suffering costs so that others may prosper. Some simple examples are a soldier giving up his or her life in combat or a mother running into a burning house to save her child. Exchange theorists would point out that this is a problem of attribution or inference. All we have really observed is the behavior (and not the motive), and we incorrectly attribute an "other-directedness" to an act that was actually calculated to yield profit. Thus, the mother is acting in the least costly way if she regards the death of her child as more costly than the personal risk she incurs by her attempt to save the child. The soldier who refuses to fight faces court martial, humiliation, and shame. On the other hand, critics might argue that these people are not acting rationally at all, but emotionally.

The assumption of a rational actor provides further difficulties, especially in the study of the family. The family is often considered to be a social group characterized by intense loyalty and emotions. Most police officers will tell you that domestic quarrels are often emotional and potentially explosive situations due to their irrational nature. Furthermore, the institution of marriage has long been viewed as "till death do us part," which flies in the face of the exchange view "till profitability declines." And, of course, children do not choose their parents, nor is the family they enter representative of the voluntaristic ideal of unfettered choice needed for the optimization of profit. Thus, it seems natural to question whether the assumption of rational actors calculating their most profitable choice makes sense in the context of the family.

One of the most basic questions in the study of the family is, "Why do people have children?" Exchange theory should treat this choice as bearing profit for the parents. But as most economists and parents will attest, children are expensive. Conservative estimates for raising a middle-class child today are usually above a quarter of a million dollars. Furthermore, the decline in the norms regarding filial care of the aged, coupled with social security and institutional care, make returns to the parents in old age unlikely. Nye (1979) attempts to answer this question by saying there is a form of intergenerational norm of reciprocity. You feel an obligation to pass on what your parent did for you to the succeeding generation. But people who are childless by choice can pocket the quarter of a million dollars and seemingly feel little remorse in not passing on the favor. It may be that having children is not a rational decision.

There is a problem of weighing costs and rewards. We have previously mentioned that the salience, or importance, of rewards and costs must be examined to understand a choice. Of course, theorists would like to believe that some costs and rewards have roughly similar value across actors. If this were not so, then it would be unlikely that we could develop a successful microeconomics. Even the symbols and meaning associated with economic units may be unstable, however. In our society, there are symbols of wealth and success. Increasingly, these symbols may be attained by both the wealthy and the indebted. These symbols may vary across cohorts and periods. We know of a very wealthy man who insisted on driving himself in a 10-year-old vehicle. His offspring all had fancier new cars with chauffeurs. And the meaning of rewards and costs changes more drastically once we move our comparisons to other cultures. In Tikopeia, a man's wealth was based on the number of wives he had. But number of wives did not just reflect material well-being. Daughters could be traded for wives and therefore daughters were a means to wealth and status.

Turner (1991) argues that exchange theory can be accused of tautological reasoning. In essence, a *tautology* exists when terms are all defined by one another and there is no possibility of disproving the statements. Turner argues that reward is defined as that which is valued by the person. The choice that a person makes is the maximization of profit. Thus, all actions are rewarding and the reason we undertake an action is that it brings rewards. For example, we may ask, "Why did Tiffany get married?" Some exchange theorists would answer that Tiffany got married because it was a more profitable choice than remaining single. But we may ask, "How do the exchange theorists know that this maximized Tiffany's profits over remaining single?" If the exchange theorists responded that we know because people always choose those behaviors that maximize their profits, then we have just completed a tautological circle. Turner believes that this circular logic is often found in deductive theories. We do not disagree that deductive systems can be self-referential and closed systems of definitions, but we do disagree that deductive scientific theories are ever like this. Indeed, the hallmark of a scientific theory (as opposed to a theory in general) is that some of its concepts are tied to empirical measures. We may define force (f) as $f = ma$, but we have standard empirical measures for mass (m) and acceleration (a). A problem with utilitarian theories is that they often seem to lack this mooring to the concrete empirical measurement system.

Conclusion

Despite the criticisms, utilitarian, or exchange, theory is one of the most popular social science theories applied to the family. One reason for this popularity is that exchange theories typically have great scope and breadth. The notions of reward, cost, and profit are sufficiently abstract and content free that the researcher may fill in the content from any number of contexts. The assumptions of rational actors calculating profit provides some problems, as does the inadequacy of the theory for explaining how and why institutional and normative constraints operate on choices.

Food for Thought

1. A mother returns home to find her house on fire, and although the fire fighters attempt to stop her, she runs into the house in an attempt to rescue her infant. Is this a "rational choice"? To see this as "rational," what emotional variables, such as "guilt," would have to be added to the theory?
2. Where is the line between "rational" actors and "irrational" actors? Is someone who we perceive as "irrational" simply attempting to maximize different values or is his or her ability to rationally "calculate" impaired?
3. Early economic theorists stressed that for economic choice to be rational, actors' choices must not be constrained or limited by society. In contemporary society, how constrained or unfettered are our choices?

Suggested Readings

Haveman, R., & Wolfe, B. (1994). *Succeeding generations.* New York: Russell Sage.
   This is a sophisticated but very readable application of microexchange economics to an extremely important area of discourse.

Sabatelli, R. M., & Shehan, C. L. (1993). Exchange and resource theories. In P. Boss, W. Doherty, R. LaRossa, W. Schumm, & S. Steinmetz (Eds.), *Sourcebook of family theories and methods: A contextual approach* (pp. 385-411). New York: Plenum.

This is a good general introduction. The authors introduce the macro-micro distinction as "collectivism"-"individualism" and do not demarcate the theories quite as sharply as we do in this regard.

4

The Symbolic Interaction Framework

Nicole, Michael, and their teenage son, James, have agreed to participate in a social survey about family life. Survey officials requested that all three of them participate in answering questions. The doorbell rings and they meet the interviewer, a young woman named Kim. Kim asks that each of the family members fill out a section of the questionnaire independently of other family members. James takes his questionnaire to his room, Michael fills his out in the kitchen, and Nicole completes hers in the living room, where Kim is waiting. After all three family members have completed their questionnaires, Kim briefly examines them. She pauses and then says, "Gosh, all three of you answered the question about how traditional or nontraditional your family is in very different ways. Would you folks mind discussing this with me for just a moment? We are supposed to discuss differences of opinion as part of the survey, and if you don't mind, I'll take notes occasionally." The family agrees.

It turns out that James believes that his family is fairly traditional. Nicole believes the family is very traditional. And her husband, Michael, thinks the family is extremely nontraditional. Nicole says that she thinks the family is traditional because she feels she has to do all of the cleaning up after the "guys." Michael says he thinks they are nontraditional because his mother never worked outside the home. He points out that his wife earns more money than he does. James believes they are fairly traditional because he has a mother and father that aren't divorced. Finally, Michael asks Kim, the researcher, what the survey means by *traditional*. After the family is told the meaning, Kim asks if that information would change their answers. All three family members say, "Yes," and that the survey meaning is not very close to what they think of as traditional.

Contemporary social science applied to the study of groups such as families is for the most part concerned with people's behavior. Much of the media through which we communicate is taken for granted. For example, questions on a questionnaire are usually assumed by the researcher to hold the same meaning and to be interpreted in the same way by all of the respondents in the survey. The variation in answers to questions is supposed to reflect differences in behavior, not in the interpretation of a question. If we ask a husband and wife how many times they quarreled during the past week, we assume that they label the same events as quarrels. Yet, even between husbands and wives who must both have been present for a "quarrel" to take place, we find differences in responses. We must conclude that differences in counting quarrels is either a difference of interpretation in what constitutes a quarrel, difference of memory, or both. In an even broader perspective on diversity of meanings, we know some of the persons responding to our questions may have another mother tongue, the families in which they are raised are different, and they have diverse education levels and abilities. How then can we assume that they will interpret and understand our questions in the same way? Maybe their responses are based not on different reactions to the question but very different interpretations. Symbolic interactionism, more than any other of the family theories, calls for paying attention to how events and things are interpreted by actors.

Some social scientists have divided the subject matter of human behavior into disciplines studying personality (psychology), culture (linguistics and anthropology), and social behavior (sociology, economics, and political science). At the base of these distinctions is the assumption that a culture is composed of commonly shared signs and symbols from which actors construct the meanings found in the culture. Many social scientists approach the meaning of symbols and signs in a culture as being relatively uniform and therefore the words on the questionnaire are viewed as commonly and uniformly understood. But some social scientists have argued that we cannot understand a behavioral response (including answering a questionnaire) unless we know what meaning the situation and the stimulus has for an actor. In broader terms, these social scientists believe that to understand social behavior, the researcher must understand the meanings actors assign to the situation and action. This uniting of the study of cultural meanings with social behavior is the prime focus of theories of symbolic interaction.

Intellectual Traditions

The symbolic interaction approach has a rich and complex history. Today, the term *symbolic interactionism* represents a diverse family of theories, and it can be difficult to detect what many of these variants now have in common that unites them under a single banner. The common threads that exist are perhaps best highlighted by understanding the common progenitors from which the current variants developed.

Without a doubt, the greatest single influence on social science thinking in the 20th century has come from Charles Darwin. Darwin (1880) provided a concrete and biologically rooted approach at a period when *idealism* (e.g., Hegel) was in philosophical favor in Europe. To intellectuals in North America, this more concrete approach emphasizing the "adaptation" of organisms to their environment was much more attractive. In North America, three scholars were particularly influential in generating ideas that would become incorporated in symbolic interactionism. Charles S. Peirce developed a theory of signs and symbols, William James developed a notion of self in relation to environment, and John Dewey developed the concept of mind. As Charles Morris points out in his preface to Mead's (1934) *Mind, Self and Society*, pragmatists saw no sharp distinction or conflict between science and philosophy. Together, these scholars represent the foundation of the philosophical school called *pragmatism,* from which symbolic interactionism sprang.

The philosophical foundation for symbolic interactionism is complemented by advances in social science thinking occurring in the first two decades of the 20th century. Charles Horton Cooley (1902, 1909) expanded William James's idea of the self into the more elaborate social science concept of the *looking glass self.* The importance of Cooley's (1909) notion is that it conceptualized part of the self as capable of reflection on its own behavior. This later became incorporated in Mead's (1934) conception of the self. W. I. Thomas and D. S. Thomas (1928) expanded on the pragmatic premise formulated by Peirce (1905) that the conception of an object is wholly given by the conception of all possible effects. Thomas and Thomas (1928) reinterpreted the pragmatic maxim as the important social-psychological principle: *What humans define as real has real consequences* (p. 572). This has become known as the *definition of the situation* and provides a linkage between how we perceive our environment and how we act in it. Both of these notions guided the early formulations of symbolic interactionism.

Despite these important earlier influences, it is really the work of George Herbert Mead that most scholars identify as the start of symbolic interactionism. Mead's thinking is, for the most part, only accessible through the lecture notes of his students, compiled and edited by the linguist Charles Morris (e.g., *Mind, Self and Society,* 1934). Indeed, Morris (1934) points out that although Mead's students took notes, Mead never even used lecture notes and his thinking was constantly evolving. Yet Mead's influence and contribution have been sufficiently strong to establish him as the paternal figurehead of symbolic interactionism.

Central to Mead's approach is the idea that by sharing common symbols, humans can adapt to and survive in their environment. He was especially interested in the process by which the flexibly adaptive infant came to share the conventional understandings in any society. His work incorporated the idea of stages of interactional learning through play and games, an especially important perspective for the study of socialization in the family.

Although Mead is an important beginning point, numerous scholars have contributed to symbolic interactionism and it would be misleading to portray the development of symbolic interactionism as monotonic and united. In fact, scholars have quarreled bitterly about the relative emphases and interpretation of ideas. Most secondary sources record an original bifurcation of symbolic interactionism into the Chicago school (Blumer, 1962, 1969) and the Iowa school (Kuhn, 1964), but we see more variants than just these two. We discuss many of these in the variants section below. We believe it is also important for the student to gain some notion of the unifying elements in this theoretical perspective and here focus on the common ground we think exists in this approach.

It is easy to say that symbolic interaction theories focus on meaning but quite a different and more difficult task to explain what that "means." To understand this complex issue, we must return to the seminal work of Peirce and later Charles Morris. Humans have the ability to mentally form invariant associations. For example, when Event A is associated with Event B, we could say that A is a *sign* for B. Where there is smoke, there is fire. Smoke is thus a sign for fire. An octagonal traffic sign is a sign to stop. A sign is the necessary ingredient for the development of a *symbol*. A symbol is any sign that is agreed on by convention. Now, although there are several important aspects to these distinctions, the question symbolic interactionism poses is, "How do we agree upon (convention) the sign?" Let's apply this to language. We have sounds such as "dad" that stand as a sign for a particular person in our lives. Not only do you have a "dad," but others understand the referent of that utterance. In addition, if you think about this issue for very long, you will note that many words (both written and spoken) refer not to things but to other clusters of symbols. The complexity of human symbolism and meaning as we now know it escapes any simple notion that every sign has a referent, because words can stand for other symbols as well as things.

To understand the term *meaning* in a social context, symbolic interactionists focus on the idea of how these complex symbol systems are shared. Indeed, for communication to take place, symbols must be shared or commonly agreed on. Thus, the focus for Mead and many other interactionists is on the process by which the infant comes to acquire the symbol system of the society.

The symbolic content of any culture is constantly changing. Words such as *limn* leave our system through disuse and abuse and new words such as *groovy* come into use. Even though the symbol system must be relatively stable for the achievement of agreement and convention, it nonetheless changes. But it changes within the rules of the system. As Chomsky and other linguists have pointed out, a key ingredient to understanding a symbol system and therefore meaning is that users of the system adopt rules that allow the generation of new and meaningful utterances based on these rules, or *syntax*. This insight is responsible for a second focus for interactionists. That focus is on the process by which meanings are constructed through interaction with both the environment and other people. In fact, most human symbol systems are so complex as to allow the generation of meanings for specific contexts and environments.

The general focus of symbolic interactionism can be summed up to be on the acquisition and generation of meaning. It should not be forgotten that in the study of the family and other social groups, we are assuming that actors think about and act according to the meanings they attribute to their actions and context. For example, a 3-year-old may show no interest in a particular toy doll. But when an older sibling plays with the doll, it suddenly takes on new interactional and situational meaning. Now, the doll is desired. The meaning of the toy is constructed by the situational interaction of the two siblings. Symbolic interactionism is not simply a motivational theory (as exchange); it is much broader. Certainly, symbolic interaction posits that humans are motivated to create meanings to help them make sense of their world. In addition, it encompasses actors' motives as constructed from the meanings available to the actor and relevant to the situation in which the actor is located.

Focus and Scope Assumptions

Human behavior must be understood by the meanings of the actor. The most basic assumption in symbolic interactionism is that the explanation of human behavior is impossible without knowing the meaning such behavior holds for the actor. Interactionists believe that to be human is to use symbols. Indeed, they would say we live in a largely symbolic world. Our language structures the way we perceive and the way we think. Material objects, such as jeans and cars, not only perform functions (utility) but have symbolic significance aesthetically, religiously, and socially. Humans live in a symbolic world, and our actions have both physical and symbolic import. If we were to attempt to understand behavior simply from the physical side of the equation, we would miss the mark of understanding. For example, if we were to describe to you a man in the woods cutting down a tree, you would not understand that behavior unless we discovered the actor's meaning (e.g., he is employed as a lumberjack, he is getting a Christmas tree, or he is a vandal). To understand behavior, we must understand the meaning that an action has for the actor.

Actors define the meaning of context and situation. The assumption that actors define the meaning of the contexts and situations in which they find themselves is in some ways an extension of the previous assumption. If humans live in a symbolic world, then the context in which humans find themselves will be both physical and symbolic. This assumption is only fully understood, however, by returning to Thomas and Thomas's (1928) maxim that what humans define as real has real consequences. Imagine that a terribly inebriated person hallucinates a herd of pink elephants charging down the street toward where he or she is standing. In response to the hallucinated charging elephants, the person begins to run down the street. Regardless of the fact that no elephants exist, the fact that the person defines the situation as dangerous is important in understanding why the person runs down the street. How we define the situation in which we find ourselves explains what problems we define and what actions and solutions we undertake. The fact that some definitions may be entirely mental rather than physical constructions makes our understanding of the actors' definitions of the situation even more important.

Individuals have minds. Another basic assumption of symbolic interactionism is that humans have minds. This may seem a trivial assumption unless we examine it more closely. All of us recognize that we have an organ of the body that sends and receives electrochemical impulses. But the idea of an individual mind presupposes an individual self that perceives, reasons, senses, and imagines. The notion of mind includes memory and willing actions as retrospective and prospective operations. Whether there is one organ or a system of interconnected organs that give rise to these complex operations is not totally resolved, even in the neurosciences. Yet it is the assumption in symbolic interactionism that the human mind acquires, integrates, and processes information. At the same time, the mind is capable of reflecting on its own processes so that the individual can develop a self as both actor (I) and object (me).

Society precedes the individual. When symbolic interactionists assume that humans live in a symbolic world and use their minds to manipulate and interpret these symbols, it is tempting to ask, "When did this all begin?" At some point in evolutionary time, we as a subhuman species lacked these talents. The problem with asking when we gained the abilities is that it was such a gradual process that there was no single point in time. Indeed, it might be considered a moot question whether symbols, social organization, or mind came first, as they are so strongly interdependent. But because we cannot conceptualize without symbols, and symbols are shared, society in rudimentary form must precede the individual mind and self. The single most important point to understand about Mead's conception of mind is that individual minds are results of the society and not vice versa. As Morris (1934) says,

> Instead of beginning with individual minds and working out to society, Mead starts with an objective social process and works inward through the importation of the social process of communication into the individual by the medium of the vocal gesture. The individual has taken the social act into himself. Mind remains social. (p. xxii)

Probably the best known empirical cases illustrating Morris's point would be the two cases of infant isolation documented by Kingsley Davis (1947). In both cases, children lacked socialization and failed to develop language and social skills. The assumption that society precedes individuals leads interactionists to focus on the process of socialization.

Concepts

SELF AND MIND

The notion of self is pivotal in symbolic interactionism. But our understanding of this concept is not well served by translating Mead's

(1934) concept of self as that which we commonly understand as our identity. For Mead, self, mind, and symbol developed concurrently. Our notion of self is founded on symbols and consciousness. The essence of symbolic interaction is that the self is a symbolic representation of that which did an act (I) and that which was acted on (me). In other words, we may represent ourselves as both subject and object. This means that humans can look at their own behavior as an object (me) and as such take the "role of the other." The concept of taking the role of the other is directly analogous to what Cooley (1902) had called "the looking glass self." Mead (1934) extended this concept from looking at our actions as a specific other (How would my father see my action?) to looking at our actions as a "generalized other" (How would others in society look at my act?). The self, then, is constructed by our consciousness from the two perspectives of I and me. The self as object contains the perspective of specific others when we take on the role of particular persons to see ourselves as they might, and it is constructed from the perspective of generalization of roles, or generalized other.

SOCIALIZATION

Socialization is the process by which we acquire the symbols, beliefs, and attitudes of our culture. Although the notion of socialization is central in symbolic interaction, Mead (1934) did not use it as a concept. Rather, Mead talked about this process as the "importation" of social symbols into the mind as part of the development of the generalized other: "Mind is nothing but the importation of this external process into the conduct of the individual so as to meet the problems that arise" (p. 188). For the child, the process of socialization is marked by two stages. First is the *play stage,* in which the child plays at being something like a police officer or mother. The play stage incorporates Mead's notion of taking the role of the other. Second is the *game stage,* in which the child must be able to incorporate his or her self in an organized activity through the generalized other. As Mead says,

> If we contrast play with the situation in an organized game, we note the essential difference that the child who plays in a game must be ready to

take the attitude of everyone else involved in that game, and that these different roles must have a definite relationship to each other. (p. 151)

Thus, the play stage assists in the learning and practice of *role taking*, whereas the game stage assists in the more complex task of learning the rules governing all social actors in the game. It is the game stage that is most similar to the complex social game we play as adults with our ability to "play a role" in society.

ROLE

Although the concept of role does not originate with symbolic interactionism, it is without a doubt one of the most basic concepts in symbolic interactionism. It is also the concept that has proved most problematic, because Mead (1934) uses the term throughout his work but seemingly takes its definition as self-evident. Probably the closest passage to a definition comes in a footnote in which Mead identifies social intelligence as depending on "the given individual's ability to take the roles of, or 'put himself in the place of,' the other individuals implicated with him in given social situations; and upon his consequent sensitivity to their attitudes toward himself and toward one another" (p. 141n). From this, we can clearly see that a role must be the "place of an actor." Mead also dealt with roles as rules to be learned in the game stage of a child's development. *Role taking* then is to put oneself in the place of the actor, and it includes the rules that the actor is expected to follow. The sketchiness of these references and lack of a clear definition has fueled bitter debates among later symbolic interactionists.

There are several dimensions of the concept of role that are significant in explaining family phenomena. If we assume that roles have the two characteristics alluded to above—rules of behavior for positions—then we can see how these rules also provide others with expectations for what someone in that position is to do. For example, the general norm, or rule, for a person who is "it" in the game of hide-and-seek is to close one's eyes and count to 10 while others hide. If the person who is "it" does not do this, he or she has not performed the role as others expected. Note that the others' behavior is predicated on the expectation of how "it" would behave. Thus, one important dimension of roles is the *expectations* that both the actor and others have about the performance of the role.

The *clarity* of the role expectations or rules of the role are another important dimension. Without clear expectations shared by both the actor and others, it is impossible for the actor to perform the role or for others to know how their behavior articulates with that of the actor. Returning to the game of hide-and-seek, if "it" only counts to. five but others expect "it" to count to a higher number, their behavior cannot be successfully meshed and the game carried on.

Role strain is an important dimension of roles. Role strain is where the actor does not have sufficient resources to enact a role or roles. When there are multiple roles, the overload of expectations may be so great as to create role overload or strain. A corollary to role strain is the special case in which the expectations of one role contradict or conflict with the expectations of another role. This *role conflict* usually produces role strain because the actor cannot enact the contrary roles simultaneously.

DEFINITION OF THE SITUATION

The concept of the definition of the situation originated with W. I. Thomas (Thomas & Thomas, 1928) but is also implicit in Mead's (1934) work in his emphasis on the social situation and taking the role of the other and the generalized other. The definition of the situation refers to the dictum that what we define as real will have real consequences. The definition of the situation sensitizes symbolic interactionists to the role of perception in forming our behavior. Mead, however, seemed wary about an approach that was too perceptually oriented and lacked focus on humans as problem solvers interacting with their environment. He stated,

> This process of thinking, which is the elaboration of our responses to the stimulus, is a process which also necessarily goes on in the organism. Yet it is a mistake to assume that all that we call thought can be located in the organism or can be put inside the head. The goodness or badness of the investments is in the investment, and the valuable or dangerous character of food is in the food, not in our heads. (p. 115)

Thus, Mead, in a manner consistent with Thomas and Thomas's (1928) dictum and Dewey's pragmatism, focuses us once again on the problem-solving interaction with the environment rather than on isolated internal mental processes.

Propositions

Although numerous authors have employed a symbolic interaction approach in the empirical study of the family (e.g., LaRossa & LaRossa, 1981), none of the contributions to date have equaled the theoretical presentation by Burr and his colleagues (Burr, 1973; Burr, Leigh, Day, & Constantine, 1979). They focus on the general propositions that are directly relevant to understanding families and, in our opinion, provide the most elegant and systematic statement of symbolic inter-actionism applied to families. For this reason, much of the clarity and power of the theory to explain family behavior and processes origi-nates in the propositional inventory provided by Burr, Leigh, et al. (1979). Here we discuss a few of the propositions that we regard as among the most useful for understanding families:

The quality of ego's role enactment in a relationship positively affects ego's satisfaction with the relationship. (Burr, Leigh, et al., 1979, p. 70)

Although most of us assume that our satisfaction in a relationship such as marriage is "made" by the other person, this proposition states a person (ego) is more satisfied in a relationship when he or she is doing a good job of enacting the role in that relationship. For example, a wife would feel more satisfied about her marriage when she feels that she is doing a good job in the role of wife. Burr, Leigh, et al. also offer a proposition regarding the role performance of the other, but that would be more expected. The proposition regarding ego's role enactment is a little like the homilies, "You like what you're good at" or "The more you put into something, the more you get out of it."

The greater the perceived clarity of role expectations, the higher the quality of role enactment. (Burr, Leigh, et al., 1979, p. 74)

A role is defined as the normative expectations attached to a specific position in a social structure. For example, the role of mother is defined by the social norms or expectations of nurturance and protection of her young. The more clearly defined these are to any person occupying the position of biological motherhood, the easier it is for that person to perform the role in a socially acceptable way. Obviously, a lack of clarity could result when biological mothers receive unclear or no anticipatory socialization as to the expectations of motherhood, or if the society lacks clear expectations and this lack of clarity is passed on through socialization to mothers. In either instance, the result would be decrements in the role enactment of the young mother. For example, 20 years ago breast feeding of infants was not as socially expected as it is today. Today, the normative expectations for breast feeding are gaining increased force and clarity as role expectations for mothers.

The more individuals perceive consensus in the expectations about a role they occupy, the less their role strain. (Burr, Leigh, et al., 1979, p. 79)

As Rossi and Berk (1985) have pointed out, one critical aspect to a role is that expectations are shared or consensual. Indeed, Mead (1934) argued that all social symbols are the result of consensus. If a person perceives that there is a social consensus on a norm or expectation, then the role as an instruction for behavior is clearer. As we have seen with the second of our propositions, the clarity of such prescriptions facilitates enactment of the behaviors. Thus, if a young mother believes that there exists a broad social consensus that mothers should breast-feed their infants, they are less likely to feel that expectation is vague or ambiguous. Vague and ambiguous role prescriptions cause people to feel uncertain about what the prescriptions are and whether or not they can meet those expectations. This is the experience of role strain. Burr, Leigh, et al. (1979) define role strain as the felt stress generated when a person has difficulty complying with the expectations of a role (see p. 57). The mother who is uncertain as to the socially approved pattern of infant feeding would undergo role strain.

The greater the diversification of a person's roles, the less consensus the person will perceive in the expectations about those roles. (Burr, Leigh, et al., 1979, p. 80)

When a person plays multiple roles, there are multiple expectations. At the very minimum, the multitude of expectations may become murky, and, at worst, contradictory expectations may lead to conflict between the expectations of roles. In both situations, it is difficult for the person to perceive clearly that there is a consensus about the expected behavior. For example, a working mother with an infant may feel that among nonworking mothers and health care professionals there is a consensus preferring breast milk for infants. Among fellow workers she may feel that there is a consensus that expressing milk in the office situation is unprofessional and shows a lack of commitment to work. Among working mothers, there may be no consensus, some siding with fellow workers and some with health care professionals. Clearly, the stay-at-home mothers (without role diversification) perceive greater consensus.

The greater the perceived role strain that results from performing a role, the less the ease in making a transition into the role and the greater the ease in making a transition out of the role. (Burr, Leigh, et al., 1979, p. 86)

Naturally, most of us avoid feeling stressed, and it seems reasonable that roles that are perceived as producing stress are regarded as requiring a more difficult adjustment than roles perceived as carrying little stress. For example, the perceived role strain of motherhood suggests that although becoming a mother is a biological function, it is not an easy transition. As a result, we have developed elaborate rituals and forms of anticipatory socialization in attempts to clarify the role expectations and ease the transition. Prenatal classes for expectant parents are one example of such anticipatory socialization.

The systematic propositions above are only a few examples of the many proposed by Burr, Leigh, and colleagues (1979). These authors presented these propositions as part of a deductive formalization of symbolic interactionism. As you may recall from the introductory chapter of this book, one of the strengths of a deductive theory is that propositions can be chained together to produce new and informative propositions. If we assume that the propositions are conceptually equivalent and transitive, we can put them into deductive chains. For example,

The greater the diversification of a person's roles, the less consensus the person will perceive in the expectations about those roles. (Burr, Leigh, et al., 1979, p. 80)

The more individuals perceive consensus in the expectations about a role they occupy, the less their role strain. (Burr, Leigh, et al., 1979, p. 79)

lead to the deduction that

The greater the diversification of roles, the greater the role strain.

This deduction provides an illustration of how the propositions developed in symbolic interaction theory may be used to produce theoretically derived propositions important in guiding empirical research on families. Let's now turn to some of the variants of symbolic interaction theory.

Variations

After Mead's death in 1931, two major schools of thought within symbolic interactionism emerged. One of these is known as the Iowa school and is associated with the work of Manfred Kuhn (1964). The other is known as the Chicago school and is identified with the position of Herbert Blumer (1962, 1969). Briefly, Kuhn's Iowa school is more positivistic and based on more structural and normative determinism and less interactional creativity than Blumer's Chicago school. Although many authors, such as Turner (1991), continue to focus on the disagreements and intellectual battles between the two schools of thought, we see this as a useless emphasis. Indeed, although the warriors may still be fighting on the battlefield, the castle has quietly been occupied by noncombatants from elsewhere. Many contemporary family scholars spend no time on the metaphysical questions raised by Kuhn (1964) and Blumer (1962, 1969), such as the nature of causality, the truthfulness of observational versus quantitative methods, and the nature of sociological theory. Many of today's family scholars have returned to the pragmatic roots of symbolic interactionism and use whatever methods are most appropriate to the research question they are asking.

The debate between Kuhn and Blumer served to focus interpretations of symbolic interaction on one or the other of these two, with the unfortunate consequence of deemphasizing the important and considerable contributions of predecessors such as Dewey and Peirce. It must be recalled that symbolic interactionism was formulated by the pragmatists, including Mead. Yet this has all but been lost in the continuing interest in the two warring factions that still battle over problems, many of which were resolved by Dewey, Peirce, and James. The focus on these two schools has often forced new scholars to take sides, even though the debate is no longer particularly relevant or sophisticated. Many times, it would be far more helpful to examine advances in *semiotics* (a study founded by Peirce) or *structural linguistics* (such as the work of Noam Chomsky) to see how these might further basic concepts in symbolic interaction such as gesture, sign, and symbol and their relationship to social behavior. But such influences and advances have been neglected because of the narrow focus of scholars on the two schools.

A central issue that divides most symbolic interactionists is whether interactions between people are (a) a product of the expectations residing in the social structure or (b) created and negotiated by the actors in each interaction. We use this issue as a theme in exploring the unique contributions of four variants of symbolic interactionism. In the study of the family, four relatively recent major variants of symbolic interaction theory have evolved. We identify these four as the "structural" approach, the "interactional" approach, the "micro-interactional" approach, and the "phenomenological" approach. Although each could be related to the schools of thought represented by Kuhn and Blumer, we believe these variants are sufficiently well formulated to deserve to be considered on their own merits and that little clarity is gained by forcing them into the restrictive categories of belonging to either the Chicago or Iowa school.

STRUCTURAL APPROACH

We begin by examining the structural approach. Although many family scholars align themselves with this approach, it is probably most identified with the work of Sheldon Stryker (1964, 1980). Others who have made significant contributions include Nye (1976) and Burr, Leigh, et al. (1979). We intend a general characterization that does not focus on any one scholar but on the group of scholars who assume that social roles are learned and then enacted by people when they occupy positions in a social structure. The focus of the structural approach is so much on the concept of role that many scholars call themselves *role theorists* rather than symbolic interactionists.

The three most basic notions in this approach are position (or status), norm, and role. A position, or status, is seen as embedded in a social network of interrelated positions. Each position has associated social norms or expectations. In our society, as in most societies, a woman in the kinship position "mother" is expected to behave nur- turantly toward her infant. A social role simply represents the com- plete cluster of the expectations or norms for any status, or position. A person may occupy several positions and therefore roles at any one time or across the life span. For example, the young mother may also be a teacher. Much of the research emphasis of the structuralists derives from the fact that an individual may play multiple roles at any one time and thus be exposed to role strain and role conflict.

Jonathan Turner (1991) points out that the metaphor for the structuralists is clearly that of "actors on a stage." Indeed, one ap- proach within symbolic interactionism in which this metaphor is emphasized is Goffman's (1974) "dramaturgical" approach. In the most general terms, the structuralists think that the scripts for the roles are passed down to the actors from society, which "precedes the individual." The actors' performance of the roles is largely a matter of how well they have learned their roles through primary and anticipatory socialization. And although the actors' role performances vary somewhat, the actual normative content of the roles changes very little from actor to actor. According to this view, despite decades of talk about equal participation by both spouses in household chores, chores remain largely the province of wives rather than husbands because the norms are deeply embedded in the social structure and are not strongly affected by the whims of individual actors.

The structuralist perspective has produced an impressive array of theoretical propositions (Burr, Leigh, et al., 1979) as well as an impressive amount of empirical research on such topics as role strain. It nonetheless has garnered some rather severe criticisms, especially from the "interactionist" wing of symbolic interactionism. Most significant among these criticisms is the argument that the structural perspective provides a deterministic view of humans being poured into the molds of the social system. This "oversocialized" self has little freedom to adapt to or change the environment. The problem-solving and adaptive nature of humans stressed by both Mead and Dewey seems lost within the structural symbolic interaction perspective. As a result, the view the structuralists have concerning social change is that it is at best slow and phlegmatic.

INTERACTIONAL APPROACH

The interactional variant of symbolic interaction is most closely associated with the work of Ralph Turner. Turner (1970) focuses on individual families. He is not concerned with aggregate patterns for families or cultural patterns. Instead, he focuses on the patterned processes within the family as a small group. Turner, unlike the structuralists, believes that many of these patterns are developed through interaction. Rather than seeing social structure as encompassing and monolithic, Turner believes social structure and culture provide a broad, vague, and often ambiguous outline for behavior. The individual's role taking is not simply the enacting of a well-defined role but is "making" the role through interaction with others and the context. Individuals have the freedom to make roles and communicate the role they are playing to others. Thus, Turner emphasizes the creative and problem-solving dimension of roles that is neglected by the structuralist symbolic interactionists. Whereas the structuralists emphasize how humans are constructed by their culture and society, the interactionists emphasize how culture and society are created by interacting actors.

After Ralph Turner's (1970) work *Family Interaction,* he continued to refine and formalize his thinking on role theory. The formal propositions that Turner and his associates (Turner, 1980; Turner & Colomy, 1987) have developed have led them into more and more structural terrain. For example, Jonathan Turner (1991) describes Ralph Turner's recent deductive system as containing some laws: "Functionality is, therefore, one of Turner's 'laws' of social organization, at least among 'roles' as a basic property of all patterns of social organization" (p. 439). Although it would be inaccurate to describe Ralph Turner as straying far from interactionism, his program to develop a nomothetic deductive role theory is bound to lead to more general statements. He increasingly focuses on the explanation of more aggregate phenomena than any one family or situation (e.g., Turner, 1987). It probably is not unfair to say that interactionists may have assumed too much power for the individual to "role-make" and they may have failed to adequately consider the constraints of the preexisting social structure and its tenacity in maintaining the status quo.

MICROINTERACTIONAL APPROACH

The microinteractional perspective is not so much a coherent school of thought as an extension of interactionism focused mainly on the individual and self. Certainly, the influence of the early work by Ralph Turner resides within this approach, but if we were forced to identify one major progenitor for this approach, it would be Erving Goffman. In his first major work, *Presentation of Self in Everyday Life*, Goffman (1959) elaborated the "dramaturgical" metaphor as central to his approach. This metaphor returns to the notion of role as it is found in stage productions. In contrast to the type of influence Goffman's work has exerted on structuralists, a different dimension of Goffman's work has affected the microinteractionists. Microinteractionists emphasize the fluidity and contingency of roles. Actors play roles with scripts and props; there is a backstage reality and an onstage reality. Roles are contingent on the interactions with other actors and thus are organized by systems of rules, such as rules about talk and rules of relevance. The self is relatively fluid and defined by the interactional context and the way in which the person frames or schematically understands the context and the rules. Microinteractionists view Goffman's work as focused exclusively on microinteraction and make no attempt to extend their explanations to a macroscopic level.

Although Goffman did not directly apply his work to the family, his influence is nonetheless present among family scholars studying family microprocesses, for example, LaRossa and LaRossa (1981), in their study on the transition to parenthood and the ways in which "parents" formulate "accounts" of their parenting contributions. New fathers were found to have a greater number of socially available accounts to justify noninvolvement in child care duties than mothers had. LaRossa and LaRossa's work relies heavily on an analytic strategy centered on the way people frame their behavior. This strategy is closely aligned to the microinteractional approach with an emphasis on roles being contingent on other interactions and the context and the frame that the actor is using.

PHENOMENOLOGY OF THE FAMILY

Of the many "postpositivist" schools, phenomenology has received the greatest attention and application in the work of family scholars. Although phenomenology originated in Europe, it has found a North American home within the broad framework of symbolic interaction. The term *phenomenology,* which means the "study of phenomenon," had circulated in philosophy for centuries (e.g., Kant, Hegel) before the French philosopher Edmond Husserl (1859-1938) applied the name to an entire philosophy. Husserl's work was applied to the social sciences by his student Alfred Schutz, who along with the ideas immigrated to the United States in 1939. Schutz's ideas and the more general paradigm of phenomenology landed on fertile ground among the microinteractionists and symbolic interactionists of North America. As Turner (1991) notes, however, "Husserl's ideas, then, have been selectively borrowed and used in ways that he would not condone to develop modern phenomenology and various forms of interactionist thought" (p. 383). This statement is certainly true of the way in which phenomenology has been developed and applied to the study of the family. Even the most accurate applications of Husserl's project, such as by McLain and Weigert (1979), also include other diverse sources of influences, such as the psychoanalytic theory of R. D. Laing and the work of ethnomethodologists such as Garfinkel. It seems doubtful that this work can be conceived of as part of Husserl's original project to discover the underlying essences of consciousness by a radical stripping away of associations (phenomenological reduction) that are unnecessary to the way something appears in our consciousness.

Rather than pursue Husserl's philosophical phenomenology with its technique of phenomenological reduction, most North Americans and many Europeans (e.g., Schutz, Habermas) have pursued a sociological phenomenology focused on the *taken-for-granted everyday lifeworld* and the ways in which these taken-for-granted meanings are maintained.

The major thrust in sociological phenomenology of the family is to identify the assumptions and *typifications* that enter into the construction of the everyday life of families (McLain & Weigert, 1979). For example, phenomenologists insist that families are different from the general taken-for-granted everyday world even though they are part of it. Families share in the "public" dimension of the common everyday world, but they also generate their own "private" understandings. The larger everyday public world acknowledges the family as a relatively private sphere in which many things happen (sexual intercourse, wife assault, intense emotions) that do not routinely occur outside of the family. The private understandings constructed by family members are based on their shared history, perspective, and interpretation of events. Dating and marriage are viewed as a process by which separate individuals "fuse" into a common living arrangement and worldview. On the other hand, children gradually separate from their parents' world (fission) and eventually construct their own families (Berger & Kellner, 1964). The focus in phenomenology of the family is to find out how, at any point in history, the "public" typifies families and how, for any family, family members typify and understand their family activities.

Each individual's report of subjective experience must necessarily contain *intersubjective* components—components that are shared with and communicable to others. These intersubjective meanings are the foundation of the social world. It is these intersubjective components that are the "data" for most social analyses by ethnomethodologists and phenomenologists.

Intersubjective meanings are shared in a set of actors, whether it be a subpopulation such as convicts, an ethnic group, or the more general society. These meanings compose the commonly held and understood meanings of our everyday life, or lifeworld (e.g., McLain & Weigert, 1979; Schutz, 1967). Sectors of these commonly held meanings in our common lifeworld represent frames of reference, or *provinces of meaning*, in which we operate in a more restricted sense.

Within each frame of reference, or province of meaning, such as art, science, and family, there are more restricted shared assumptions and meaning constructions that guide and form our experience. For example, the family domain contains a sense of shared history and future and a sense of "biography." When we marry, we enter a process of "biographical fusion" in which we not only share experiences but increasingly share a common way of typifying and explaining those experiences (Berger & Kellner, 1964).

The way actors explain or *typify* (e.g., Schutz, 1967) their experience, both in the lifeworld and in the more restricted frames of reference, is the subject matter for the social analysis of meaning. These typifications allow us to understand (*verstehen*) the way meanings are constructed and explained to others in the shared lifeworld.

The principal method of contextual understanding is not positivistic measurement but *hermeneutics*. Technically, hermeneutics refers to the interpretation of textual materials. The technique is currently applied to the contextualized actor's language reports and activities. But hermeneutics is not just a technique of analysis. In addition, it is a way the researcher can, to some degree, experience what the actor experiences:

> *Hermeneutics* is both a form of experience and grammatical analysis at the same time. . . . The quasi-inductive course of the hermeneutic sciences is based on the specific capacity of ordinary language, which makes it possible for the function of general categories to be communicated indirectly in a concrete life context. On this foundation the language of the hermeneutic interpreter adapts itself in the course of interpretation to the life experience concentrated around individual meaning. (Habermas, 1970, pp. 162-163)

Thus, hermeneutics offers an openness, sensitivity, and adaptability to the meanings in ordinary language and context of the actor as opposed to the rigidity of a priori techniques such as used in positivism.

Because the focus is clearly on the ways in which actors typify and construct meanings for their family activities, quantitative, statistical data are viewed as largely useless. Quantitative approaches involve use of previously established categories and counting of frequencies within ranges of those categories (strongly agree, agree somewhat, etc.). The result is only mildly interesting to the phenomenologists, to the degree that those categories are indeed the constructs or typifications used by actors. For the "public" everyday world, it is the role of the sociological phenomenologists to discover the typifications used by actors so that they may then be investigated by sociologists. In the more "private" realm of the family, other more open and sensitive approaches must be used to discover the typifications and understandings employed by the family members.

In the past 20 years, it appears that phenomenology of the family has increasingly merged with the microinteractionist approach to the family (e.g., Gubrium & Holstein, 1993). Sociological phenomenologists, ethnomethodologists, and interactionists view theory not as a deductive tool but as an open and sensitizing set of concepts that initially guide the researcher but are constantly altered as interactional research proceeds.

Empirical Applications

We examine two areas of study in which symbolic interactionists have contributed to an explanation. The first area entails research on the proposition we earlier derived that "The greater the diversification of roles, the greater the role strain." We examine this proposition as it applies to working mothers' role strain. The second area of application is the study of aggression in dating.

ROLE STRAIN AND WORKING MOTHERS

As a research question, our derived proposition is of some interest. Indeed, it provides one of the two major perspectives on the role strain experienced by working mothers. In the study of working mothers, two relatively simple minitheories have been developed. One is called *enhancement theory* (Marks, 1977). Enhancement theory is based on the assumption that multiple roles lead to an enhancement of role performance in any given role and to lower role strain. The logic behind this claim is that multiple roles allow the person to gain more skills, experience, and coping strategies. These greater skills can be transferred by a person from one role to another so that the ability to competently perform any role is enhanced. As people gain increased competency in their roles, role strain is decreased. The minitheory that fits with the derivation from symbolic interaction—that role diversification is positively related to role strain—is called *role overload*. This theory is based on the assumption that the more roles one has, the greater the strain. Clearly our deduction fits better with the role overload perspective.

Research on role strain among working mothers provides a less-than-clear resolution between the competing perspectives of enhancement and role overload. The dominant finding seems to be that whether a mother is working or not is not strongly related to her report of her feelings of well-being (Menaghan & Parcel, 1990). This research has not resolved our deduction so much as shown us that there are more variables relevant to the question than suggested in our initial derivation. Some of the most salient of these are whether the mother desires to enter the labor force or not, whether her husband supports her work and family intentions, and the amount of spousal support in household and family tasks. These variables are called *moderating* because they change the effect of maternal employment on role strain.

In addition to learning that more variables than simply the number of roles are necessary to explain role strain, researchers have created some valuable theoretical insights to add to our theory. Voydanoff (1987) has proposed that a more processual and dynamic approach is useful for examining the relationship between employment and mother roles. She argues that there are various paths by which families may articulate the relationship between work and family roles and that these change over time. For example, the demands of small children may be so great as to create role strain with most types of employment. As the children become more self-sufficient, maternal employment may have a salutary effect. Thus, Voydanoff argues that the time dimension should be incorporated. Menaghan (1989) correctly cautions us that not all roles are equally demanding and that motherhood is especially demanding. Role diversification is affected by the differing strengths and extent of role demands. Other researchers caution us that both minitheories may apply. Tiedje et al. (1990) propose that every set of roles probably has some areas of enhancement and some areas of strain and overload. This dynamic interchange between empirical research and symbolic interaction theory leads us to some wariness regarding our derivation, yet we are far from obtaining a definitive resolution to its truth or falsity at this time. This area of application provides a clear and important example of how theory guides research and research clarifies and extends theory. This interchange between theory and empirical research provides us with an illustration of the very heart of the process of rational-empirical social science.

DATING AGGRESSION

The study of aggression in dating is one that is particularly salient for university and college students. It is easy to assume that such acts occur in groups less privileged than university students, but, as recent research has shown, this would be an incorrect assumption. In addition, the notion of a hurtful act deliberately aimed at a dating partner, a person that is supposedly liked, seems almost a contradiction. How can we explain why such acts occur among university student couples?

Jan Stets (1992) attempts to explain dating aggression in university couples using concepts and propositions from symbolic interaction theory. Stets proposes that interactional rather than demographic variables can explain date aggression. She argues that taking the role of the other entails putting yourself in that person's place and feeling and understanding the other's emotions and actions. She states that role taking has been previously related to relationship satisfaction and to the use of less abrasive styles in interaction. It appears that as role taking increases by both partners in a relationship, the chances of conflict leading to aggressive acts would decline. Following this logic, Stets predicts that where at least one person is low in role taking, there is a higher probability for aggressive acts in dating relationships.

The findings in Stets's study offer considerable support for this theoretical perspective. First, interactional variables explain more of the variance in dating aggression than do demographic variables. This leads Stets to cautiously conclude that interaction is probably more important in explaining and producing date aggression than background variables such as age, race, gender, and socioeconomic status. Role taking is related not only to aggression in dating but also to the seriousness of the aggression. The less the role-taking ability of one partner, the greater the seriousness of aggression when it occurs. Although complete prediction of dating aggression would require additional variables, this research supports the contention that symbolic interaction propositions and concepts must be part of any such explanation.

Implications for Intervention

Although symbolic interaction theory has been used in many intervention contexts (e.g., Boss, 1993), one of the major uses of symbolic interaction theory currently is in the area of family life education. Family life education is a professional field in which our knowledge about families is used to better educate family members. It is the belief of family life educators that by establishing more realistic expectations and enhancing the skills needed in family life, families will become more stable and healthy (e.g., Arcus, Schvaneveldt, & Moss, 1993). This perspective fits well with the basic notions of symbolic interaction.

Most of the developed world has relatively high divorce and remarriage rates. For many, remarriage is not as simple as a first marriage. Although one can divorce one's spouse, parental and kin roles and responsibilities are not so easily sundered. Indeed, many remarriages incorporate parental roles from previous families in addition to any children born into the remarriage. These stepfamilies have obstacles and stresses unlike those encountered in first marriages. One focus of family life education has been to better prepare people for the strains encountered in remarriage.

Kaplan and Hennon (1992) developed the Personal Reflections Program to assist in preparing people for remarriage. The program is intended to assist those entering a second marriage in identifying unrealistic or potentially stress-producing expectations by means of self-reflection. The theoretical orientation of Kaplan and Hennon is symbolic interaction: "Grounded in symbolic interactionism, the program includes exercises that emphasize bringing into awareness and sharing self and partner's expectations for playing roles within the structure of a remarriage and/or stepfamily" (p. 127). Thus, concepts such as self, role stress, and role enactment are central in developing this intervention program.

Critiques and Discussion

Although symbolic interactionism enjoys great popularity among both sociologists and family scholars, it is not without its detractors and critics. Most interesting in this regard is that some of the more vicious attacks on parts of the theory have come from those whose work is included under the same theoretical umbrella. The critiques of structural interactionists offered by microinteractionists and vice versa contain some of the most devastating criticisms. We regard some of these as red herrings and begin this section by identifying those criticisms we believe are relatively baseless.

The branching of symbolic interactionism into the structural and interactional perspectives derived from profound differences, but with time and academic progress, we believe that at least some of the differences between these schools no longer represent valid criticisms. First, is social behavior mainly created by social structural norms or by interactional role making? To a large extent, the contemporary interactional theorists (e.g., Turner & Colomy, 1987) have moved to increasingly include macrostructural elements in their theories, and the macro theorists have witnessed the interactional emergence of relatively new social structures, such as cohabitation. We think it is now clear to most scholars that there are some norms and roles in every society that are clear and strictly sanctioned and as a result provide little room for role making. There are many other roles and norms that are less clearly defined and are sanctionless (e.g., grandparental roles, mother-in-law role), providing room for individuals to make roles. Thus, we see both perspectives as valid and necessarily complementary for a truly useful analysis of social behavior. The two major critiques associated with this debate have been that the structuralists put forth an oversocialized conception of humans and that the interactionists overestimate the actor's influence in creating roles and downplay structural constraints. In our view, for any given social role, there are degrees of truth to each of these criticisms based on the clarity and strength of the norms for the role.

A second area of disagreement between these two perspectives that we believe fails as a valid criticism of either is the argument about qualitative versus quantitative methods of data collection. Again, we see this dispute as being resolved by the earlier pragmatists, such as

William James (1975). Indeed, this argument is only unresolvable when it becomes a metaphysical argument about which method is "true," similar to asking how many angels fit on the head of a pin. Most researchers now agree that there are research questions that are best addressed by qualitative methods and those that are best addressed by quantitative methods. If we are interested in how people in specific situations feel, perceive, and experience, then qualitative methods are appropriate; if we ask questions about how many people behave in a certain way or what most people do, then quantitative methods are appropriate. If we want to know why young people find cohabitation appealing as an added step toward marriage, we would start with in-depth observation and talk. But if we want to know what proportion of young people who finish university then cohabit, we would use quantitative methods. Many times both methods can fruitfully be used in a multimethod approach to answer a research question. Thus, we see no critique of substance for either school of thought.

One of the principal criticisms of symbolic interactionism as a whole is that the concepts it offers are vague and poorly defined. Although this may be a problem in some cases, researchers such as Burr, Leigh, et al. (1979) are careful to define and elaborate their terms. Still others, such as Turner (e.g., 1970), have argued that some terms such as role should not be defined at the outset, but rather one should allow definitions to arise from how the terms are used. Certainly, such a strategy has a long history in mathematics, in which certain terms are considered "primitive" or are defined as tautologies, such as "equals" and "identity."

Symbolic interactionists in the family field no doubt sometimes offer vague and ill-defined concepts. But the root of this criticism probably lies in the fact that symbolic interactionism is so fecund. It has given birth to many variants. Critics would say that some of this richness is supplied by vagueness and ambiguity in the original concepts. There is some truth to that claim, but today's symbolic interactionists seem to be on the way to rectifying this shortcoming. Indeed, it may be that every theory starts out containing ambiguity and vagueness, and it is the task of future theorists to refine the efforts of the forebears.

Another major question about symbolic interaction theory is whether or not a symbol-specific theory can ever be nomothetic, or cross-

culturally relevant. The interpretation of behavior in symbolic interactionism relies in large part on the meaning of symbols and context
to the actors. Not only does the actor's interpretation depend on his
or her culture and situation, it is also subjective. If our explanations
are always subjective and context and symbol specific, can symbolic
interactionism ever amount to more than low-level interpretations
constrained by the culture and time in which they occur? Another way
of posing this question is to ask if symbolic interactionism can generate
statements such as the general laws associated with scientific theory.
This criticism is a fairly easy one for symbolic interactionists to answer,
because the propositions provided by scholars such as Turner (e.g.,
Turner & Colomy, 1987) and Burr (e.g., Burr, Leigh, et al., 1979) are
clearly not culture or period specific. In addition, social psychology
has a long history of scientific (and objective) study of the uniformities
in subjective interpretations, such as attitudes and attributions.

The problems surrounding the concepts of mind and self are more
serious. The concept of mind incorporates aspects of neurophysiology
that are not rooted in the organ of the brain. Indeed, even Mead
(1934) was aware of the reflex arc (muscle memory) and the problems
it provided his concept. The fact is that the mind, like our notions of
group and society, turns out not to be a "thing" or "organ" but a
complex system for which we have a name. Most social scientists have
not had to confront this conceptual problem, but when they do they
will find that it provides the same problems inherent in the question,
"Are families just a collection of individual members or are families
something more than just the individual members?" This is a very old
question in philosophy and social science. The early pragmatists,
especially William James, paid a great deal of attention to this question. We do not pretend that others or even ourselves have resolved
this question to the satisfaction of those who believe that a function
must be attached to an organ that performs that function.

The problems with the concept of mind carry over to the concept
of self as a construction of the reflexive activity of the mind. Just
because humans act (I) and are able to see themselves as actors (me)
does not necessarily imply the existence of self. Because the mind is
unidentified and self is a construct of mind, self raises the same
problems as our concept of mind. Particularly when you add in the

notion of developmental change and maturation, the notions of self and identity become difficult to pin down. At least one symbolic interactionist, Turner (1970), does not use the concept of self but prefers the concept of *self-conception,* for it appears more fluid and less of an immutable structure than does the concept of the self.

LaRossa and Reitzes (1993) mention the criticism that symbolic interaction theory has failed to deal effectively with emotions. The absence of emotions, feelings, and affect as major concepts has in some ways limited the theory's conceptual utility. Symbolic interactionists invariably discuss an actor's feeling as part of the definition of the situation but leave the details of conceptualizing the type and degree of the actor's emotional experience to psychologists and psychotherapists. LaRossa and Reitzes express some optimism that this oversight is being addressed, but we do not share their opinion. None of the major contemporary theorists, such as Turner (1970), seem inclined to tackle this question. Furthermore, it may be that dealing with the subject of emotion would move symbolic interactionism into a more subjectivist position.

Some critics of symbolic interactionism see the theory as too focused on the individual and "self as agent," ignoring social institutions. Although some of these criticisms can be dismissed as more feuding between the structuralists and interactionists, some of the critiques apply to both schools of thought. For example, the notion of norms is central to both the structuralists and interactionists, but neither examine the development and change of institutional norms. The structuralists take institutional norms for granted with the axiom that "Society preceded the individual." Interactionists see norms as emerging from interaction but fail to explain how it is that social institutions exist with relative permanence.

Lastly, we could accuse symbolic interactionists of losing their way. The early pragmatists and Mead (1934) took the interpretation of sign and gesture as central to their study of human behavior. Among today's symbolic interactionists, we seldom hear theoretical discussions about the nature of signs and gestures. Today, in discussions of interpretation and meaning it might be needed to incorporate *schematic processing* from psychology into the concept of *framing* as well as the work of linguists and contemporary semiotics.

Conclusion

There can be little doubt that symbolic interactionism has had an influence on how we study families. Both role theorists and interactionists have contributed greatly to our understanding of families. Thus far, however, although interactionists' claims about the symbolic nature of human interaction have sensitized researchers, they have not tackled many critical questions, such as how patterns evolve as lasting rather momentary and idiosyncratic. Within symbolic interactionism, role theory undoubtedly offers the most formal theoretical propositions and conceptual definitions; all four variants that we have discussed offer promise as we move away from dogmatic divisions toward a more systematic and thorough investigation of which and what type of family interactions lead to and sustain longer-term social patterns of behavior.

Food for Thought

1. Suppose a grandparent and grandchild have difficulty understanding each other. Why might this be the case? What could they do to increase a sense of shared meanings?
2. Do you think families have emotional climates or moods? Can you think of many individual attributes or variables (like health or happiness) that are also attributes of the family group?
3. Try to think of examples of "private" meanings that you share within your family but that do not represent family meanings in general. Do these meanings direct or explain behaviors within your family?
4. If you were invited to someone's home, what objects would you notice that might have special symbolic significance for the family that lives there? What inferences about the family might you be willing to make based on the kinds of objects you see and the way they are displayed?

Suggested Readings

Burr, W., Leigh, G., Day, R., & Constantine, J. (1979). Symbolic interaction and the family. In W. Burr, R. Hill, I. Nye, & I. Reiss (Eds.), *Contemporary theories about the family* (Vol. 2, pp. 42-111). New York: Free Press.

This is an excellent propositional approach to symbolic interactionism. The diagrams within this chapter should assist anyone in thinking about role variables.

LaRossa, R., & Reitzes, D. C. (1993). Symbolic interactionism and family studies. In P. Boss, W. Doherty, R. LaRossa, W. Schumm, & S. Steinmetz (Eds.), *Sourcebook of family theories and methods: A contextual approach* (pp. 135-163). New York: Plenum.

This more recent chapter on symbolic interactionism is especially good on the micro-interactional variants.

5

The Family Development Framework

Tim and Rebecca are expecting their first child. They have just attended their first prenatal class and are driving home in their car discussing what they learned. At one point in the class, the instructor divided the class by gender and asked the prospective fathers and mothers to write down on a piece of paper three things that they thought about on hearing that they were to become parents. Tim says to Rebecca, "You know, I was surprised that every one of the guys had thought of taking out life insurance or getting more life insurance!" He continued, "Some of those guys are barely shaving and a few must be around 50 years old. Yet they all said life insurance." Rebecca replied, "I guess a really important part of being a father is still being a 'provider.'" "Yeah," said Tim, "but what I was astounded by was that these guys are all different ages, races, and backgrounds, yet they all had similar ideas as to what becoming a father means."

Tim has discovered an important element in what family development scholars study as the "transition to parenthood." For years, scholars thought variables like "taking out life insurance" were predicted by

119

the age of a person. What Tim (and family development theorists) noticed is that it is not the age of the person that matters but where the person is in his or her family development. Young children are dependent and require lots of parental time. The loss of one spouse's income would represent a severe burden for most families. But the impact of this loss of income is dramatically different at each stage of family development. For families with infants, the loss might mean reliance on day care and less parental attention from the remaining parent. For families with adolescent children, it might mean restrictions in teenage recreation and the necessity for after-school work to help the family. In other words, it is the family stage that is important, not the chronological age of the family members.

Family development theory focuses on the systematic and patterned changes experienced by families as they move through stages of their family life course. Family development theory is not to be confused with theories about individual development, such as those offered by psychologists (e.g., Erikson, Freud, Piaget). Although family development theorists acknowledge the importance of individual development, the development of the family as a *group* of interacting individuals and organized by social norms is their major focus.

Of all the theories you will find in this book, family development theory is the only one that developed out of a restricted interest in families. All the other theories have broader applications to other social groups and social structures. For example, both exchange theory and conflict theory can be applied to competition between labor and management as well as to husbands and wives. Family development theory, on the other hand, has focused exclusively on the family.

As a theory, family development has several other unique dimensions that characterize its focus. Family development theory incorporates time and history as major components. Although other theories may include time in the measurement of change, they do not involve discussion of the theoretical nuances of the conceptualization and measurement of time. Family development theorists have discussed time as measured by clocks, social processes, and event histories (Rodgers, 1973). A second unique dimension of family development theory is the focus on forms of family change. Family development deals with the changing content of social roles in the family as well as macroscopic changes in the membership structure of the family. Of all the current theories about the family, family development theory is unique in emphasizing the dimensions of time and change.

Intellectual Traditions

Family development theory has gone through three distinct phases of maturation. The first phase was characterized by the rise of the idea of the family life cycle. Researchers viewed families as having a life course, or what in biological studies was commonly referred to as a *life cycle.* Similar to a biological organism, the family group went through analogous processes of birth, growth, maintenance, shrinkage, and eventually death. We do not know the exact origins of the family life cycle concept, but we do know it has a long history. Mattessich and Hill (1987) supply a genealogy that traces the rudiments of the notion back to 1777. The idea of the family life cycle appears in the work of rural sociologists such as Lively (1932) and Loomis (1934) during the Great Depression. Through the work of Paul Glick (1947), the notion of family life cycle entered social demography as a descriptive tool. This first phase was the descriptive phase of the theory's maturation.

The second phase of the theory's maturation was characterized by the conscious formulation of the contemporary theory. This phase began after World War II with work on family stress by Hill (1949) and a textbook by Duvall (1957). But it was the chapter by Hill and Rodgers (1964) that truly provided the first systematic statement of the approach. In their statement, the family is composed of social roles and relationships that change with each stage of the family. Hill and Rodgers also identified three levels of analysis for the study of families over time: the individual-psychological, the interactional-associational, and the societal-institutional. The approach first systematized by Hill and Rodgers, received further expansion in Rodgers's (1973) book. He suggested abandoning the family life cycle concept in favor of a concept oriented toward the life course, the *family career.* Aldous (1978) further developed the notion of the family career. She conceptualized the family career as containing subcareers such as the sibling career, the marital career, and the parental career, all influenced by careers external to the family such as the educational and occupational careers. This middle phase could be characterized as the phase in which the theory was first systematized and the family career concept emerged as preferable to the family life cycle concept.

The third and most recent phase of theoretical development may be viewed as a reaction to new techniques for data analysis and some strong critiques of the theory. In 1979, several scholars launched critiques of the family life cycle concept (Nock, 1979; Schram, 1979; Spanier, Sauer, & Larzelere, 1979). Note that Rodgers (1973) and Aldous (1978) had already abandoned the family life cycle concept in favor of the life course oriented family career concept. Klein and Aldous (1979) represent the lone response to these critiques. In 1980, Holman and Burr relegated family development theory to the status of one of the "minor" theoretical approaches in the study of the family. Holman and Burr (1980) argued that what little theoretical formulation had been achieved in family development theory in the 1960s had been largely subsumed under the aegis of life course analysis in the 1970s (p. 733).

Despite the epitaph by Holman and Burr (1980) and the critiques by Nock (1979), Schram (1979), and Spanier et al. (1979), Mattessich and Hill maintained the notion of family development unfolding through invariant and universal stages linked to some inherent family dynamic. Although the conception of development proposed by Mattessich and Hill (1987) has met with great criticism (Bengtson & Allen, 1993; Rodgers & White, 1993; White, 1991), it nonetheless provided some basis for Aldous (1990) to argue that family development theory and life course analysis could not be considered to be the same. Aldous (1990) analyzes differences between the life course and family development approaches and argues that the major difference is that the life course approach is focused on the individual whereas the family development approach is focused on the family level of analysis. According to Aldous, neither approach deserves to be called a scientific theory.

Contrary to Aldous (1990), White (1991) argues that family development is a scientific theory containing definitions and general propositions implying a formal model of the process of development. He couples methodological distinctions in *event history analysis* (Allison, 1984; Tuma & Hannan, 1984) with an expanded conception of levels of analysis in his formalization of the theory. Most recently, Rodgers and White (1993) argue that the "old" perspective of families moving through deterministic, invariant stages is moribund. They revise and simplify the concepts in the theory and produce formal propositions. In this latest phase of theoretical development, family development scholars have attempted to revise and reconstruct the theory so as to answer the relevant comments of critics as well as incorporate new methodological techniques. This latest phase can be characterized as the "formal" phase of the theory's maturation.

In summary, the major focus of family development theory is on the patterned changes in family life over time. The theory has gone through three phases of maturation: a descriptive phase in which stages of the family life cycle were used to study families; a systematizing phase in which the theory received its first conscious statement as a theory; and an ongoing, formal phase in which, as a response to criticisms and new methodologies, the theory has been formally stated as propositions and formal models. Although each phase may have slightly different emphases, the overall thrust of family development theory has remained uniform and unchanged in seeking to explain family change over time.

Focus and Scope Assumptions

Many theories require basic assumptions about the nature of individual motivation (exchange theory) or about human nature (conflict theory). Family development theory relies on basic assumptions about the family. These assumptions are not restricted to the family group but extend to the broader fabric of the social institution of the family. Here, we enumerate the basic assumptions that provide the foundation for family development theory. These are the assumptions of multiple levels of analysis, the definition of the family group as a semipermeable unit, and a multidimensional view of time.

Developmental processes are inevitable and important in understanding families. This assumes that individual family members, the interaction between family members, the structure of the family, and the norms composing expectations about family roles all change with the passage of time. Individuals age, relationships have duration, family stages are traversed, and family structure changes. The changing roles and expectations for different stages of family are viewed as essential to an understanding of the family.

Family developmentalists, from the first systematic statements (Aldous, 1978; Hill & Rodgers, 1964; Rodgers, 1973), have suggested that *families be analyzed on different levels.* This is not just a simple micro-macrosocial distinction that most theorists make but a realization that family as a phenomenon resides at different levels of analysis in different forms. If we leave out a level of analysis and form of family, then the resulting picture we develop is flawed. Most theorists start with the family as a *social group.* Below the family as a social group are subgroup *relationships* such as the husband-wife relationship and the sibling relationship. And below the relationship level is the *individual* family member who experiences his or her family and the relationships in it. If we move up a level from the family group, we find relatively homogeneous *aggregate clusters* of families and social norms that are structured by social class and ethnicity. And moving up levels once again, we find that each social system maintains general norms and conventions about the family. Some of these norms are codified as legal expectations such as those found in child neglect or child abuse laws, but more often the norms are less formal. These general social norms represent the level of analysis of the family as a *social institution.* The institutional level of analysis is generally the one we refer to when we talk about "the family."

A third major assumption that family development scholars make is that *the family group is affected by all the levels of analysis,* including the social norms of the larger society and the social norms of clusters such as social class. For example, the norms about techniques of child discipline are related to social class as well as to the codifications of the larger social system. The family group is also affected by its component lower levels, such as the nature of a sibling relationship or an individual disability.

The family is a semiclosed or semipermeable group. The intermingling and integration of effects on the family group has led family development scholars to adopt a definition of the family as semiclosed and semipermeable. Although the family group sets up distinctive boundaries usually demarcated spatially by household or domicile, these boundaries are permeated by the effects of the larger society. This semipermeable nature of the family group is directly cited in some definitions of the family (Aldous, 1978; Rodgers, 1973) and is referred to indirectly by others who incorporate social norms both external and internal to the family group. For example, Rodgers and White (1993) and White (1991) define the family as a social group that contains at least one parent-child (intergenerational) relationship and is organized and governed by social norms.

All family developmental theorists assume that *time is multidimensional*. To understand this assumption, we need to examine our notion of time. Time is a monotonic process—once a moment in time is gone, it doesn't come back. Time is measured by the *periodicity* of some recurring event. In ancient Greece, time was measured by a sundial. During the Renaissance, time was measured by the dripping water in water clocks. During the industrial revolution, time was measured by gears turning in mechanical clocks. Today, time is measured by the entropy, or decay of an element, in an "atomic" clock. All of these ways of measuring time are attempts to make sure that there is an equal interval of time between each event on the clock. For example, the gears in your wristwatch are the same distance apart. The problem is that there is absolutely no guarantee that time is so orderly. Furthermore, because all our methods of measuring time rely on recurring discrete events, there is no guarantee that time is continuous. Even the assumption that time moves at a uniform rate, such as measured by gears in your wristwatch, is counter to much of our experience. Most of you have experienced an hour spent in an enjoyable pursuit as flying by or an hour spent in a dull and boring pursuit as dragging on. In other words, your experience of time is perhaps not as regimented as your wristwatch would lead you to believe. Not only does your experience of time deny the orderliness of your wristwatch, but most of us use our family experiences as a separate way to divide up time. Thus, we might discuss with our family what we did in 1990 and 1991. More likely, we might abandon the calendar notion of time in favor of listing events, such as "when we first married," "before your sister was born," or "just after your father died." Interestingly, these events lack periodicity for any one family (you only expect your sister to be born once), but these experiences are commonly understood "markers" on the family calendar because they happen to most families over time (family career).

This alternative conception of time is called *social process time* (Rodgers, 1973). Social, or family, process time is an important dimension of our conception of time for family scholars because social norms are tied more closely to this social process dimension of time than to calendar or wristwatch time. For instance, "when you get married" is tied to "finishing school" more closely than to any given calendar date, such as 1999. Other social and biological dimensions of time are age and period. Fortunately, because time is monotonic and only flows in one direction, all of the different ways of conceptualizing time can be organized into temporal maps of our life course and that of our family. A socially important stage can be identified by the events such as "after our father's death" but "before our sister got married." Because family members usually recall the calendar dates of such major events, we can trace the multiple timelines of calendar and family process time. For family development theory, the family process dimension of time is critical to understanding and explaining family change.

It is interesting to note that of all the family theories, family development theory makes few if any basic assumptions about the individual. Rather, family development theory is true to its focus on the family group. Individuals are viewed as subcomponents of the family group, which is not merely the aggregate of individual members. The family group is affected by institutional and aggregate clusters of norms that along with the characteristics of individual family members and their relationships determine the social organization of the family group.

Concepts

FAMILY CHANGE AND DEVELOPMENT

Early family developmentalists were not clear about the distinction between change and development. Indeed, some seem to have used the two terms interchangeably. But with the rise of child development theory in the 1940s and 1950s came a new concern among family developmentalists that development meant more than all of family change. Child developmentalists such as Piaget brought the notion of *ontogenetic* change to the forefront of their discipline and likewise raised the issue for family development scholars. Although the exact nature of family development has been a long-standing issue, recently the notion of developmental change has received significant scholarly attention (e.g., Baltes & Nesselroade, 1984; Dannefer, 1984; Dannefer & Perlmutter, 1991; Featherman & Lerner, 1985; Mattessich & Hill, 1987). The outcome of all this attention is that two distinct versions of development have emerged. Child development focuses on *ontogenetic development,* which is founded on the genetic capacity of the species to progressively learn language and thought. A second, sociological meaning of development is focused on the traversing of normatively expected family events. Although there have been some attempts to unite these two versions, such as the definition of development proposed by Mattessich and Hill (1987), most developmental scholars shy away from the teleological and moralistic overtones inherent in an ontogenetic view of family development.

Both White (1991) and Rodgers and White (1993) argue for the sociological view of development. They incorporate the proposal by Featherman (1985) that development is linked to the stage of the family and the duration of time the family has been in a certain family stage. White (1991) defines development similarly, arguing that family transitions are dependent on the stage a family is in and the duration of time they have been in that stage. According to the sociological approach, family development is a process following age- and stage-graded social norms. Unlike the rigid stage sequencing of Piaget, family developmental stages may be sequenced in a variety of ways, however, and family developmental change is only one type of many possible changes a family may experience. Of course, family development theorists believe that developmental change is an important form of family change.

POSITIONS, NORMS, AND ROLES

We cannot forget that our families are embedded in kinship structures. Indeed, it is the positions in the kinship structure that supply our relatives. A *position* in the kinship structure is defined by gender, marriage or blood relations, and generational relations. The basic positions within the family are husband, wife, father, mother, son, daughter, brother, and sister. From these basic positions other society-specific positions can be defined. For example, the North American term *uncle* usually refers to brothers of either your father or mother (fabr, mobr).

Norms are social rules that govern group and individual behavior. For example, the incest taboo is a strong and pervasive social rule forbidding mating between certain family members. Norms may be rules about the way something is to be accomplished at various stages of the family and at various ages for an individual. Thus, many norms are age and stage graded. For instance, you do not apply the same rules to a toddler that you do to a teenager.

A family *role* is defined as *all* the norms attached to one of the kinship positions. In most societies, the role of mother, for example, entails the norm of nurturance of the young. Because positions are defined structurally, however, the content of a role (the norms) may change from society to society or ethnic subculture to ethnic subculture. And like the norms that compose them, social roles may be age and stage graded. For example, the nurturant role for a mother with an infant is quite different than that for a mother with adolescent children.

A *family stage* is an interval of time in which the structure and interactions of role relationships in the family are noticeably and qualitatively distinct from other periods of time. A stage at the group level represents a pattern of role interaction between family members distinct from those stages that precede and follow it. The stage is usually inferred from events that indicate a change in the membership of the family or the way in which members are spatially and interactionally organized. For example, launching a child into adulthood does not mean the end of the parental role but a change based on the spatial and interactional organization of members.

TRANSITIONS

Transitions are shifts from one family stage to another. A family's career is composed of many such transitions between stages. Magrabi and Marshall (1965) were the first to conceptualize family transitions as a branching process; others such as Klein, Borne, Jache, and Sederberg (1979) have further developed the notion. The concept that has emerged is that family transitions viewed over time consist of paths taken and not taken. For example, at any one time a married couple may stay married or get divorced, one of the spouses may die, or they might have a child. Each of the possible events would move the family to a new series of possible alternative transitions. The process charted over time would look like a tree with many branches; the path that any one family takes would be one series of branches.

Transitions from one family stage to another are indicated by the events between stages. Family stages and events are experienced as "on time" or "off time" with the expected timing for these events. For instance, giving birth to a child when your postadolescent children are leaving home would be "off time." In general, the age- and stage-graded social norms supply timing expectations. Not only might events be "off time," but sequences of events and stages might be "disorganized." For example, the sequence of getting married before the birth of your first child is normatively organized, whereas a premarital birth would be departure from the normative expectations for sequencing marriage and births.

DEVELOPMENTAL TASKS

Early developmentalists thought transitions were linked to *developmental tasks* that arise in the life course of individuals and families. The successful achievement of these tasks was thought to lead to happiness and success with later tasks (Havighurst, 1948). The notion of developmental tasks was an attempt to integrate age- and stage-graded social norms with the ontogenetic maturation of individual family members. However well intentioned the concept, it has fallen into a myriad of difficulties. The notion of developmental tasks has been criticized as making nonscientific value judgments about what constitutes "success." In addition, the notion of developmental tasks is tied to a preformational, ontogenetic view of child development that has largely been rejected by those studying the social group of the family. As a result, researchers early on redefined the concept as a set of norms (role expectations) arising at a particular stage of the family career (Hill & Rodgers, 1964; Rodgers, 1973, p. 51). Rodgers and White (1993) believe the concept is redundant with the age- and stage-graded notions of norm and role and no longer include it among the core concepts of the theory.

FAMILY CAREER

The concept of the *family career* replaced the earlier concept of family life cycle. The notion that family life somehow "cycled" was not the meaning developmentalists meant to convey. Rather, development as a process is viewed more like a career, in which current stages are affected by the past, but there is no teleological end to the process that would bring it full circle. A family career is composed of all the events and periods of time (stages) between events traversed by a family. For families in any one society, such as North America, we find that stage-graded norms are indicated by the sequence of events followed by most families. For example, the great majority of people get married before having a child, and for most people a premarital birth is considered out of the normative sequence. This is not to say that there are not variations and deviations.

VARIATIONS AND DEVIATIONS

Variation in family careers indicates the strength of the norms within any given birth cohort and historical period. The difference between variation and deviation at the aggregate level of analysis is that variation about a measure of central tendency (mode or median) is random, whereas deviation is nonrandom and systematic. *Deviation* by large numbers of families from a normative career sequence is viewed as a source of social change. Clearly, people only deviate from the normative path when they perceive that there are rewards for doing so. Once an individual or family is out of sequence and off time, however, it is difficult to resume a normative course. Sometimes, such situations arise from individual mistakes; these would be random. Other times, large numbers of families seem to deviate from social norms, such as at present with premarital cohabitation. If such deviation becomes systematic (it is one as opposed to many forms of alternatives to marriage) and a larger and larger numbers of people follow this "new" path, at some point the social norms shift so that it becomes deviant *not* to live together before marriage as part of mate selection. The reason such deviance comes about is to align family timing and sequencing norms with those of other institutions such as education and work. In the past two decades, there has been increased pressure from the labor force for higher skills and more education. This pressure to get more education coupled with the sequencing norm of "finish your education before you get married" has resulted in the delay of marriage for younger people. But with the delay in marriage another problem arises. A dominant norm in mate selection is that females seek mates who are the same age or older. Because older males have a higher probability of marriage, there are fewer of them available for younger females. This is called the "marriage squeeze." As both genders delay marriage to finish school and start careers, cohabitation represents a way to enter an intimate relationship with a potential spouse but without the constricting roles of husband and wife and without pressure to have children. Indeed, the norms would suggest that before people would ask, "When are you two going to have a child?" they would ask, "When are you two going to get married?" Thus, social change comes about because families seek to align their sequencing of stages with the sequencing and timing norms of nonfamily institutions (such as education and occupation). These cross-institutional norms, such as "finish your education before you get married," create the need for systematic deviation in family careers and ultimately social change.

Propositions

Rodgers and White (1993) caution that propositions that might be reasonable for one level of analysis might not be as accurate for other levels of analysis. For example, we can reasonably talk about an individual's "motivation," but it might be unreasonable to assume that groups or social institutions are "motivated" in the same way as individuals. It is usually more appropriate to move propositions from higher to lower levels of analysis than the reverse. Thus, we focus our examples of propositions from family development theory on the more general institutional and group levels of analysis.

Family development is a group process regulated by societal timing and sequencing norms.

This proposition asserts that family development is a process defined by social norms. Because norms are different from culture to culture, the process of family development may be different from culture to culture. We have used the North American norm regarding premarital births as an illustration of a sequencing norm. In many cultures, such as the Polynesian culture, a premarital birth was expected before marriage and considered a necessary step in mate selection. How could a prospective husband discern the reproductive capacity of a woman if she had not demonstrated her fertility? This proposition also asserts that because family development is regulated by social norms, the central focus for understanding this process must be on the institution of the family. The institution of the family is composed of all those norms that regulate and define family life within a culture or social system. The assertion that the process is governed by social norms involves the assumption that family development is not a form of biological preformationism or ontogenesis. Rather, social systems are viewed as defining the norms of family development, and like all social norms, those regulating the process of family development change over historical time.

Although timing and sequencing norms are interrelated, research suggests that the sequence (order) of stages or events is more strongly regulated than the timing of stages or events (Hogan, 1978; Modell, 1980; White, 1987). People appear more likely to attempt to maintain the order of events, such as "first comes love, then comes marriage, then comes Suzy with the baby carriage," than they are to maintain a set number of years between these events. What this suggests is that the family career as a sequence of stages or events is probably more important in explaining family behavior than is the timing. Indeed, military men returning after World War II were conscious of needing to compress the timing of family events but did not change the order of events or subtract events. Those pursuing advanced education, such as medical doctors, may also delay family events and then compress the time between events without changing the order.

If a family or individual is "out of sequence" with the normative ordering of family events, the probability of later life disruptions is increased.

A society must be organized. A significant part of social organization is the age and stage grading of various institutions. An often-overlooked dimension of the social fabric is that timing and sequencing norms, such as those regarding education, must be synchronized with norms in other institutions, such as work and family. If a person or family gets out of sequence within one institution, the result is that they are more likely to be thrown out of synchrony with other institutions. Most of the research in this area has suggested negative consequences for families and individuals, such as higher rates for marital disruption. There is, however, the argument that when the norms are changing, successive cohorts pursuing what is originally deviant behavior and suffering the consequences of being out of sequence or off time gradually come to represent the new dominant norm (normative succession). This new dominant norm gradually synchronizes with other institutions as they realign. A useful example of this process of normative succession is premarital cohabitation. During the 1980s, researchers invariably demonstrated negative effects for premarital cohabitation on later marital stability (e.g., Teachman & Polonko, 1990). Gwartney-Gibbs (1986) suggested that premarital cohabitation was on its way to becoming a normative stage in family development. By 1992, evidence surfaced that the most recent cohorts of cohabitants seemed to have less probability for marital disruption than their non-cohabiting counterparts (Schoen, 1992).

Within the family group, family members create internal family norms.

Within the family group, each family creates social rules such as bedtimes, rules about how much TV can be watched and rules about staying out late. The institution of the family provides the broad parameters within which families can interactively create their internal rules. For example, in North America, there are few parents that would suggest to their children that they have multiple premarital births. The internal family norms or rules are further circumscribed by the institution of the family in that internal rules must not overly threaten institutional functions of the family. For example, parents who do not want to educate their children would probably find their children declared wards of the state. Although many of the internal family norms are not developmental in the sense of timing and sequencing norms, some clearly are. For instance, when a parent says to a child, "You can go in the canoe when you can swim," the parent is stating a sequencing rule. Many such norms in the family rest on the stage of individual development of the members, such as, "When you can accomplish this" or "Your grandmother can't do that for herself anymore." Thus, some of these internal norms are developmental, but some are simply nondevelopmental rules (e.g., "Always tell your parents the truth").

Interactions within the family group are regulated by the social norms constructing family roles.

Family interactions are predictable and uniform across families due to the institutional norms and expectations regarding family roles. As we indicated previously, these norms provide the parameters within which family members can create rules unique to their family. The parameters for roles such as mother and father of young children are especially restrictive because the society at large has a tremendous stake in the reproduction and socialization of new members of society. Indeed, when mothers and fathers fail to meet these roles, emissaries of the state step in to supervise or seize the children from the parents. For example, mothers are expected to be nurturant of the young. Failure in this regard can show up in behavior disorders in the children and more seriously in an infant's failure to thrive. Less codified norms exist about parental disciplinary techniques such as spanking and control of the children. Even the method of infant feeding—breast or bottle—has become the focus for normative pressures and informal sanctions from health care professionals and resource groups. In addition to the regulation of parent-child relationships, there are general social expectations regarding other family relationships, such as the sibling relationship. Siblings are expected to care for and watch out for each other. The norms constructing this sibling relationship extend into old age, when siblings rely on each other for support.

Transitions from one family stage to another are predicted by the current stage and the duration of time spent in that stage.

Although families move through their life course making what seem to be individual decisions about when to get married, have a child, and so on, there is a high degree of predictability for families in general. This is not surprising as this process is largely formed by social timing and sequencing norms. Couples who are recently married have a high probability of having a child, whereas the longer the couple stays in the childless stage, the less the probability that they will have a child. These patterns of family development vary from culture to culture. Even within one culture there may be variation. The variation within one culture demonstrates the strength of family timing and sequencing norms. For example, in at least one totalitarian state, the government has attempted rather successfully to control family size. The norms are very formal and enforced with strict sanctions. In North America, our norms are less formal, and people respond more strongly to the need to be articulated with the timing and sequencing of educational and work careers.

Individuals and families systematically deviate from institutional family norms to adjust their behavior to other institutional norms, such as work and education.

The timing and sequencing norms for family development do not stand in isolation from other major social institutions. Indeed, in the past, religious institutions reinforced and strongly sanctioned the norms about family life, and religious organizations organized their own normative content to be in conjunction with family norms. Today, the family is less buttressed by institutional religious norms but strongly forced to articulate family sequencing with sequencing in work and education. Indeed, the conjunction of timing and sequencing norms from various institutions constructs the normative life course for individuals and families. For example, an educational norm such as "Get more education" in conjunction with a cross-institutional sequencing norm such as "Finish your education before you get married" and "Get a job before you get married," all conjoin to form the normative life sequence of "Finish your education, then get a job, then get married." Although there are no formal sanctions for not following this sequence, there are informal ones. The informal sanctions are subtle, as they derive from the fact that all social institutions are age and stage graded. In work, as in family, there are stages of development, such as "formative" and "consolidation" stages of career development (e.g., Voydanoff, 1987). If an individual or family becomes off time or out of sequence within one institution, its members find it increasingly difficult to meet the timing and sequencing expectations in other institutions. For example, a premarital birth does not just put one out of sequence in family life but also has distinct ramifications for meeting the timing and sequencing norms in education and work. The resulting modifications in the family, work, and educational careers make for difficulties and hardships associated with being out of synchrony with the social fabric of society and its reward systems. Of course, deviance is necessary as part of social change and adaptation to a changing society. As with premarital cohabitation, however, those in the vanguard of such adaptive deviance suffer to bring in the new normative order.

Variations

There are three major variants of family development theory, each on a specific level of analysis. The structural perspective represented in the work of White (1991) and Rodgers and White (1993) is focused on the institutional and cross-institutional processes affecting family development. The interactional perspective represented in the work of Aldous (1978, 1990) is focused on the relationships within the group and the construction of unique family norms and roles. The third variant of family development theory is life course analysis, represented in the work of Elder (1974) and Bengtson and Allen (1993). The life course approach is focused on the individual rather than the family group. It is especially concerned with the life course from the individual's perspective rather than an institutional family perspective. Thus, the three variants represent the institutional and group levels of analysis (structural), the group and relationship levels of analysis (interactional), and the individual and institutional levels of analysis (life course).

STRUCTURAL PERSPECTIVE

In the structural approach, commonly shared social timing and sequencing norms in a social system are emphasized. Although the structuralists admit that norms internal to the family can emerge through the interaction of family members, they emphasize the societal timing and sequencing norms that constrain any idiosyncratic emergent norms or roles. They argue that what family social scientists should be concerned with are the aggregate patterns and variations of family development within societies. Furthermore, the structuralists argue that a focus on the aggregate patterns also provides a way of addressing social change within the institution of the family as well as other institutions. The principal concept structuralists use to explain social change is cross-institutional adaptation of the timing and sequencing norms of one institution with the norms of other institutions. In their view, the institution of the family is continually adapting to align and synchronize with other institutions. Deviance from the timing and sequencing norms of one institution (often to conform to the norms in another institution) is the mechanism by which social change occurs.

As you might expect, theorists following the structural perspective of family development are also concerned with stating theoretical propositions and definitions that are cross-culturally applicable. They argue that family development is social in nature and thus varies between societies. The aggregate patterns of family development from each society provide a window on the society-specific timing and sequencing norms for each society (e.g., Kumagai, 1984). The degree of random variation in each society indicates the relative strength of the norms; the degree of systematic deviance demonstrates the direction and intensity of normative social change in each social system.

The structural perspective is more formal in its approach to family development theory, as is evident in the propositional statement of the theory by Rodgers and White (1993) and the use of formal models by White (1991) to model the transitions from one family stage to another. The structural school provides a readily accessible theory for demographers and cross-cultural researchers in part because the formal and abstract nature of presentation is relatively free of the cultural contents of any one society. This great strength is also a weakness in that scholars as well as students of the family typically find more immediate relevance from theories constructed about and within their own culture.

INTERACTIONAL PERSPECTIVE

The interactional approach to family development theory is identified with symbolic interaction, especially the approach proposed by

Turner (1970). Essentially, those adopting the interactional perspective maintain that the norms constructing social roles in the family can in large part be created by the individual family members and their interactions. Contrary to the structuralists, interactionists maintain that emergent norms and roles are not just idiosyncrasies of one family within the constraints of the larger society's timing and sequencing norms. The interactionists argue that family members can construct social roles (role making) and thereby set the course for social change. For example, there are many ways in which a mother may "nurture" children. Some mothers may take their infants to work, other mothers may stay home, and still others may judiciously select a warm and nurturant caregiver. The interactionists argue that all of these "behaviors" fit within the broad framework of being a "nurturant mother," but there is sufficient scope for the individual to construct her own norms and rules about "mothering." Furthermore, the interactionists argue that such role making and norm making is how social change comes about. First, the individual family constructs its norms and roles to adapt to the social and economic situation. As larger numbers of people join in similar adaptations, the norms and roles become more common and acceptable until these norms eventually become the new norm.

In the interactional perspective, the internal dynamics of the family are emphasized. The consensus family members reach on norms and roles provides an understanding of family behavior and possible directions of normative change. The interactionists view family development as a process governed by the interactions of family members. Family developmental stage is defined similarly to the structuralists' definition, but the emphasis is somewhat different. The interactionists emphasize that each stage of family development represents a qualitatively distinct pattern of interaction between family members. Whereas the structuralists define stages mainly by the more cross-culturally relevant dimension of group membership, the interactionists use more qualitative assessments of interaction. For example, in North America, the age of the oldest child's entry into school has been used to demarcate a change in family interaction because the child is now away from home for extended periods of time and integrated into the community (e.g., Aldous, 1978; Rodgers, 1973). Structuralists would point out that incorporating such society-specific content in the theory makes it less cross-culturally applicable. On the other hand, interactionists would argue that the qualitative interaction patterns need to be studied in each society without imposing a predetermined definition of stage on these diverse families.

The interactionists' perspective on family development remains a vital part of family development theory. Not only does the interactionist perspective support research more sensitive to the definitions and processes used within each family (Klein et al., 1979), but the interactionists have throughout the history of family development theory provided the most popular North American formulations of the theory (e.g., Aldous, 1978; Duvall, 1957).

INDIVIDUAL LIFE COURSE ANALYSIS

The past three decades have witnessed the emergence of a type of analysis of individual event histories referred to as *life course analysis*. Although this form of analysis has largely been developed independent of family development theory, much of life course analysis is focused on family events. Family development theory has both contributed to these formulations and received impetus from this approach to expand developmental theory by incorporating some of the methods used in life course analysis. Indeed, Mattessich and Hill (1987) criticize family development theorists for not incorporating the effects of the timing of nonfamily life events on family development. Rodgers and White (1993) and White (1991) expanded family development theory to incorporate these other institutional events (e.g., education and work) in the developmental paradigm as "cross-institutional" timing and sequencing norms. Bengtson and Allen (1993) argue that life course analysis is a theory in its own right. They endeavor to produce a set of propositions unique to life course analysis. It is our opinion that many of their propositions are long-standing ones in family development theory and thus life course analysis is a form of developmental analysis of individual cross-institutional event histories.

Life course analysis, like family development, incorporates the historical dimensions of change: period, age, and birth cohort. Besides the recognition that timing and sequencing norms are affected by and change with historical period, the age of the individual experiencing events, and the norms carried by the birth cohort, life course analysis appears to rely mainly on methodological innovations in studying the sequencing and timing of events (e.g., Allison, 1984). Similar historical dimensions and event history methods also show up in the work of family developmentalists as early as Glick (1947) and as recently as White (1991). White treats event sequences such as the event ordering of marriage, first job, and first child as independent variables predicting marital disruption. Although prior to Mattessich and Hill's (1987) call for developmental theorists to incorporate these cross-institutional events in developmental theory there was perhaps more reason to consider life course analysis as an independent school of thought, the current situation seems to evidence that this type of analysis is now within the scope of family developmental theory.

A contrary view is proposed by Aldous (1990). She argues that because family development theory is focused on the family group and life course analysis is focused on the individual, the two approaches are not the same. But more recent contributions, such as Rodgers and White (1993), suggest that because in both variants explanations rest on institutional and cross-institutional timing and sequencing norms, the variants are the same. What little difference there is can be attributed to the emphasis on individual units of analysis rather than the family group. As we have seen, that emphasis is a matter of the level of analysis selected by the researcher rather than a substantive theoretical difference.

The most recent example of the approach used in life course studies is provided in the collection of chapters, edited by Glen Elder, John Modell, and Ross Parke (1993), titled *Children in Time and Place*. These authors and their colleagues from the social sciences undertake an ambitious project to unify historical, psychological, and sociological approaches to the study of the life course. For example, using two longitudinal cohort studies, successive authors demonstrate age; age and cohort; and age, cohort, and period effects on such diverse topics as children's aptitudes and anorexia nervosa in females. In the end, the ontogenetic explanations of the life course seem difficult to incorporate into social explanations much as they had provided difficulties for the concept of developmental task discussed earlier. Much of life course analysis remains moored to the notions of age, cohort, and period that are also important in family development theory (e.g., Rodgers, 1973; White, 1991).

Empirical Applications

STRESS IN FAMILIES

One of the major empirical applications of family development theory has been in the area of stress. One of the "fathers" of family development theory, Reuben Hill (1971), was originally responsible for the theoretical formulation in this area. Boss (1988) argues that although individuals experience stress as a felt inability to cope with change, families are organized units that also demonstrate group symptoms of stress. She defines family stress as a disturbance in the organization and process of family life. Although individuals "perceive" and react to stresses, it may be the resources of the family that explain the successful management of stress. Furthermore, individuals' perception of what is a stressor is guided by their understanding of timing and sequencing norms for family development. For example,

> The event of pregnancy is viewed more positively by the families of a couple in their thirties than by the families of a couple still in their teens. The different levels of family stress caused by the same event (in this case pregnancy) can be explained by developmental context. (Boss, 1988, p. 32)

Accordingly, family stress and individual stress must be explained by using multiple levels of analysis focusing on both the individual and family resources and coping skills.

The study of stress and recent therapeutic applications of family development theory (e.g., Carter & McGoldrick, 1988; Falicov, 1988; Klein & Aldous, 1988) have emphasized significant events and "pileup" of events in the individual and family history. For example, we all consider that a recent event such as a divorce places family members under significant stress by requiring emotionally intense adjustments. In recent analyses, researchers have examined not just such events but where the event falls in the family's event history. A family may have moved to a new house, then experienced a prolonged illness of a family member, and then undergone a separation and then a divorce. Clearly, each event alone would be considered stressful, but the compression of the events in a brief time span also must be considered in an analysis of stress on individuals and family members.

TRANSITION TO PARENTHOOD

Family development scholars have also turned their attention to the stress attached to particular transitions in the family life course. Hill and Rodgers (1964) argued that particular transitions from one family stage to another might be stressful. Menaghan (1983) examined the stress associated with the transition to parenthood. She argued that the stress on individuals of assuming the roles and norms of parenthood was mitigated by anticipatory socialization and coping skills. Belsky and Rovine (1990) documented that many families suffered declines in marital role relationships during the transition to parenthood. The transition to parenthood continues to occupy developmental researchers as they incorporate events such as prenatal preparation, infant-feeding practices, and the timing of work-related events in their analyses. For example, Bulcroft, Forste, and White (1993) argue that the decision to breast-feed an infant must be studied as part of the transition to parenthood because the choice of infant-feeding technique is linked to strains on the marital relationship that are elevated by breast feeding. Although we do not as yet know whether all family transitions are stressful for family members, we do have an indication that the birth of the first child and transition to parenthood is fraught with potential strains for individuals and relationships in the family.

Implications for Intervention

Family development theory is rich with implications for interventions and policy. The notion of the family career and its stages alerts policymakers to the fact that there is not "a" or "the" family but myriad family patterns and paths. Indeed, family development as a perspective sensitizes policymakers as to some of the more salient dimensions of these patterns, such as age and membership structure. For example, Aldous (1994) recently discussed how developmental insights shed light on the issue of family caregiving:

> In the formation and child-rearing stages, families are the most hard pressed with respect to caregiving resources. Trying to maintain marriages, starting parenthood, divorcing, remarrying, and preparing youths to leave home in the economic context of stagnant or falling wages and

troublesome unemployment rates make these family stages careseeking rather than caregiving periods. (p. 61)

Policymakers must take into consideration not only what is happening in any one stage but also the dynamic process as families move from stage to stage. Such general insights are not simply restricted to policy made in one culture but may be used to address policy questions in cultures other than North American.

The concepts of normative and nonnormative timing and sequencing of family career events and the synchronization of these family events with work and educational careers has proved useful in family and individual therapy. Carter and McGoldrick (1988) argue that the family career is a useful framework for family therapy. They and others have pointed out that the family context of stress and coping change throughout the family's stages. Falicov (1988) focuses more on the concepts of off time and out of sequence as important constructs for the therapist. Finally, Russell (1993) notes that the stage formulation presented by Rodgers and White (1993) has already been used by therapists as a form of genogram analysis that includes the household. Russell (1993) notes that the move away from developmental tasks to a more probabilistic approach to family development (Rodgers & White, 1993) will help both family practitioners and their clients accept "a realistic level of unpredictability in family life" (p. 257), and this in turn assists in addressing both long- and short-term problem solving for families.

Critiques and Discussion

One of the outstanding problems for developmentalists is the conflict between the interactional and structural perspectives within family development theory. The interactionists assume that individuals and families have great efficacy in constructing their own family norms. The structuralists assume that institutional timing and sequencing norms so constrain family members that there is limited room for such constructions. This conflict between these two perspectives is an old one. Both are probably correct but not as correct as each one would prefer. We want to share with you an anecdote from our teaching. We were discussing this topic in a graduate seminar when one of the students said, "Why is it that we are all dressed in dark colors—greens, blacks, browns?" She went on to state the crux of the problem: When she goes into a shop, she is free to choose from among the styles that are stocked in the store. But if she really wanted something in bright orange, it would be almost impossible to get from any shops in the early 1990s because "earth tones" are in vogue. From the perspective of most individuals, they have all the choice they want even though that choice is severely constrained to one set of colors by popularity and fashion.

The conflict between the interactional and structural viewpoints is analogous. The interactionists perceive that there is freedom to "create" norms and roles; the structuralists view the situation as constrained by existing family timing and sequencing norms and family members' inclusion in other age-graded organizations such as the school system. If, for example, your child wanted to concentrate on studying music to the exclusion of mathematics and English studies, the authorities would have something to say about this. In the final analysis, the interactionist perspective is most appropriate for the relationship and group levels of analysis, and the structuralist perspective is most useful for the institutional level of analysis. In this sense, we can regard these approaches as complementing one another rather than competing. Indeed, in Aldous's (1996) revision of her 1978 *Family Careers,* much of the friction between these points of view is minimized by attention to levels of analysis.

Another problem area for family developmental theory is the identification of the process of development. Mattessich and Hill (1987) offered a definition of family development that was influenced by the thinking of scholars in child development. As a result, their definition contained elements such as *progressive structural differentiation.* But family groups are more social and less biological in their development than are individuals. For individuals, developmental scholars argue that there are ontogenetic, or biologically based, stages of development. But for the family, the argument about a biological basis doesn't stand up. The only established biological parameters are fertility, and with the onslaught of fertilization technology, that may not last long as a parameter of family life.

White (1991) suggested that family development theory should explain the transition from one family stage to another. As a result of that emphasis, White's definition of development is that it is a process in which the probabilities of a transition change according to the family's current stage and how long it has been in that stage. For example, usually newlyweds allow themselves a period of adjustment before having a first child. The probability for a first child peaks during the early years of marriage; after 5 years the probability of a birth rapidly declines. The developmental process is where a transition to a family stage, such as parenthood, is dependent on the current stage (childless marriage) and the duration of time in that stage (less than or greater than 5 years). This view of family development relies on the behavior of individuals and families as being guided by social norms rather than ontogenetic causes.

The ontogenetic-sociogenetic argument will continue to plague family development theory until there is a clear theoretical link with ontogenetic child development theories. There can be little doubt that the maturation of children makes for large changes in interaction in families, but family developmentalists have not studied these interactions longitudinally to discover which norms and patterns change and which do not. On the other hand, child developmentalists have largely ignored the family context of ontogenetic development, and we have little idea of the interactions between a child's development and family norms and patterns. The only conclusion we can reach is that the goal of a theoretical linkage between individual and family development remains elusive.

Although newer versions of family development theory (Rodgers & White, 1993; White, 1991) address the "old" problems of normative descriptions and cross-cultural relevance, new problems have arisen. Most substantial is the problem of using behavior to infer norms. Marini (1984) argues that norms cannot be inferred from behavior. She states that norms always carry sanctions and are part of a group. The aggregate patterns of family development cannot be used to infer social norms because there is no demonstration that these norms are carried by group members and have sanctions. White's (1991) response to Marini's (1984) argument is that she fails to incorporate the many levels of analysis appropriate for analyzing norms. He states that Marini's definition is suitable only for the group level of analysis, not for the institutional level of analysis. Marini's argument, however, raises important questions about the conditions under which scholars may validly infer norms from patterns of family behavior.

A long-standing critique of the stage concept is that it cannot incorporate all of the myriad family forms. This criticism was first made about the absence of single-parent families as a stage. Today, we must wonder whether there is so much diversity of family forms that the stage concept cannot work. This criticism is appropriate for earlier versions of the theory in which stages were given culture-specific content but inappropriate for the recent versions of the theory in which stages are based on either possible membership structure or patterns of families. Indeed, family development stages are appropriate as long as there are patterns of family life.

A more serious criticism of the theory is that many of the changes viewed in family development theory as discrete jumps associated with changing family stages are more realistically conceptualized as gradual, continuous changes. For example, critics would argue that the preparation and anticipation for a first child are more continuous than discrete. Even among family developmentalists, there is the view that transitions are not a point in time but a process (e.g., Aldous, 1978; Bohannan, 1970; Klein et al., 1979). The rebuttal is that no matter what the preparation, if the relatively discrete event of the birth of the first child does not take place, then we cannot say that a transition has taken place. This rebuttal relies on the fact that transitions are usually tied to a relatively discrete event and that such events are turning points for the family.

Another problem we see for family development theory is its scope. Family development theorists attempt to explain the uniform and patterned ways in which families develop not only within a society but also from society to society. Much of family development theory, however, has been focused on family development during the decade of the 1960s within middle-class U.S. families. Although older versions of the theory appear to lack cross-cultural applicability, there is some cause for optimism with the newer theoretical versions. The generality of the newer theoretical propositions and the specification of events hold greater promise for cross-cultural researchers than did the older culture-specific stages.

Conclusion

Family development theory is the only theory covered in this book that focuses exclusively on families. Thus, it is unique. Family development theory provides a broad theory to explain the patterns of family formation and dissolution (e.g., Rodgers & White, 1993). Family development theory has grown and matured throughout the second half of this century. We have little doubt that it will continue to provide both students and scholars insight into the ways families grow and change over time.

Food for Thought

1. Think back about major changes in your family. What sorts of events or variables seemed to be responsible for these changes? If you were to draw a family life line for your family, which events would you use to mark off transitions? Can you classify events as expected or unexpected, on time and off time?

2. Think about a stage, such as early years of a couple with their first infant. Even though we are all different, what things would you expect to be relatively similar across couples in North America? The world?

3. Every family career has a beginning, a middle, and an end. Thinking about your own family and others similar to yours, indicate what particular event or set of events would be the best indicators of the "beginning." Then, do the same for the "end"—although this may not have occurred yet in the case of your own family. Based on your judgments about the length of a family career, try to identify the middle or halfway point. We ask this because some scholars use such ideas as "the second half of life." Does such an idea make sense when we think of families? How would we ever know if we have reached the halfway point in a family's career?

Suggested Readings

Aldous, J. (1996). *Family careers: Rethinking the developmental perspective.* Thousand Oaks, CA: Sage.

This is a revised and updated version of one of the most popular undergraduate texts on family development.

Rodgers, R. H., & White, J. M. (1993). Family development theory. In P. Boss, W. Doherty, R. LaRossa, W. Schumm, & S. Steinmetz (Eds.), *Sourcebook of family theories and methods: A contextual approach* (pp. 225-254). New York: Plenum.
This is a thorough sketch of the newer, structural version of the family development theory.

6

The Systems Framework

Today is Jack and Jan's 10th wedding anniversary. For the past 10 years, Jack has always presented Jan with a dozen yellow roses. When he gives her the roses this year, Jan makes a funny face. She says thanks and puts the roses aside while she finishes reading a newspaper article. Jack is disappointed that Jan did not respond more positively to his gift. He asks Jan what is wrong. She informs him that she has an allergy to roses. Jack says that he remembered her liking them even before they were married. She says she has always been allergic but received them enthusiastically because of the "thought." Jack responds that the thought is still there. Jan counters that after 10 years of marriage she had hoped that his knowledge about her would grow deeper. Jan said that she has sent a number of messages that not only does she not like roses but some variety would show more thought on Jack's part. Instead, all she receives is the message that their marriage has sunk into thoughtless routine. After all, says Jan, variety is the spice of life.

Let's take a closer look at this example, for it illustrates some general principles about a communications system. First, Jack inferred from Jan's premarital behavior that she liked roses. He then incorporated this in his conception of his wife. Jan is "disappointed" that Jack does not know her better, but unless Jack asked Jan about her flower preferences or had occasion to observe Jan being disappointed previously, he would have no reason to doubt the validity of his premarital inference. Indeed, the only reason Jack would change his inference would be if he received new information. Jan on the other hand thinks Jack's perceptions are shallow. She thinks he should have been sensitive to her subtle cues that she liked the thought but not the flowers without her having to say it. She feels she provided sufficient nonverbal cues to alert her husband and he is simply insensitive to the information she sends (e.g., Gottman & Porterfield, 1981).

In general, then, we can see both spouses as being linked in a system in which one person's behavior becomes the other person's information. In turn, this person's information provides the beliefs and basis on which future actions are taken. Those actions become evidence that the other spouse doesn't understand him or her and has not received the more subtle messages. Jan is thus disappointed in what she believes is her husband's insensitivity to her behavioral cues. In a distilled sense, this interactional spiral, composed of behaviors between the spouses and each one's perception and reception of the information carried by those behaviors, captures the notion of a marital interaction system.

In this chapter, we address the question, "What is a system?" rather than examine marital communication. Through defining and discussing the properties of a system, we will become more adept at analyzing cases such as that of Jack and Jan. Indeed, the study of marital and family interaction has been an important component in the recent development of systems theory in the social sciences. What we now call *general systems theory* does not have a simple pedigree or lineage, however. Originally, systems theory evolved from a set of diverse influences, such as biology, robotics, and mathematics. Of all the theories we consider in this book, systems theory is certainly the most recent. Most if not all of its evolution has taken place within the 20th century.

Intellectual Traditions

Prior to the beginning of the 20th century, there were two major sources of influences that were to prove foundational for systems theory. One of these influences was the "organic" and "evolutionary" perspective on society launched by Herbert Spencer (1880). Spencer's belief that the same basic processes operated throughout the universe led him to assume a set of principles that would apply within biology, psychology, and sociology. He viewed the universe as a continual process that forms and dissipates structures. Spencer's work is one of the major contemporary sources for the idea of *emergence* and the notion that aggregations may come together to form "more than the sum of their parts." Of course, this notion was voiced by the ancient Greek philosopher Democritus (460-360 B.C.) and after the turn of the 20th century was tied up with the notion of *vitalism* in biology and the process cosmology of Alfred North Whitehead (1929). Spencer's work also rekindled the age-old quest for unity among the sciences. This quest for universal principles common to all domains of study reached an apex during the 1950s and 1960s as evidenced by the publication of the *International Encyclopedia of Unified Science* with such illustrious contributors as Charles Morris (see Chapter 4), Rudolph Carnap, Niels Bohr, and Carl Hempel (see Chapter 1).

The second major influence came from the emerging science of information and automata. Along with the invention of the telegraph and telephone, new ways of conceptualizing and measuring the flow of information developed. This was the start of communications theory. The digital codes that could be sent on telegraphs were the subject of early research that culminated in the study of digital computers. At the same time that the study of these message systems was evolving, new technologies for control and guidance were being developed. For example, the servomechanism used on ships' rudders incorporated the ideas of error detection and feedback. But the greatest single impetus for the growth of information theory came from technological demands during World War II. For example, with the increase in the ability of aircraft to fly faster came a need for antiaircraft guns to anticipate the position of such fast-moving targets. Probably one of the more familiar examples is that of the early rockets developed by Germany. The first V1 rockets were notorious for having a guidance system as rudimentary as a skyrocket's—point and ignite. Although these rockets were aimed at London, they probably terrorized more cows in rural Britain than Londoners. The subsequent version of the rocket, the V2, incorporated an error detection and trajectory correction feedback loop that increased the accuracy. Fortunately, these advances occurred only as the war was coming to a close.

The technological developments during the war created a need for theory to unite areas such as guidance systems and information flows. This need culminated in a series of academic developments. Soon after the war, Norbert Wiener (1948) published what became acknowledged as the seminal work on cybernetics and control systems. At about the same time, C. E. Shannon, a research scientist with Bell Laboratories, developed a mathematical theory of information and coding that he subsequently published with W. Weaver as *The Mathematical Theory of Communication* (1949). This theory consolidated the measurement of information (bits) in a way that we still use and offered several propositions regarding coding and error detection. From Shannon and Weaver's (1949) work, we find that the amount of information carried on a channel is inversely related to the amount of redundancy used for error detection. Another important postwar development was the founding of the Society for General Systems Research in 1954 by such notable social scientists as James Miller and Margaret Mead. And it is at this point that systems theory started to gain a particular focus among those using it to study families.

The way in which systems theory evolved in the study of the family is especially interesting because its application to families preceded its entry into more established domains such as sociology (Buckley, 1967). This was principally due to the influence of a small group of researchers in San Francisco. Gregory Bateson, an anthropologist and the second husband of Margaret Mead, had explored both psychiatry and systems theory during his postwar years at Harvard University. Don Jackson was a psychiatrist who along with Bateson forged the early entry of systems theory into the study of the family. These scholars founded the Mental Research Institute (MRI) in 1958 after Bateson, Jackson, Haley, and Weakland (1956) published their influential paper "Toward a Theory of Schizophrenia."

In this and subsequent papers, Bateson and his colleagues argued that the family represents a communications system in which, if double binds occur, one member may show signs of schizophrenia. The notion that the schizophrenic individual is a symptom of a family system pathology rather than an individual pathology gave rise to terms such as *dysfunctional* family. This view is seductive to many even though decades of research have failed to produce any substantial empirical support for the double-bind hypothesis (e.g., Mishler & Waxler, 1968; Olson, 1972; Schuham, 1967). The view of the family as a system, however, continues to operate as a strong metaphor within family therapy circles. For example, Kantor and Lehr's (1975) book *Inside the Family: Toward a Theory of Family Process* typified the family as being a self-regulating system in which members control each other's access to meaning, power, and affect. The applications of systems type thinking in the realm of family therapy has become identified as one of the major variants of general systems theory and is commonly known as "family process theory" (see Broderick, 1993).

The initial entry of systems theory into the subject area of family through practitioners and therapists was closely followed by more formal statements from disciplinary scholars. The impact of von Bertalanffy (1968) in biology and Buckley (1967) in sociology was complemented in the social sciences by the more traditional "functionalist" approach used in anthropology, biology, and sociology. In all three of these disciplines, researchers had made arguments that when we observe a structure it must exist because it either presently or at one time performed functions for the organism or society. Thus, when we examine what seem to be nonfunctional organs in the human body, such as the appendix, we argue that the structure (the appendix) must have served some function at a previous time or it wouldn't exist. These *structural-functional* arguments reached a theoretical zenith in the work of Talcott Parsons (1951). Although Parsons used the systems metaphor and even incorporated some systems notions such as "hierarchy of control," most scholars would not classify him as a general systems theorist. But the similarities between these two approaches in part explain the enthusiasm for systems theory found in the social and biological sciences.

General systems theory is sufficiently abstract and general to be applied to both animate and inanimate objects. We can speak coherently about "planetary systems" and "family systems" even though the two subject matters differ dramatically in many regards. Indeed, this great generality is one of the compelling points of the theory and is tied to the unification of science movement. Yet several systems theorists (e.g., Buckley, 1967) have noted that although nonliving systems tend to follow the second law of thermodynamics and exhibit increased states of randomness (*entropy*), living systems tend to increase in order and differentiation (*negentropy*). As all physical matter emits radiation, it loses energy used to organize its structure. This loss of energy creates the dissipative process of entropy. But as Toffler points out in his foreword to Prigogine and Stengers's (1984) book, biological systems do not seem to follow the same pattern as physical systems:

> Evolution proceeds from the simple to complex, from "lower" to "higher" forms of life, from undifferentiated to differentiated structures. And, from a human point of view, all this is quite optimistic. The universe gets "better" organized as it ages, continually advancing to a higher level as time sweeps by. (p. xx)

The diametrical opposition of these processes gave rise to the suggestion that the processes of living systems must be studied separately from nonliving systems. This view is most thoroughly explored by James G. Miller (1978) in his book *Living Systems*. Miller provides a classificatory view of living systems based on subsystems functions, such as "reproduction," that are necessary for living structures. Each subsystem function is examined at various levels of analysis. For example, the subsystem function of "reproducer" at the cellular level is performed by the chromosome and at the group level by the "mating dyad." The taxonomic approach used by Miller bears some resemblance to functionalist theory in sociology and has led at least one scholar (Turner, 1991) to discuss systems theory as *general systems functionalism*. Regardless of Miller's (1978) similarities to Parsons and other functionalists, one critical dissimilarity is that he presents some general theoretical propositions that go beyond mere class inclusion. Also, Miller represents the currently dominant view that living, as opposed to nonliving, systems are driven by different negentropic and organizing processes.

This dominant view of living systems—one of which would be the family—as characterized by processes atypical of nonliving things has recently been challenged within biology. Researchers in the natural science of biology assume some continuity with other physical sciences, such as chemistry and physics, and this has perhaps made the disjunction with the physical science perspective more sharply felt. The idea that there are two distinct processes at work, one for living and another for nonliving systems, threatens the continuity of science as well as the unification of science envisioned by Spencer and others. Recently, two biologists, Brooks and Wiley (1986), have argued that the contradiction between nonliving systems being entropic and living systems being negentropic can be resolved by sorting out the level of analysis. Brooks and Wiley propose that the problem is largely resolved by clarifying levels of analysis. Their argument is too complex to present here in full, but the essence is that they suggest that what might seem "organizational" at an aggregate level of analysis may be entropic at a microlevel of analysis. The importance of their claim for us is that we are cautioned that the division in systems theory between living and nonliving systems may not be as clear and obviously acceptable as claimed by many authors in the social sciences. This caution leads us to present the concepts and propositions of general systems theory rather than only those deemed appropriate for living systems.

Focus and Scope Assumptions

All parts of the system are interconnected. Although the assumption of interconnectedness in a system seems obvious, it is far from trivial. Burr, Leigh, et al. (1979) state, "The discovery by the family process group that changes in one part of a system influence all other parts of the system should be greeted with as much enthusiasm as the observation that people talk and think" (p. 98). We would agree with this comment if this assumption were to be treated as a claim to knowledge rather than as a basic orienting assumption. But this assumption is a basic epistemological statement announcing that systems theory is not concerned with isolating Cause A and Effect B from the environment in which they occur. In this sense, the assumption is a statement about the ecological validity and inclusivity of systems theory.

Understanding is only possible by viewing the whole. The assumption that one must consider a system in its entirety serves a similar epistemological function to our first assumption. This assumption in systems theory largely resulted from the "vitalism" tied to the discovery that when some animals, such as the paramecium, were sliced in two they would grow a new half. Clearly, these animals were "greater than the sum of their parts" because when you divided them they would replicate. This assumption was immediately relevant to sociology and family studies. Indeed, the argument that social groups such as families were "real" and greater than just a collection of individuals had raged in these fields for a considerable time (White, 1984).

A systems' behavior affects its environment and in turn the environment affects the system. Some of the output of a system becomes input of the system (*feedback*). The notion of feedback is both a concept and an epistemological assumption. The most simple of systems may not incorporate direct feedback loops, but this assumption serves to sensitize us to the fact that even the most simple systems affect and are, in turn, affected by their environment. In this sense, all systems have some form of feedback. This is the epistemological assumption, and it coheres nicely with the previous two assumptions of wholeness and connectedness. In the study of the family, we are usually concerned with the type of feedback whereby some of the output of a system becomes input to the system. In this sense, feedback represents a particular type of system operation that can be specified and measured. This second meaning of feedback does not refer to the assumption but to the concept.

"Systems" are heuristics, not real things. Systems theory is a way of knowing, not reality. This fourth and last major assumption is one that has only recently been formally recognized in systems theory. The assumption is that defining an object as a system composed of subsystems, inputs, and outputs is just one among many possible ways we might study the object. The systems perspective offers no special claim to veracity. But most of all, to say something behaves like a system is a model or metaphor, not the thing itself. Ernst von Glasersfeld (1987) has summed up this *constructivist* perspective as the "view that knowl-

edge must not be taken to be a picture of objective reality but rather as a particular way of organizing experience" (p. 10). It follows from this perspective that we should not consider the "model" to be the "thing." Indeed, the systems model becomes a heuristic for understanding our world. If we attribute reality to a family system rather than see it as a heuristic device, we make the mistake commonly called *reification,* or what the philosopher Alfred North Whitehead (1929, p. 11) called the "fallacy of misplaced concreteness."

In summary, there are four basic assumptions underlying the systems perspective: (a) system elements are interconnected, (b) systems can only be understood as wholes, (c) all systems affect themselves through environmental feedback, and (d) systems are not reality. These four assumptions are necessarily broad but represent the foundation on which the architecture of concepts and propositions rest.

Concepts

SYSTEM

Almost every discussion of systems begins with Hall and Fagan's (1956) now-classic definition of a system as a set of objects and relations between these objects and their attributes. This definition is useful for those who understand the formal set theory behind the definition, but for many students this definition doesn't seem to say much. For this reason, we characterize systems in a more familiar and, we hope, approachable manner. At minimum, a system is a unit that affects its environment. This is a "minimalist" definition and usually we would say additional things, such as that a system has exchanges with its environment and has internal elements. But the only characteristic needed to identify something as a system is that it has an effect on its environment. That effect may only be that the system requires energy as input from the environment, such as a black hole, or it may only be that the system has output that affects the environment, such as a perpetual motion machine. In both cases, the system is a system because it affects its environment and can be distinguished from its environment.

BOUNDARIES

All systems have some form of boundaries. A boundary is a border between the system and its environment that affects the flow of information and energy between the environment and the system. Boundaries can be measured on the dimension of permeability to the environment as running from "closed" boundaries, through which nothing goes in or out, to completely "open" boundaries, in which there is no impediment to energy and information transfers of any kind. Clearly, a completely closed system can only be imagined (as in mathematics) and a completely open system would lose most of its identity as a system as it would be difficult to separate from its environment. Fortunately, most systems occupy a position between these two ideal types. This means that the great majority of systems can be categorized by their *degree of permeability*.

RULES OF TRANSFORMATION

All systems have internal rules of transformation. A rule of transformation represents a relationship between two elements of the system. For example, a husband and wife are both elements of the marital system. A rule of transformation for the marital system would be the *quid pro quo* rule that whenever the husband is nasty to the wife, the wife is nasty in return. One of the major functions of a rule of transformation is to transform inputs to the system from the environment into outputs from the system. For example, if a family's house is on fire and the smoke alarm goes off late at night, this information is transformed by the family into output as behavior that may doom or save them.

FEEDBACK

We previously developed the idea of feedback as an epistemological assumption. Now we turn to feedback as a concept in systems theory. Feedback refers to the circular loop that brings some of the system's output back to the system as input. Feedback can be of two types. On the one hand, it may be *positive,* or *deviation amplifying*. Do not confuse positive feedback with the concept of positive reinforcement from psychology—the two are very different. Positive reinforcement makes the goal behavior more likely, whereas positive feedback (deviation amplifying) may make reaching the goal less likely. On the other hand, *negative feedback is deviation dampening*. This categorization of feedback relies on the identification of either the past output or the goals of the system. With higher-order systems that monitor error from their goals, feedback is invaluable in error correction, as when you get a poor grade on an exam. In lower-level systems that lack error correction or monitoring, feedback can either increase the amplitude of output or decrease the amplitude. In families, we are mainly concerned with goal-oriented systems.

VARIETY

All systems have degrees of variety. Variety in a system refers to the extent to which the system has the resources to meet new environmental demands or adapt to changes. Some systems may lack the requisite variety to adapt to changes. For example, a family with very rigid rules may lack the flexibility to adapt to changes such as a daughter wanting to marry someone from another religion or race. The lack of variety in such a rigid family might result in a rupture to the family system because it is unable to adapt to this change.

EQUILIBRIUM

Even systems with sufficient variety may be in a state of equilibrium. Equilibrium refers to a balance of inputs and outputs. For example, most families require a balance of income and expenditures. A family system can also be described as *homeostatic*. A homeostatic system dynamically maintains equilibrium by feedback and control. A physical example of a homeostatic device is a thermostat; an organic example is the dynamic maintenance of your body temperature within fairly limited parameters. A family may maintain its dynamic equilibrium by using its resources to maintain its rules. For example, a family that goes camping in Alaska might purchase sleeping shades so it can maintain the rule that everyone is to go to sleep by 8:30 p.m. even in the land of the midnight sun. As you can see, homeostasis is neither inherently good nor bad but describes the manner in which equilibrium is maintained over time.

SUBSYSTEMS

Systems have various levels or subsystems. For example, one way of viewing the family system is that it contains sibling subsystems, marital subsystems, and parent-child subsystems. Each of these subsystems could be further analyzed in terms of subsystems. In general, a subsystem is a part of a system that is analyzed separately as to its exchanges with the system and other subsystems. Some system characteristics, such as "control," can only emerge with a system that has two subsystems, one containing rules of transformation and the other comparing output with the goal of the system. For example, a thermostatic system can be broken into one subsystem that performs heating, including elements such as the furnace and ducts, and another subsystem that senses the air temperature and turns the heater on if the temperature is not within the goal parameters. In a family system, we might see the parental subsystem as the control subsystem. It must be kept in mind, however, that subsystems, like systems, are intellectual ways of understanding and analyzing our world. There are many ways to conceptualize subsystems and systems in families, and some serve one purpose better than others, but none are "true." They have heuristic value but no *ontological* reality.

Propositions

Systems theorists such as Mesarovic (1970) and Miller (1978) have offered general propositions regarding the behavior of systems. These propositions, because of their necessary abstractness and generality, are less immediately applicable to the study of the family than are several applications of systems theory to the family, such as Kantor and Lehr (1975), Wilkinson (1977), Burr, Day, and Bahr (1993), and Broderick (1993). In this section, we incorporate some of the more abstract propositions but especially concentrate on examples of propositions that are directly applicable to the study of the family.

As far as we know, all family systems theorists conceptualize the family as a goal-oriented system with a control subsystem. Broderick and Smith (1979) talk about this as a Level 2, or cybernetic, system.

Most scholars conceptualize the family as having many more levels of control than just one. Perhaps an example will make this more clear.

Jack and Jan now have a 3-year-old who is in the process of developmentally "dropping" her afternoon nap. This has made the family rule of a 7 o'clock bedtime even more important for both Jack and Jan. Jack is putting his overtired and cranky daughter to bed when she rebels and begins to throw a screaming tantrum about not going to bed. Jack first tries to manage the rule breaking by increasing the level of threats and punishments, threatening to close the door if she doesn't settle down. The tantrum continues until Jack realizes that by continuing to escalate the conflict he is getting farther from the important goal of making sure his daughter gets some sleep. He takes his daughter out of bed. Holding his daughter in his arms, he rocks and sings to her, and the exhausted little girl is asleep in a few seconds.

This example illustrates the notion of goals and control. The initial rule of the system was set by the first-order goal of "7 o'clock bedtime." But this first-order goal was actually deduced from a higher-order goal of "ensuring their daughter gets sufficient rest." Likewise, "ensuring the daughter gets sufficient rest" is deduced from a much higher-order goal of "being good parents." What happened in the example is that Jack attempted to correct the negative feedback (error from the initial 7 o'clock bedtime), but his correction by enforcing the rules produced positive feedback (amplified the deviation from the goal) and more error. As a result, Jack changed control levels to "check" what was wrong. What was wrong was that with an overly tired child, tantrums are positive feedback loops, and the way to break those loops is less enforcement of the Level 1 rule. In other words, the way you achieve the goal of rest for the child is by not enforcing the Level 1 goal of the 7 o'clock bedtime. This example also shows that if Jack lacked the requisite variety to change behaviors in midstream, he would have been trapped in his daughter's positive feedback loop.

What theoretical propositions does systems theory supply to help us understand our example? Miller (1978) suggests that the greater the number of channels for processing information in a structurally differentiated living system, the less the strains and tensions among subsystems. Miller's proposition would seem to illustrate just one advantage to variety in a system, however. Wilkinson (1977) states a similar proposition using the concept of variety:

The adaptability and therefore viability of a (family) system (as contrasted to rigidity and vulnerability) is positively related to the amount of variety in the system.

and

The adaptability and therefore viability of a (family) system (as contrasted to rigidity and vulnerability) is related negatively to conflict and tension in the system.

These two general propositions help us identify that in Jack's family system variety is related to the dampening of tension. This general proposition does not, however, entirely capture the process in our example whereby Jack reassessed and corrected his behavior by reference to higher-order goals. Both Mesarovic (1970) for general systems and Broderick (1993) for family systems clarify this point, and Broderick adds a further proposition that is useful in this regard. Broderick believes family goals are organized into hierarchies:

Higher level goals define the priorities among lower level goals and are intrinsically less likely to be revised and abandoned. (p. 43)

According to this proposition, the variety of a system is positively related to the number of levels of the system. This explains why Jack was guided by one set of goals over another and suggests how he could reassess the utility of lower-level goals by comparing them and the output to the higher-level system goal of sleep for his daughter.

It would be somewhat misleading to portray most of the explanatory work by systems theorists as being incorporated in theoretical propositions such as the ones we have identified above. Much of the "explanation" provided by systems theorists is by means of flow charts or diagrams. Despite the often-heard claim that systems theory provides an approach that is nonlinear, most of the diagrams and the solutions to systems equations are by means of either linear algebra or linear programming.

Figure 6.1 represents a simplified comparator, or control, system. In this figure, information is expressed as signal quantities, and these

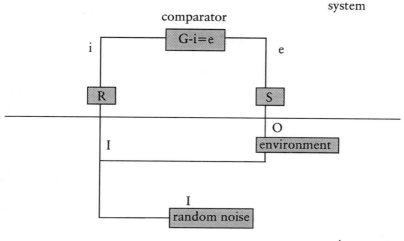

Figure 6.1. Simplified Comparator System

signals are transformed by transformation functions (in boxes). We could also express what is going on in this system as a series of functional transformations of the initial signal entering the system from the environment. When the environmental signal (I) enters the system, it is transformed by the receiver (R). After the receiver function, the signal becomes system input (i) rather than environmental input (I). The system input enters the comparator where the system input is compared or subtracted from the goal signal (G). Returning to our example of Jack and his daughter, this is where Jack compared his perception of his daughter's tantrum to the goal of bedtime. A positive or negative result from the comparator is error (e). Error is then transformed by the sender function (S) for certain channels and enters the environment as output (O) from the system. At this point, Jack decided to enforce the bedtime by threats and punishments. The environment transforms the output (O) so that it is changed to another quantity (I). The child, already in an irrational state, saw Jack's behavior as further reason to be upset. The environmentally transformed output of the system is joined with other systematic signals from the environment (I) and random noise to compose the totality of the environmental input back into the system (I). The example of Jack and his daughter did not contain a lot of other systematic signals (such as visitors in the house), and other sorts of random interferences were not a question. Most of the environmental input (I) was the daughter's tantrum.

To use a diagram such as in Figure 6.1 to explain higher-order goals, we would have to add a linkage where the error signal (e) becomes input to an even higher-level comparator containing a higher-order goal that is not included in the simplified version in Figure 6.1. In our example, the higher-order goal was getting sufficient rest for the child. The lower-order goal was a 7 o'clock bedtime. When the higher-level comparator compares the error with its goal, it may send an error message to change the lower-order goal in the lower-order comparator. This is commonly called recalibration. Every time you turn the heat up on the thermostat in your house, you (a higher-order goal system) recalibrate the goal in the lower-order thermostat in a way similar to what Jack did.

There are differences in the type of explanation afforded by using systems diagrams rather than systems propositions. Although much of the thinking and analysis are similar, the two provide very different explanations because the questions each addresses are distinctively different. The systems diagrams address the question of how the process works whereas the system theory propositions address why the system works as it does. In general, this is the distinction between modeling, which supplies an analog of how things operate, and theory, which explains why things work in this way. Systems diagrams have proven popular because they allow us to visualize and simplify very complex processes. According to one theory of knowledge (*epistemology*), the operations, or how, question is all we need to know, and the why question represents a very limited "billiard ball" understanding of causation. As we shall see, von Glasersfeld's (1987) catholic, *constructionist* view of knowledge as multiple models fits this operationalist epistemology. This basic distinction, however, gives rise to some significant variation among systems theorists as to the type and form of the explanation. Furthermore, as we will find later, this operational epistemology is a prime target for critics of systems theory who say that systems theory is not a theory at all but simply a general model.

Variations

This section will cover three of the major variants in family systems theory. There are many variants of systems theory, but we limit our discussion to what we regard as the three dominant approaches. The first of these three is a general systems approach to the family. This approach tends to include use of the full arsenal of systems concepts and tools. Second, we examine family communications theory. And last, we examine family process theory, in which unique constructs for extending and modifying the systems approach have been developed, particularly for the use of family therapists. Although there are many other ways to cluster the theoretical variants in family systems, such as those using mechanical, organic, or cybernetic analogs, we feel that these other approaches would less accurately represent the true nature of the variation in family systems theory.

GENERAL SYSTEMS THEORY

Broderick and Smith (1979) provide a sound introduction to the ways that family systems might be applied to the study of the family. Their presentation can be characterized as "cautiously optimistic." These authors suggest that family systems are minimally cybernetic, or control, systems with two levels. They provide an introductory analysis of family systems as a four-level system in which the first level has an environmental feedback loop, the second level (cybernetic) has a comparator for error detection and correction, the third level (morphogenesis) has a higher-level comparator allowing for control of lower levels, and the fourth level (conversion) is the highest-level goal system—if goals are changed at this level all lower-level systems are changed. More detailed models might have six or seven levels, as William Powers (1974) found necessary in his application of systems theory to individual psychological systems. Broderick and Smith (1979) are cautious to make limited claims for the application of general systems theory. They call it an *approach* rather than a *theory*, responding to the perception that it largely offers models rather than theoretical propositions. They view attempts to produce propositions from systems theory, as by Wilkinson (1977), as "premature." In part, their caution and judgment are due to the point in time at which they

Sender	Message	Receiver
Meaning - - -► Encoding ⌐--►	Verbal & - - - - -└►Decoding - - -►	Meaning
Selection	Nonverbal	Selection
	Channels	

Figure 6.2. Sender-Receiver Communications Model

authored their contribution. But subsequent developments have not provided much more than was available in 1979 (e.g., Miller, 1978; Wilkinson, 1977). Moreover, Broderick and Smith (1979) seem to approach systems theory with the positivistic, axiomatic notion of theory rather than the operationalist view currently touted by most systems theorists. This undoubtedly adds to their caution in regard to the promise of systems theory. Yet, to date, Broderick and Smith's (1979) statement remains one of the better outlines for the application of general systems theory to the family.

COMMUNICATIONS THEORY

Communications theory originates with the work by Shannon and Weaver (1949) entitled *The Mathematical Theory of Communication.* The mathematical theory of signal communications is complemented and extended by work in the area of automata and cybernetics. The particular path on which this work entered family studies was mainly from the concerns about family communications raised by Bateson, Jackson, and others at the Mental Research Institute (MRI) in Palo Alto, California, during the late 1950s (Bateson et al., 1956). Family process theory, our third variant, shares this common ancestry with family communications. Unlike family process theory, the study of family communications largely became the focus of those in the new academic field of communications studies.

The field of communications uses a basic sender-receiver model of communications. Although there are many variants of the model, the basic elements are contained in Figure 6.2.

To understand Figure 6.2, let's follow a simple message through the model. Jack wants to tell Jan that he loves her. Of all the possible messages he could send to Jan, the meaning he selects to send is "I love you." The next step is that Jack must select the type of encoding most appropriate for the message. There are two types of codes, *digital* and *analog*. An analog message "bears a resemblance" to that for which it stands. Thus, analog codes have a degree of *isomorphy,* or similarity, to the object, idea, or feeling they represent. For example, in many film or theater productions actors "fool" you by making their behavior similar to a person in love. A "picture of an apple" is an analog code for an actual apple. Digital codes, on the other hand, are "arbitrary assignments" that receive their communications effectiveness by consensus or agreement. For example, children often play games with the arbitrary character of language by getting everyone to agree that no means yes and yes means no and "Now, let's ask Dad for ice cream cones." Arabic numerals provide another example: "2" bears no resemblance to two things nor does the sound have any inherent "twoness" to it. If Jack selects a digital code, it will most likely carry accurate commonly agreed-on information but will probably not carry much of the affect intended in his sentiment of "I love you." Indeed, imagine a completely digital message such as Morse code carrying the message "I love you"—not much affect there! If Jack is an effective communicator, he will select either both types of encodings or the more affectual analog codes.

The selection of the code directly affects Jack's choice of channels. Nonverbal channels are most appropriate for analog codes (Gottman, 1979; Mehrabian, 1972). Verbal and written channels are most appropriate for digital codes. If Jack is going to write Jan a letter saying "I love you," he will most likely embellish it with metaphor and other techniques to carry more affect or rely on Hallmark to come up with the correctly packaged digital communication. On the other hand, if Jack sees Jan face to face, he will probably use analog and digital codes carried on nonverbal and verbal channels simultaneously. Not only does this multiple channel carry both affective and cognitive dimensions of a message, but it provides message "redundancy" so that if noise interferes with one channel the message will get through on another channel. For example, if Jack is holding Jan's hand, gazing lovingly into Jan's eyes, and smiling, the fact that an airplane flying overhead obliterates the sound of his words "I love you" may not result in the loss of the message.

Jan must have the appropriate sense receptors to receive the channels on which the message is sent. For example, if Jan hears a noise and is distracted from Jack's nonverbal message and in addition the noise drowns out Jack's verbal message, then much of the message is lost because of poor reception. Once the channels are accurately received, to get the message as Jack sent it, Jan must decode in the same way in which Jack encoded. A far-fetched example of decoding error would be if Jack meant his eye gaze to carry the analog affect of "love" but Jan decoded his "blinking" as something caught in his eye. Once the decoding occurs, then Jan must select from among the repertoire of possible "meanings" of messages she expects from Jack. If Jack and Jan had been married only a short time, the probability of decoding and selecting the message "I love you" might be fairly high. Lastly, feedback in this model is simply where Jan becomes the sender and Jack the receiver. Perhaps in response to Jack's message of love, Jan will send Jack the digital message "ditto."

The complexity of the processes in the basic communications diagram is enormous. Most scholars focus on the most directly measurable and observable part of the process, which is the message. Great strides in the study of marital interaction have been made by studying gender differences in decoding verbal and nonverbal messages. For example, Gottman and Porterfield (1981) report that dissatisfied husbands are poor decoders of their wife's nonverbal messages. Many researchers have also worked on the sequential dependencies between husband and wife messages (Gottman, 1979). The research in this area has reached such a magnitude that there are several excellent reviews of the marital interaction literature, such as Noller and Fitzpatrick (1993). This area continues to be one of the most active and encouraging areas of scientific research of all the variants of systems theory.

FAMILY PROCESS THEORY

Family process theory, for the most part, can be identified with the more applied practitioners and therapists studying the family. As we have previously noted, scholars such as Bateson and Jackson had very tangible concerns, such as the treatment of schizophrenia (Bateson et al., 1956). The tangible interests giving impetus to such scholars should in no way demean their theoretical contributions, however. After all, before a therapist can effectively treat a psychopathology, he or she must have some idea of the causative factors.

The most recent statement of family process theory is by Broderick (1993), who, like other family process theorists (e.g., Kantor & Lehr, 1975), views the family as a goal-seeking system. Much of the family system, however, is devoted to maintaining social and spatial relationships within the family and between the family and the environment. Within the family, social and spatial relationships between dyads must be managed so that individuals are protected from each other's demands (buffering) and individuals are linked to each other (bonding). The relations between the family and its environment are composed of transactions that bridge and link the family to external systems while maintaining the boundaries of the family system. Broderick's (1993) view of the family system is one of the most ambitious to date because he seeks to identify both internal and external relationships.

Because many family process theorists are also immersed in the treatment of psychopathology, in some senses the theories they were constructing are more theories of family therapy than of the family. The emphasis to scientifically test claims may seem less important than if the theory "works" in the therapeutic situation. This has led to family process theory being considered metaphorical. Because so much of family process theory is concerned with applications, much of it strays from the precision we would seek in scientific theory and is more focused on guiding metaphors. For example, Minuchin (1974) developed the notion that boundaries are critical in distinguishing pathologies in families. He pioneered aspects of family process theory linked to distance regulation and closeness and coined the term *enmeshment* to describe these processes. Nowhere, however, did Minuchin provide a systematic definition of his idea of boundaries. Indeed, terms such as enmeshment, bounding, and buffering offer sensitizing metaphors for the clinician (e.g., Rosenblatt, 1994). These metaphors are similar to the ones offered by psychotherapists such as Carl Rogers, Jung, and Freud. They may prove useful in the formulation of more rigorous scientific and theoretical concepts, but this development will never happen if family process scholars are content to view these collections of metaphors as "theory."

Empirical Applications

MARITAL AND FAMILY COMMUNICATIONS

Systems theory has proven to be the major conceptual framework used in the study of marital interaction and family communications. As we have seen, the systems approach first entered family studies through the work of therapists such as Don Jackson who were very concerned with the family system of communications. This impetus later bifurcated into the two variants of communications theory and family process theory. It is in the study of marital and family communications that systems theory research seems to have made the most scientific progress. In this section, we examine only a few of the many contributions made by researchers in this area.

From the outset both systems ideas and ideas from communications theory were fused because a communications system is simply one type of general system. Researchers in the 1960s had been guided by the early work of Bateson et al. (1956). Following in this tradition is the work by the MRI group of Watzlawick, Beavin, and Jackson (1967). This book goes far beyond earlier explorations into systems theory by Jackson (e.g., 1974). The major contribution of this work is to introduce family scholars to communications theory and to establish a systematic approach to the encoding and decoding of both nonverbal and verbal messages. Many of the suggestions in this work regarding nonverbal communications were simultaneously developed by an independent group of scholars in psychology led by Mehrabian and Wiener (1968).

In 1968, Mishler and Waxler published their now-classic study on family processes, *Interaction in Families*. In their research, they examined patterns of marital and family communications and the possible linkage to schizophrenia. Their empirical work raised significant doubts about the "double-bind" hypothesis (Bateson et al., 1956) but at the same time demonstrated how complex questions about family communications patterns could be scientifically studied. Indeed, their finding that families containing a schizophrenic child showed more orderly patterns of interaction than the chaotic patterns of interruption and lack of rule following demonstrated by "normal" families turned previous suppositions on their head. Mishler and Waxler's

(1968) conclusions exemplified scientific caution in that they pointed out that in their research they could not determine whether the interaction patterns in the families with a schizophrenic child were the cause of the child's problem or the effect of the family's adjustment to the child's problem.

Building on the contributions of Watzlawick and colleagues (1967) as well as Mishler and Waxler (1968), in *Communication, Conflict and Marriage,* Raush, Barry, Hertel, and Swain (1974) developed the sender-receiver model as a system of contingencies. These authors proposed that marital interaction was a system in which the next action of the husband toward the wife was contingent on the previous message the wife sent to the husband. Because messages are behavior, this model could be examined as a time series of spousal behavioral contingencies. A simplistic example of this process is if a husband is nasty to a wife, the "reciprocity" model of contingencies would predict that she would be nasty in return.

Although this notion seems somewhat obvious common sense, it turns out to be largely untrue. It is addressed in a much more sophisticated formulation by Gottman, Markman, and Notarius (1977) and later by Gottman (1979). Their approach is to test the contingencies between spousal verbal and nonverbal messages over time using a series of contingent probabilities (a discrete-state Markov chain). Their findings are important. They found that the emotional affect carried in nonverbal messages is a better discriminator of distressed from non-distressed couples than more traditional verbal measures such as spousal agreement. Second, they found little support for a simple *quid pro quo,* or spousal reciprocity, hypothesis. The patterns of marital interaction over a series of time points showed that research in this area is both complex and worthwhile. For John Gottman, this has become a programmatic theme in his research, culminating in the identification of specific patterns of interaction that lead to couple disintegration and to the specification of causes for these patterns (Gottman, 1979, 1993; Gottman & Krokoff, 1989; Gottman & Levenson, 1992; Gottman et al., 1977; Gottman & Porterfield, 1981; Levenson & Gottman, 1983).

Although much of Gottman's work is focused on the message or behavior, he has largely ignored questions about message reception and perception. Mary Ann Fitzpatrick (1988) in her book *Between*

Husbands and Wives studies some of the verbal and nonverbal codes tied to disclosure and intimacy for traditional and nontraditional marriage. Her work and that of her colleague, Patricia Noller (1984), has culminated in a joint project providing a systematic overview of communication in the family (Noller & Fitzpatrick, 1993). Although there remain significant unresolved theoretical problems, there can be little doubt that scholars studying communications systems have provided the clearest example of the force and utility of a systems approach for the scientific study of the family.

Implications for Intervention

One cannot think of the usefulness of systems theory for intervention without at once thinking of family therapy. Family therapy is not the only area for which there are applications for systems theory. Anderson (1993) suggests several implications for family policy studies. But systems theory has provided at least four decades of family practitioners and therapists with the basic tools for theorizing about their interventions. This history of application is far from a monotonic, progressive march forward but might be better viewed as a tree with numerous branches. Undoubtedly, some of these branches of family systems therapies may not bear fruit and some might.

Broderick (1993) and others see family systems theory and theories of family therapy as united in what he terms *family process theory*. The history of this linkage between systems theory and therapy is usually traced to the work by Bateson, Jackson, and their colleagues (1956) at the MRI in Palo Alto, California. This group of scholars popularized such notions as *homeostatic family patterns* and *dysfunctional family systems*. The legacy of their work is with us today in explanations of various individual psychopathologies (e.g., anorexia nervosa) by family system characteristics, even though empirical support for pathogenesis and family patterns has been weak (e.g., Mishler & Waxler, 1968; Olson, 1972; Schuham, 1967).

The application of systems theory to family therapy is not guided by simply one theory. General systems theory may serve as an overall metaphor, but various scholars have focused on different dimensions of the metaphor. For example, Minuchin (1974) focuses on the maintenance of system boundaries and Bowen (1978) focuses on the individual's differentiation of self.

Among the more prominent contributions to systems approaches to the family is that of David Olson (1995). Over the past three decades, Olson has complemented his therapeutic approach with rigorous scientific research. He has developed a systems model called the *circumplex model,* according to which he categorizes families by their degree of adaptability and cohesion. Some families are high in cohesion (enmeshed) and low in adaptability (rigid); other families may be low in cohesion (disengaged) but high in adaptability (chaotic). Olson views normal families as occupying a range in which cohesion and adaptability are balanced rather than at the extreme points of the continuum. His system approach can incorporate the changes in the balance that families experience over time. The therapist addresses imbalances in the system by helping families move to more balanced distributions of cohesion and adaptability. For some families, this might entail learning to regard family rules as less important. In other families, it might entail helping the family to become more organized. Olson's systemic approach has a broad range of applications running from dating to elderly families, including families of orientation as well as procreation. Certainly Olson's work stands as one of the most popular of the systems approaches and one of the better examples of the fusion of science with therapy.

Critiques and Discussion

Without a doubt, the criticism of systems theory that has the potential to be the most damaging is that systems theory is in truth a "model" or "flow chart approach" but not a theory. Critics charge that even the concepts in systems theory, such as variety and feedback, are more methodological than theoretical. These concepts lack any real substantive content, compared to concepts like *power.* Critics also argue that systems approaches using mathematical models may seem to provide "prediction," but they do not succeed. The critics make a distinction between "forecasting," which as in weather forecasting is simply based on past records, and "prediction," which is a deduction from a set of substantive theoretical propositions. Systems theorists point to the few propositions that Wilkinson (1977) has offered in regard to the family, but critics are quick to point out that these are vague and there are no guidelines for what constitutes variety or even feedback.

Systems advocates argue that the accusation that the systems approach is a model and not a theory is only tenable if one adopts a specific view (epistemology) of how science works. The traditional model of science is called the *hypothetico-deductive* model in that a set of propositions is logically linked to produce a deduction that can then be empirically tested. In this view of science, whichever theory produces the most efficient explanation is the best theory. In this sense, theories are in competition with one another. This hypothetico-deductive perspective is based on a viewpoint (epistemology) that is counterpoised to the *constructivist* position. You may recall that according to the constructivist position different models may be useful for different purposes. Even models intended to explain the same phenomena may illuminate different aspects, as in the parable about the blind men feeling the elephant in which no one description was an accurate description of the whole elephant but all of the descriptions were true. Thus, systems theorists do not see themselves as playing by the same competitive rules as traditional science. This is not to say that systems theory is less scientific in the broad sense, but it does adopt a less competitive view of scientific theory.

A second criticism that has plagued systems theory is that it is too abstract and global to be of much use. The ideas in systems theory are so general as to be almost meaningless. In their quest to unify the sciences, systems theorists have abstracted to a level in which there is little meaning. Critics claim that when systems theory is applied to concrete empirical situations, the generality of its concepts trivializes and glosses over important distinctions. Turner (1991) gives the example that "notions of 'information' do not communicate the properties denoted by more traditional concepts like norms, values, beliefs, ideology, etc." (p. 130).

Systems theorists say that what most of these critics miss is that it is always easier to apply "general" ideas across diverse contexts then to apply "specific" ideas. For example, the "information processing" of crustaceans provided a basic analog for Gottman's (1979) work on marital communication. Although no one doubts that discipline-specific concepts and theories are important, it is increasingly difficult to see parts of the natural and social world as not being tied together. Naturally, systems theorists would argue that the only way we can move between diverse contexts and species is by utilizing a common set of concepts that will help us see the connections and similarity of processes.

Another criticism is that family systems theorists tend to reify the idea of system. This criticism is perhaps aimed more at the family process variant of systems theory. For example, family therapists who claim they are using systems theory in simply calling a family a system of interrelated parts or interacting personalities are attributing reality to a heuristic model for understanding. Family process theorists, like many other scientists, would like to see their knowledge benefit humankind. But in their attempts to apply systems theory to the family, family process scholars seem prone to slip from viewing the family *as* a system to the view that the family *is* a system. This slippage from an epistemology favoring knowledge as possible heuristic models to a way of knowing that clearly makes ontological claims about the nature of family reality is a prime example of reification, or what Whitehead (1929, p. 11) called "the fallacy of misplaced concreteness." In the social sciences, this is always a threat. Hard on the heels of this threat of mistaking knowledge claims for ontological claims are the arguments that what is ontologically given represents the correct moral order. This argument from "what is in reality" to "what should be" is typical of 17th-century "natural law" arguments. The following quote provides a vivid example of how clinicians, scholars, and practitioners may get caught in reification and moralism:

> In reviewing this attempt to summarize how family systems *do* operate, I am struck by how clinicians spend a good deal of energy trying to get families to operate as they believe a good family system *should* operate— that is by establishing joint goals and monitoring progress toward them, These clinicians work hard to make family members more aware of the dynamics of their previously unmediated escalating cycles so that they can bring these cycles into line with their intentions. In short, such clinicians do all they can in their power to make families more cybernetic, less reflexive, and less opportunistic. (Broderick, 1993, pp. 85-86)

Clinicians and systems theorists might respond that this criticism can be substantiated by an ample number of instances in which scholars make such incautious claims in almost every area of science. Systems theorists would argue that every field contains its proportion of naive participants and outrageous claims. The rejoinder that systems theorists offer is that reification is totally inconsistent with the constructivist epistemology according to which systems models are not models of "reality" so much as heuristics for different purposes. Therefore, systems theorists feel that their area is no more prone to reification than any other theory. Furthermore, systems theorists would argue that the constructivist epistemology militates against such abuses more than is the case in the traditional theoretical approaches.

Conclusion

Family systems theory has proved useful in two areas of family studies. One of these areas is family therapy. Family process scholars have found systems theory to be a useful metaphor in guiding inter-vention and interpreting the complex relationships between indi-viduals and their families. The second area family systems theory has proved useful in is the area of marital and family communications and interaction. Communications theory is properly a form of systems theory as it incorporates many of the basic concepts such as feedback and variety (see Shannon & Weaver, 1949). It has proven a most useful approach for the scientific study of the family. The conflict, if any, between these two variants is whether or not systems theory is both metaphor and science. A clear understanding of the constructivist epistemology behind systems theory allows both interpretations. The same model may be used for different purposes and in different ways.

Is the future of systems theory in the study of the family a bright one? Turner (1991) is pessimistic because he feels the concepts and models in systems theory do not fit well with social phenomena: "For example, efforts to adopt decision theory, game theory, information theory, analysis of servomechanisms, and similar bodies of precise concepts have never proven very useful" (p. 130). The experience of family scholars appears to be at odds with this assessment. Further-more, Turner's view of what has "proven very useful" may be at odds with the more open perspective assumed by systems theorists. In the final analysis, optimism or pessimism about systems theory may largely depend on how scholars view the noncompetitive epistemology of constructivism. Von Glasersfeld (1987) ends his essay with the warning of a true believer: "Looking at the world today, one must conclude that this way of thinking, rather than fostering competition, may be the only way to maintain human life on this planet" (p. 11).

Food for Thought

1. Can you explain what the difference is between thinking of a family *as* a system versus thinking the family *is* a system?
2. "Feedback" is one of the more important concepts in systems theory. Would a poor grade from your teacher be "positive" or "negative" feedback?
3. One criticism of systems theory is that it is a "mechanistic" rather than "organic" theory. Do you think this is an accurate criticism?
4. Is it possible to apply theories to solve concrete everyday problems without "reifying" the concepts?
5. Using Figure 6.1, can you draw what your family system might look like?

Suggested Readings

Broderick, C. (1993). *Understanding family process.* Newbury Park, CA: Sage.
> This is an excellent introduction to family process theory that nicely unifies both scientific and therapeutic contributions to the theory.

Whitchurch, G., & Constantine, L. (1993). Systems theory. In P. Boss, W. Doherty, R. LaRossa, W. Schumm, & S. Steinmetz (Eds.), *Sourcebook of family theories and methods: A contextual approach* (pp. 325-352). New York: Plenum.
> This chapter provides a good general history and survey of systems theory.

7

The Conflict Framework

Bill and Mariel have been living together for about a year. They have decided to get married. They both wanted to have a church wedding. The minister they contacted told them that the church requires all those wanting to be married to attend a marriage preparation course offered by the church. Tonight, they are attending the first of the marriage preparation classes. Bill is quite skeptical of the course. He believes that because he and Mariel have lived together for almost a year, they should know a lot about what to expect in marriage. Bill and Mariel complete their answers to an inventory of questions regarding expectations for marriage before they sit down with their counselor. The counselor's first question is, "The two of you have answered the question, 'How many arguments and fights you expect per month?' in very different ways. Mariel expects about four per month and Bill only envisions one per month. Can you each explain to me how you view fights and why you have such different expectations about the number of fights?"

Bill answers that perhaps he and Mariel have a different definition of what a fight is. He defines a fight as not just a disagreement but one person being angry toward the other person. To his surprise, Mariel agrees with his definition. Bill then asks Mariel, "So, if there is no difference between our definitions, why do you think we will fight that much?" Mariel responds that her parents have been happily married for 30 years and that is about how much they fight. Bill says, "Fighting that much isn't healthy for a relationship," but Mariel counters that fighting is normal in a marriage as long as it doesn't get out of hand. The counselor then asks, "If a couple were always harmonious, what would spark them to grow and change?"

Bill and Mariel have encountered some differences in their basic expectations about marriage. Bill appears to believe that happy marriages are harmonious, with few disagreements or fights. Mariel seems to be more accepting of conflict as being "natural" in marriage. The counselor's final question about growth and change would appear to support the view that conflict in marriage might even play an important dynamic role. Bill and Mariel are faced with an important task. They are being asked to identify what they see as the role of conflict in marriage. Are good marriages free of conflict? Is conflict always destructive or could it be a source of growth and nourishment for a relationship? And how do partners in a marriage keep conflict from getting out of hand?

These questions are part of what we address in this chapter. This chapter is concerned with the way conflict theory explains family behavior. In every theory, there reside assumptions about the nature of humans and the constraints under which humans operate. In addition, we all carry around our own assumptions and expectations, such as assumptions about what our marriage will be like and what is "normal" and "not normal" in marriage. In a sense, then, this chapter on conflict theory will not "answer" the questions posed above. But perhaps more than any other of the theoretical frameworks in this book, conflict theory allows us to fully discuss and examine these important questions and assumptions about conflict.

Intellectual Traditions

The central question for conflict theory was first and perhaps most simply stated by the social philosopher Thomas Hobbes (1651/1947) as "How is social order possible?" Without an understanding of the perspective Hobbes and later conflict theorists have about human nature, the question regarding social order might appear naive. Like utilitarian theorists, Hobbes believed that the first law of all organisms is self-preservation and self-assertion. He emphasized that among humans this law is elevated to a natural right. As a result of the natural right of the human self to survive and assert itself, the first law presents us with a natural order in which people's self-interest collides with the self-interest of others. The basic state of nature then is a "war of all against all." Hobbes acknowledges that such an existence would be short, brutish, and largely intolerable. This leads Hobbes to his second law, according to which humans form a social contract whereby all humans give up some of their rights of self-interest to live in a stable and secure society of laws. Unlike the case in utilitarianism, once a society of laws is established, much of human self-interest is regulated and governed by laws rather than negotiated. Hobbes did not see all rights of self-interest being relinquished to the state, however. Human self-interest continues to provide the impetus for collision and conflict but within the framework of the laws of the state.

Hobbes and other social contract theorists set the stage for much of the evolution of conflict theory. The assumptions of human self-interest and the need for a social contract are ideas held by most conflict theorists in one form or another. But it was Karl Marx and Friedrich Engels who not only developed a more thorough and sophisticated view of conflict but directly applied their perspective to the family. Marx and Engels developed a theory of history (*historiography*) in which they envisioned social and historical change occurring by means of class conflict. Marx and Engels, like most of their cohort in Europe, were influenced by the German idealist Friedrich Hegel (1770-1831). Hegel viewed history as ruled by a dialectic of ideas (thus the moniker of idealism). According to Hegel's dialectical logic, each idea (thesis) automatically presupposed its opposite (antithesis), and out of the tension between the idea and its opposite, the mind would seek to unify the opposition, doing so by creatively moving to a more encompassing idea (synthesis). This synthesis would form a new thesis and presuppose another antithesis followed by an even more encompassing synthesis and so on.

Marx and Engels vehemently attacked the Hegelian notions (e.g., Marx & Engels, 1845-1846/1965). They argued that history was ruled not by ideas but by material production. Using Hegel's dialectic, they explained that there were in fact only two relations to production. People could either control the means of production or labor for those who controlled production. Marx and Engels then proposed a "dialectic material" explanation of history from primitive to modern times. For example, in feudal times the opposition was between the lords who owned the land and the serfs who worked the land. In the industrial era, the opposition was between the new industrialists (*bourgeoisie*) and the factory workers or proletariat (e.g., Marx, 1913). Marx and Engels envisioned an end to the dialectic of class opposition only with the development of automation and communal society.

The family occupies a unique niche in the conflict theory of Marx and Engels. They recognized that the family was rooted in biological self-interest (sex and reproduction) and yet is also a form of social organization. Engels (1884/1946), in his book *The Origin of the Family, Private Property and the State*, attributes the move from matrilineage (mother right) to patrilineage, patriarchy, and monogamy (father right) as being the result of the first division of labor, based on gender. Out of this biologically rooted division of labor came the first class conflict: "The first class opposition that appears in history coincides with the development of the antagonism between man and woman in monogamous marriage, and the first class oppression coincides with that of the female sex by the male" (Engels, 1946, p. 58). Although Engels did not see the family as a "causal" influence, he did see it as a microcosm of the conflict in the larger culture: "It is the cellular form of civilized society, in which the nature of the oppositions and contradictions fully active in that society can already be studied" (p. 58). Thus, for Engels, the family provided a microcosm of the class conflict in the larger society rather than having its own independent microsystem process of conflict. This is the first introduction to a basic question in conflict theory, which is, "Does conflict in marriage and the family simply mirror a macrosocial process or is the conflict in the family of a different kind?"

At the core of the conflict theory of Hobbes, Marx, and Engels lies a basic assumption about scarcity of resources. If there were a surplus of resources, then even if humans act out of self-interest, there would be no reason for them to pursue conflict. Indeed, Marx made this scarcity a key to the last phase of his dialectical materialist view of history in switching from resources being distributed "to each according to his work" to "to each according to his need." Later, family conflict theorists (e.g., Scanzoni, 1972; Sprey, 1979) became more conscious of this assumption as being the basic factor underlying the notion of conflict. The ideas of resources and power have become central to what many consider to be the true nature of conflict in the family.

Although some conflict scholars undoubtedly see resources as the key to understanding conflict, others believe that conflict also has a structural dimension. Georg Simmel (1904) viewed conflict as being embedded in the structure of groups. Moreover, he emphasized the positive role of conflict in achieving greater unity for the group. Sprey (1979) has a more concrete perspective on the structural characteristics of the dialectic within families. He envisions "a perpetual confrontation between the quest for autonomy and jointness as characteristic of all groups, but especially small intimate ones, such as marriages and families" (1979, p. 141). Indeed, Sprey sees this form of structural conflict as so endemic that "issues involving individual autonomy and the competition between privacy and jointness cannot be 'solved' except through the termination of the relationship" (p. 147). One of the implications of the structuralist perspective on conflict is that because conflict is endemic in the group the only alternative is to "manage" conflict so that it does not escalate to damaging levels or reduce the group to totally separate individuals.

In the century that has passed since Marx and Engels, conflict theory has developed as one of the theories in the pantheon of social science theories. The writings of Marx and Engels contained both a theory of history and what Turner (1991) calls an emancipatory call to action (e.g., Marx & Engels, 1867/1971). This emancipatory element has led some scholars to view conflict theory as essentially nonscientific:

Conflict theory tends to be only a step away from *ideology,* which may be defined as the organization of ideas for the promotion of social movements or for the defense of social institutions. An ideology is a system of ideas intended to serve practice rather than to promote the aims of understanding. (Martindale, 1960, p. 151)

On the other side, some proponents of the emancipatory vision of conflict theory argue that all social science theories are ideologies because they all defend one institution or another. Marx and Engels argued that understanding is emancipatory and that knowledge and political action are always tied together (praxis). Without pretending to resolve this argument, we should nonetheless point out that some family conflict theorists view the theory as providing both understanding and political direction (e.g., Firestone, 1970).

Summing up, the focus of conflict theory is on both conflict within groups (family interaction) and conflict between groups (class conflict). Some conflict theorists of the family view internal family interactions as being part of the larger social process (Firestone, 1970), and others view the conflict in the family as being unique because of the affectual nature of the resources (Scanzoni, 1970). Most conflict theorists accept the assumptions from Hobbes that humans act out of self-interest and that social order needs to be negotiated and ritualized. The existence of social order in the form of the state and laws does not mean that conflict is absent. Rather, conflict continues between interest groups and between self-interested individuals, and these conflicts must be managed to keep the group from the extremes of social breakup on the one hand and war on the other hand.

Focus and Scope Assumptions

Humans are motivated principally by self-interest. Individuals' self-interest is rooted in the will to survive and persevere. By extension, humans generalize this orientation of self-interest from mere survival to a more general mode of operating in the world. Thus, if one desires something owned by another who has more power or forces, the solution is to ban together with like-minded persons to gain sufficient force to realize your desires. This is the state of nature. In contrast to utilitarian theories, this self-interest is not necessarily tied to a rational faculty. This rather unbridled primitive self-interest is the source of Hobbes's "war of all against all."

Conflict is endemic in social groups. People who join together to attain a goal of common interest such as having children nonetheless have conflict because of disagreements on other issues and the structural opposition between autonomy and togetherness. Indeed, we can imagine that in those social groups (family) in which we spend the most time and have the greatest expectations for "togetherness" we might also find the greatest conflict.

Conflict is inevitable between social groups. Not only do we expect to find conflict in small intimate social groups, but we expect conflict between social groups. Individuals have "interests," but in any society those interests must be pursued by means of group affiliation. All social groups have "interests," even if only for survival. Usually, these interests are more far reaching, such as for wealth or land. Because not all groups can simultaneously achieve their goals (resource scarcity), there is conflict. The assumption is that groups and individuals must compete for scarce resources. Indeed, resource scarcity is the necessary condition for competition.

As a result of both structural conflict and competition, we find that *the normal state of society is to be in conflict rather than harmony.* Harmony is an achieved rather than a natural state. This assumption is crucial to our understanding families through the perspective of conflict theory. Accordingly, when you get married you should expect to be entering an arrangement more prone to conflict than harmony.

Because conflict is both endemic and inevitable, the primary concern in the study of social groups such as the family is how they manage conflict. If conflict is the rule, then the Hobbesian question, "How is order possible?" makes sense even in the study of such close and intimate groups as the family. Indeed, much of family conflict theory involves examination of the techniques used in marriages and families to keep these groups from either separation or war.

Concepts

CONFLICT

Of course, the most basic concept in conflict theory is that of conflict. Conflict has been variously defined as disagreement, clashes, and discordance in interests or ideas. The definition that Sprey (1979) offers is exceptional in its clarity. He says that *conflict as a process* "is defined as a confrontation between individuals, or groups, over scarce resources, controversial means, incompatible goals, or combinations of these" (p. 134). Sprey's emphasis that conflict is a process rather than a behavior is consistent with Marx and other theorists who emphasize the dialectical nature of conflict. Thus, behavior might be used to infer this process, but the process itself is not necessarily observable. For example, your parents might want you to visit on the weekend, but this clashes with your plans for a fishing trip. This particular example of parent-child conflict of goals may not be readily observable to an external observer and represents a more covert conflict. The same might be true of a clash in ideas. But the conflict between runners at a track meet attempting to be first across the finish line is readily observable and overt.

STRUCTURE

Structure has two meanings in conflict theory: the *structure of the situation* as either competitive or cooperative and the *structure of the group*. Let's examine the cooperative or competitive situational structure first.

Competition does not refer to a process but to an observable organization or structure of scarce resources. Competition is the way in which a situation is organized or structured. For example, if we tell students that we will "fit" their grades to a "normal" curve so that only 5% will receive an A, then we are structuring the learning situation in a competitive way. In this case, it makes sense for students not to assist one another because they lessen their own probability of getting an A in the course. If we tell all students what the standard is for attaining an A and that all may get As if they attain these standards, then we structure the learning situation in a noncompetitive way, a way that emphasizes *cooperation*. In this situation, the free exchange of ideas and assistance makes sense. Competition and cooperation, then, are set by the social rules, or norms, that organize an activity or social system. These rules, or norms, structure the situation so that not all parties interested in the goal can achieve it (competition) or so that potentially all parties interested in the goal can achieve it.

The second meaning of structure is the *structure of the group*, or *social structure*. There are several dimensions to the social structure of the group that conflict theorists view as salient. First, and most obvious, is the dimension of the number of members in the group. Conflict theorists from Simmel (1904) to the present recognize that group size affects the techniques with which the group can manage conflict. For example, a two-person group cannot be democratic; a dyad can only argue and negotiate. Groups of three or more can form power coalitions to get their way (e.g., Caplow, 1968). A second dimension of group structure is the age of the members. Marx and Engels (1867/1971) pointed out in *The Communist Manifesto* that children and women were subjugated to the male bourgeoisie. Later, Caplow (1968) argued that resources and power accrue with the aging of children in the family. He supposed that as children developed social skills and resources their power in the family increased. Likewise, we might suggest that aging is in part a loss of some resources and power. The third dimension of the structure of the group is gender. Marx and Engels viewed gender as important in the internal dialectic of the family in the first division of labor. Some later theorists concentrate exclusively on the issues of gender and the dialectics within the family (Firestone, 1970). Thus, most conflict theorists analyze the structure of the group by the number of members, the age structure, and the gender structure.

RESOURCES

The notion of *resources* is a pivotal concept for conflict theory. Marx and Engels viewed the basic resource as the "control of the means of production." Their focus on the material economy has proved too narrow for most current conflict theorists. The concept of resources is a broader concept, closely aligned to the notion of power. We would be less than accurate if we did not report that there exists considerable scholarly debate on the exact relationship between power, resources, and authority (e.g., Brinkerhoff & Lupri, 1989; Cromwell & Olson, 1975; Szinovacz, 1987). We present what we believe is a coherent picture of the relationship between authority, power, and resources. Resources is the broadest of the three concepts and includes the other two concepts (power and authority) as subsets. Resources include all those knowledge, skills, techniques, and materials that are at the ready disposal of a person or group. Clearly, resources provide a potential base for the exercise of power. Power, according to Sprey (1979), is the ability of an individual or group to exercise effective control over others and things. Clearly, power can only be measured by its outcome, which is control, whereas resources provide the potential for power and control. Authority is a type of resource that is constructed by the normative system of a specific culture (Rodman, 1967). Thus, for example, a woman in Greece might have more resources (potential) than her unemployed husband, but if there is a strong cultural norm for patriarchy, then the husband may have greater control (power) in the family. Under more egalitarian or democratic authority norms, the greater resources of the female would give her greater control (power) (Scanzoni, 1972). Thus, the relationship between authority and power is that the normative system (authority) can serve as one among many resources. Resources that are relevant in a situation can be used to exert control or exercise power.

NEGOTIATION

Negotiation is one of the major techniques used in families to manage conflict. Negotiation is restricted, however, to those situations in which each person or group desires a goal that cannot be attained without the assistance of other parties. A simple example of this is sexual intercourse. Although it may be one person's goal, without the cooperation of the other party it is impossible. Another example is when a mother might want to take the family on a picnic but the father prefers taking the family to the swimming pool. Behind both options is the notion of "doing something with the family," which means that willing cooperation is needed to reach the goal. Negotiation happens when both parties state their goals and then use their resources to induce or coerce the other to move closer to their goal. Argument, bribery, and deceit may all be involved in negotiations.

CONSENSUS

Consensus means agreement. It is the preferable outcome of negotiation. Consensus is achieved when parties to a negotiation agree. For example, many family members enter into temporary coalitions with a sibling or parent to achieve an end. Such coalitions rely on agreement between the coalition partners. Agreement or consensus can also be achieved in mate selection by selecting mates with the same values and orientation and by socialization of mate or children to accept the same view one holds. The opposite of consensus is disagreement. Dissension is discord arising from a disagreement. It is an interesting trademark of close relationships that we spend enormous amounts of time focused on areas of disagreement but seldom feel a need to focus on areas of agreement—because they have been successfully managed.

Propositions

Conflict theorists have often concentrated on macrosystem analysis of society and global confrontations. Some conflict theorists believe that the family is simply a microcosm of these larger processes and that what is said of the larger society is naturally also true for the family. A significant number of family conflict theorists have claimed, however, that the family (and some other small groups) is sufficiently dissimilar to the macrolevel and that they must be analyzed separately. Sprey (1979) for one argues that the autonomy-togetherness issue is atypical of macrolevel analyses and yet important in analyzing the family. Caplow (1968) argues that there are distinct and important structural differences between even two-person and three-person groups. The propositions we include below principally focus on the family. Although there are a few propositions about the distribution of resources in the larger society, here we try to focus consistently on the family.

Social groups such as the family are structurally disposed to conflict both within and between groups. This supposition implies that variables subsumed under structure of the group (membership, age, gender) and structure of the situation (competition and cooperation) are related to the degree of conflict. Even the most homogeneous group (two females of the same age) in the most cooperative normative situation would still be predisposed to conflict, because in a dyad there is the structural issue of autonomy-togetherness and in dyads all issues can only be resolved by direct negotiation (see fourth proposition below).

Conflict between groups is based on resource allocation and competitive social structure.

There exists no known society in which resources are allocated equally to all. This is not to say that resource allocation is unfair. Indeed, even Marx was not egalitarian in this regard but said "to each according to his need"—and needs are not distributed equally. Thus, the mere fact that some families have more than others ensures competition. Usually families participate in larger interest-group clusters such as Children First or other profamily or prochild groups. Regardless of the validity of the perceptions involved, the recent uproar over "family values" attests to the fact that many families see themselves competing for scarce benefits against "nonfamily" groups such as gays, singles, and even single-parent families. As a corollary to the above,

Conflict within the group (e.g., family) is due to the inequity of resources between individuals.

Resources are differentially allocated in a social system, often by group membership, age, and gender. As a result, resource differentials exist in the family so that some members have more resources than other members. This resource inequity leads to conflict to the degree that the norms internal to the family are competitive rather than cooperative. For example, females generally make less money than males, ensuring that they have fewer resources and, therefore, even in egalitarian authority structures, have on average less power in relation to their husband.

Conflict within marriages and families is minimally structural. Regardless of gender and age, dyads and larger groups are faced with the conflict of individual members over autonomy versus togetherness. This issue is especially salient for the dyad in two regards. First, togetherness necessarily involves the only other member. A family group offers several levels of togetherness (sibling, mother-child, etc.), but togetherness in the dyad always involves the other person. The second reason the issue of conflict is especially salient for the dyad is that negotiations are always against the same adversary. In families, coalitions can be formed to overpower the resources of any one individual. One implicit strength of family coalitions is that your coalition partners on today's issue might well be your adversaries on tomorrow's issue and today's enemy might be tomorrow's coalition partner. The dyad lacks this dynamic; today's adversary is also tomorrow's adversary in negotiations (Caplow, 1968).

Negotiation, as a form of conflict management, is more likely in egalitarian authority structures.

and

The outcome of negotiation is more likely to favor the person with the greatest resources in the family.

The authority pattern in the culture sets up the norms or rules as to who has authority based on age and gender. The more unilateral the authority pattern (matriarchy, patriarchy) the less room there is for negotiation. Indeed, negotiation is most likely in democratic or egalitarian families.

Negotiation involves resources; whoever has the greatest resources can negotiate the greatest rewards in a compromise.

This proposition is somewhat akin to the old saying, "Them that's got, gets." It must be remembered, however, that there are many forms of resources besides money and occupation. Indeed, personal abilities to manipulate, lie, and cajole must be counted among the resources of relevance in negotiations. Negotiations are almost invariably used in egalitarian marriages, whereas once children are present coalition formation might play a larger role than negotiation.

Coalition formation is most likely in groups (families) with democratic authority patterns.

and

In democratic groups, material resources alone do not necessarily predict family coalitions and outcomes.

In most North American families, one person does not make all the decisions. Decision making is a complex matter of consultation, coalition formation, and lobbying. Caplow (1968) points out that as children grow and mature they gain increased interpersonal competence, knowledge, and material resources. The power that they have is not sufficiently great as to countermand the father's residual patriarchal authority and greater material resources, but coupled with the mother and other siblings, children might have significant influence over decision making. Indeed, even before the children are old enough to participate in such coalitions, they are assumed to be coalesced with the mother and constitute a resource for the mother in that she might voice what is best for the children as part of negotiations.

These few propositions represent a small subset of the many that have been developed in conflict theory. These few should be sufficient to demonstrate how conflict theorists deal with the sources of conflict and the management of conflict in families. Most scholars would agree that the family is the central building block of social systems, and we might propose that the techniques of conflict management and authority patterns learned in the family influence the directions to be taken by the entire social system. In this sense, it could easily be argued that Marx's view that the family is a microcosm reflecting processes in the larger society could be turned on its head. Indeed, it is equally defensible to propose that family structure and conflict resolution formatively influence the direction of society.

Variations

There are many variants of conflict theory. Some variants involve latching on to one dimension of conflict, such as gender, and elevating that one dimension as the major explanatory variable of all conflict, much as Marx elevated the "means of material production" to such explanatory status. The four variants we focus on below we feel represent the most conspicuous schools of thought on family conflict and the most productive to date. Although these variants do not exhaust the varieties of conflict theory in general, we feel that they represent the range of work on family conflict theory.

STRUCTURAL CONFLICT

One of the acknowledged fathers of sociology is Georg Simmel. Simmel's sociology was "formal" and theoretical following the style of the formal philosophy of nature of the German philosopher Immanuel Kant. Simmel viewed conflict as a constant process of associative and dissociative forces that brought unity and coherence to society. Simmel did not identify one underlying cause of conflict such as Marx's relation to the means of production. Nor did Simmel view the processes in the family as simply a microcosm of larger-scale processes. In regard to the family, Simmel focused his attention on the formal properties of small-group structure and interaction. He viewed marriage and family as distinctly different social structures with different social properties. Marriage, because it is a two-person, or dyadic, structure, involves one individual being totally dependent on the other:

> This dependence of the dyad upon its two individual members causes the thought of its existence to be accompanied by the thought of its termination much more closely and impressively than in any group, where every member knows that even after his retirement or death, the group can continue to exist. (Simmel, 1950, pp. 123-124)

Simmel (1950) argues that marriage is unlike most dyads in one regard: "namely, absence of a super-personal unit" (p. 129). He argues that the institution of marriage seems to transcend the two individuals involved, in part because it is socially regulated. Even though marriage is different from other dyads, it lacks the structural dimensions of three-person and larger groups. Indeed, Simmel says, "a marriage with one child has a character which is completely different from that of a childless marriage" (p. 138). The critical difference for Simmel is that once the group grows beyond the dyad, "parties of interest" may form alliances. Simmel sought to characterize the types of triads that are universal to this social group. The task of fully formalizing and applying the notions of "ties" and "coalitions" to the family fell to later sociologists, however.

Caplow (1968) calls the mother-father-child triad the "primary triad." He acknowledges that there are other significant family triads, such as sibling triads, but views this parent-child triad as most basic. In Caplow's view, family members form coalitions based on each person's relative power. If the father had greater power than either the mother or child, a winning coalition between the child and mother might be possible. Caplow suggested that over the family's life cycle, the relative power of family members changes and potential coalitions also change. One of the strengths this has for families is that today's coalition partner might be tomorrow's opponent and today's opponent might be tomorrow's partner. Caplow (1968) suggests that the typical family evolves from a dyad in which the husband (father to be) usually has more power than the wife (mother to be) (F > M). As a child grows, the mother-child coalition tends to equal the individual power of father (F = M + C). This might increasingly force the father into a coalition with mother (F + M > C). Eventually, the mother-child coalition surpasses the relative power of the father (F < M + C). Because the mother would be the dominant member of the mother-child coalition, she would effectively have the greatest power in families with one adolescent child. Of course, Caplow recognizes that coalition strategies become more complex when there is more than one child or a parental member is absent. Caplow's theory is a direct extension of Simmel (1950). It adds the ingredient of the ordinal (<, >, =) computation of individual power and graph theory to the prediction of coalition formation. He acknowledges that social norms of authority and the compatibility of coalition partners play a role in coalition formations, but the initial step in the theory is to outline the logically possible coalitions. In the end, Caplow (1968) provides a systematic and scientifically measurable approach to the resolution of family conflict through coalitions.

Caplow (1968) is sensitive to criticism that he might be ignoring the emotional context of family life. He argues like Simmel, Coser, and many other conflict theorists that the "function" of conflict is "solidarity." Caplow argues that emotions are tied to coalitions because coalition partners attempt to reinforce and protect one another. Out of this coalition partner interaction come the emotions that we associate with being in a family: "Love is an intense preference for a particular coalition partner. Hate is an intense reaction against an opponent" (Caplow, 1968, p. 78). For Caplow, then, conflict and coalitions are not a sideshow in family life but compose the very essence of being in a family:

> Family life is fraught with the tension of conflicting emotions precisely because it is based on coalitions and every coalition involves an opponent. Begun with a husband-wife coalition, continued by a mother-child coalition, a family is sustained by the interlocking forces of love and hate in somewhat the same way that buildings are held up by opposing forces of tension and compression. (p. 78)

In their structural conflict approach, Simmel (1950) and Caplow (1968) attempt to provide a scholarly and scientific approach to conflict in families in which love, partnership, hate, and solidarity emerge from conflict.

MICRORESOURCE CONFLICT THEORY

It seems wise to start with the major differences between microresource conflict theory, discussed in this section, and macroresource conflict theory, discussed in the section following this one. Both of these forms of conflict theory share an emphasis on "resources." Microresource theory is unique in incorporating the giving and receiving of affection in an accounting of resources. Macroresource theory tends to be focused on larger social structures rather than the interpersonal dimension of "affect" or "expressiveness." As a result of this interpersonal emphasis, microresource is more prone to stress "negotiations" as a technique of conflict management, whereas macroresource theorists are more prone to see the need for more revolutionary forms of conflict to bring about structural social change.

Scanzoni's (1972) microresource theory eclectically draws from a diversity of theories, such as exchange theory, conflict theory, and even functionalist theory. It is somewhat difficult, not to mention risky, to identify Scanzoni's (1972) theory with any one framework. But because the basic focus is on marital conflict and its resolution through negotiations, it appears to us to best fit as a variant of conflict theory.

Although Scanzoni (1972) accepts Simmel's (1904) argument that conflict may lead to solidarity, he also shares with Coser (1956) the suspicion that this glosses over "what tears families apart." Following Coser, Scanzoni (1972) distinguishes two forms of conflict: basic conflict, which brings into question the most basic "rule of the game," and nonbasic conflict, which is played out according to the rules of the game. He provides a tidy analogy. Imagine a game of football. The two teams can conflict and yet build solidarity as long as they follow the rules of the game. But if they lack agreement on the rules of the game, then we have basic conflict. Scanzoni then portrays the basic rules of the family or marital game.

Scanzoni views the rules (norms) of the family as governing the exchange of the husband's instrumental duties for expressive rights and likewise the wife's expressive duties for instrumental rights. The husband's right is the reciprocal of the wife's duty and the husband's duty is the reciprocal of the wife's right. An instrumental activity is a means to some end, whereas an expressive activity tends to be an end in itself and carries affect or emotion. For example, the father holding a baby while the mother searches for a diaper is instrumental in the sense that a playpen might also do the job. On the other hand, holding, cuddling, and playing with a baby enjoying the simple affectual expression of love is an expressive activity. Scanzoni argues that the traditional rules for family are that the husband has instrumental duties, mainly as a provider, and the wife has mainly expressive duties, such as tension reduction, child care, and sexual services. The wife has the right to expect the husband to adequately provide for the family and the husband has a right to expect expressive services from the wife. Nonbasic conflict may occur within these marriages over the discipline of children, economic matters, and so on, but such conflict does not bring into question the basic rules of the game. Indeed, Scanzoni, following Simmel (1904), says this nonbasic conflict may enhance the stability of the marriage and the family and bring about change and growth.

Basic conflict, on the other hand, challenges the rules of the game. According to Scanzoni (1972), there are several ways that basic conflict emerges. One is if one partner fails to live up to role expectations such as provider or sexual partner. This is a key to feelings of inequity in the marriage. Other sources are exogenous, or outside of any one marriage, such as the change away from patriarchy and the increased accessibility for females to their own resources such as education and work. As these changes come about and females have greater instrumental resources, they would want to renegotiate the basic rules, because those rules are now a source of inequity for them. Wives now have instrumental resources of their own, devaluing the contribution of male resources. When females have approximately equal instrumental resources to those of the male, they may renegotiate the expressive roles they have fulfilled in traditional marriages by demanding more expressive duties from the husband as their right or reducing the expressive duties they perform, because the value of the male's provider role has been reduced.

Although Scanzoni's (1970, 1972) analysis began over two decades ago, it continues to be refined (Scanzoni & Szinovacz, 1980) and remains one of the more cogent analyses of changing gender roles in the family and the resulting conflict that surrounds such basic redesignation of family roles. Two decades later, we can see that there are a number of forces exogenous to the family that might also be responsible for the decline in male ability to fulfill the provider role. For example, the rate of increase for male earnings relative to female earnings has decreased. Furthermore, the purchasing power of families has been eroded to such a degree that most families require two incomes simply to maintain living standards equivalent to one-earner families in 1970. Female participation rates in education and the labor force have increased dramatically. Females have tended to seek work in the growing service sector (tertiary) of the economy rather than the downsizing production sectors (primary and secondary). As a result, females find themselves increasingly to be the more stable provider in a marriage. Of course, females still do the lion's share of the housework, or "second shift," compared to males. Thus, females have increased their instrumental duties for the family but with no corresponding reduction in their expressive duties. Two decades later, this inequity in the family's rules and roles seems to have become greater and still provides the foundation for the basic conflict predicted by Scanzoni (1972).

MACRORESOURCE CONFLICT
THEORY (MARXIST-FEMINISM)

Macroresource conflict theory is characterized by several distinctive components. First, like Marx, macroresource theorists view the family as simply a mirror of larger-scale processes of conflict, such as class or gender conflict. Second, macroresource theorists tend to see conflict as fomented by the inequitable allotment of scarce resources. In general, the inequity of resources is traced to structural barriers in the social system. Finally, the analysis of structural barriers provides the necessary "knowledge" for emancipatory activities. In this sense, macroresource theorists tend to view "knowledge" and "political action" as tied to what Marx called the "praxic" character of knowledge. Although there are many examples of this type of conflict theory, few have focused on the family. One contemporary variety that has focused on the family is Marxist-feminist theory. Even within Marxist-feminist theory of the family, there are some differences in approach and analysis. One of the most cogent and impressive analyses in this area is contained in the work *The Dialectic of Sex* by Shulamith Firestone (1970).

Firestone (1970) begins her analysis with an acknowledgment of her debt to Engels's (1884/1946) analysis in *The Origin of the Family, Private Property and the State* and her evaluation that Engels and Marx failed to go deep enough in their analysis:

> Engels did observe that the original division of labor was between man and woman for the purposes of childbreeding; that within the family the husband was the owner, the wife the means of production, the children the labor; and that reproduction of the human species was an important economic system distinct from the means of production. (p. 5)

Where Marx and Engels went wrong, according to Firestone, is that they did not plumb the depths of the nature of reproduction and sex but instead envisioned these as part of the underlying economic class conflict. Firestone proposes a view of history based on sex rather than economic relations. She supposes that "Unlike economic class, sex class sprang directly from a biological reality: men and women were created different, and not equally privileged" (p. 8). She argues that for most of human history, the family (and women) has been characterized

by four fundamental points. First, prior to the very recent development of birth control, women were at the mercy of their biology in
terms of pregnancy, lactation, and care of infants and thus were
dependent on others for survival. Second, human infants take a long
time to become self-sufficient and are dependent on adults for their
survival. Third, basic mother-child interdependency has shaped the
psychology of every woman and child. Fourth, and last, the basic
reproductive division of labor provides for the most fundamental class
distinction, that of sex. From these four points, Firestone (1970)
argues that sex class underlies other social divisions by economic class
or race. She suggests that male patriarchy as well as female socialization in the family have encouraged the social partitioning of labor so
as to justify not only social inequality but inequality of opportunity.
Her argument does not lack for either historical, cross-cultural, or
contemporary examples of inequity based on gender.

Firestone notes that the root source of the inequity is biological in
origin. As long as women get pregnant, bear children, and breast-feed,
they are tied to the very elements that justify the division of labor:

> Nature produced the fundamental inequality—half the human race must
> bear and rear the children of all of them—which was later con-
> solidated, institutionalized, in the interests of men. Reproduction of the
> species cost women dearly, not only emotionally, psychologically, cul-
> turally. . . . (p. 232)

Firestone (1970) suggests a program to correct the damage that has
been done to both males and females by the excessive partitioning of
sex division of labor. The central point in her program is that females
should be freed of the tyranny of biological reproduction. She argues
that only when we use reproductive technology to free women from
biological reproduction will the division into sex classes cease. She
goes even further and argues that removing biological reproduction
and creating economic independence of both women and children
"would be enough to destroy the family, which breeds the power psychology" (p. 236). Firestone's program thus envisions the reorganization of reproduction in addition to the more traditional Marxian focus
on the reorganization of production. She believes that the changes she
envisions are already under way as technology slowly replaces the

functions of the family and care of infants becomes increasingly performed by "professional caregivers." In the end, she believes that "revolt against the family could bring on the first successful revolution" (p. 274).

Firestone (1970) probably represents the more radical wing of Marxist-feminism, but other scholars have followed up on various aspects of these ideas. For example, Berk (1985) deals with the family as the major component in the reproduction of gender relations and division of labor. Ferree (1990), in her review of feminists' contributions to the family literature, cites the family ideology that can be used to legitimate appeals for female self-sacrifice (p. 870). Osmond and Thorne (1993) point out that feminist scholars have been critical of what constitutes "family" because they are "critical of that ideology and alert to contemporary disputes . . . (i.e., over surrogate mothering, the control of reproduction, child custody, and legal provisions for domestic partnerships)" (p. 618). Although all feminist scholars are not necessarily Marxist-feminist or as radical as Firestone (1970), the issues that she raises are indeed central.

DIALECTICAL DECONSTRUCTIONISM

Deconstructionism is most clearly identified with the work of the French scholar Jacques Derrida (1976). Derrida's major focus has been to use a "dialectical" method in interpreting textual materials. In this sense, Derrida represents one particular development of hermeneutics. He advocates two readings of a text. The first reading constructs an everyday interpretation of the text; the second reading "deconstructs," or is critical of, all those assumptions developed in the initial reading. The rationale behind this technique is a form of radical antifoundationalism. Following from the work of the linguistic philosophers Wittgenstein and Austin, Derrida (1978) asserts that all communication acts are inherently "undecidable," or in lay terms have multiple meanings. He argues that there is no way to exclude these several possible meanings to a communicative act. As a result, then, Derrida (1978) supposes that all possible meanings are equivalent as there is no way of definitively deciding between them. This view yields a kind of chaos or plurality of meaning for any communicative act.

The broader movement of deconstructionism has been widely discussed within the realm of literary criticism, but as yet there have been only a few applications to sociology (e.g., Game, 1991) and few direct applications to the family (Baber & Allen, 1992). Feminist deconstructionists currently focus on the deconstruction of the everyday view of female sexuality and the reconstruction of alternative meanings (e.g., Cixous & Clement, 1986). Deconstructionism is possibly the most extreme form of antifoundationalism and relativism, as Derrida and his followers feel that if one cannot nail down exactly the meaning of a communication act then all meanings are on an equal footing. There appears to be no room for degrees of "decidability" in deconstructionism.

Deconstructionism is often linked to postmodernism. Postmodernism is directly linked to Jean-François Lyotard and the publication of *The Postmodern Condition* in 1979 (English translation, 1984). This work was the result of Lyotard's investigations into the status of knowledge commissioned by a university in the Canadian province of Quebec. The conclusion Lyotard (1979/1984) reaches is that all existing perspectives (narratives) on knowledge come from the rationalism of modernity. These perspectives seek to claim "legitimacy," whether for the claims of science as objective or the claims of democracy as just, equal, and free. Lyotard argues that these narratives give "modernity" its "project." Whereas Habermas argues that the project of modernity in science and culture needs to be renewed, Lyotard (1992) argues that it is dead (p. 18). According to Lyotard, we are entering a period in which there are only a plurality of ways of knowing (paralogy), with none having greater claim to veracity than any others. Cheal (1991) states of Lyotard,

> Unlike modernist theorists of knowledge, he does not view this situation negatively, as a "paradigm crisis." Rather, as a post-modernist, he positively embraces paralogy in a celebration of pluralism, and as a way of avoiding all forms of totalitarianism. (p. 157)

It remains somewhat unclear whether Lyotard (1979/1984, 1992) views postmodernism as a philosophy or as a historical era. The descriptor postmodernist is increasingly attached to those who take an antifoundational and relativistic perspective on all knowledge. The term *postmodern* now refers to a set of terms (see Box 7.1) that may seem foreign to the uninitiated. Increasingly, these terms represent the backbone of a theoretical and methodological orientation.

Although we do not as yet have a major deconstructionist approach to the family, Cheal (1991) suggests that North American theories of the family cannot avoid being influenced by this train of thought. Gubrium and Holstein (1990) discuss their approach to definitions of the family as both phenomenological and deconstructionist. This would seem to indicate that this approach is having some impact on family scholarship. It remains to be seen if this movement, which has currently lost much of its momentum in Europe due to the rediscovery of U.S. pragmatism (e.g., Apel, 1981; Norris, 1989), will catch the imaginations of family scholars in North America.

Empirical Applications

WIFE ASSAULT

One of the major empirical areas for the application of conflict theory has been family violence. The very nature of the subject matter, family violence, immediately implies that some variants of conflict theory rather than others will be more relevant. For example, because we are attempting to explain why some husbands assault their wives, theoretical variants of conflict theory that assist in predicting "conflict" seem more relevant than those variants that deal with negotiating, conflict management, and the unifying function of conflict (Caplow, 1968; Simmel, 1904). In general, conflict theory predicts that clashes and confrontations occur when there is competition for scarce resources. One way we can determine the potential for conflict is when one person or group does not have the same resources as another person or group. For Marx, the proletariat did not have the same resources as the bourgeoisie. For Firestone (1970), patriarchy helped to ensure that men and women did not have the same resources. Thus, conflict theorists view social inequity as indicating the necessary conditions for conflict to arise.

Wife assault is difficult to observe and study. In North America, there is no uniform method for reporting and recording such incidents.

Box 7.1

An Abbreviated Glossary of Postmodernist Ideas

anarchy: disorderliness

antiessentialism: absence of necessary truths and of general laws of nature; structure is in the mind

antitheory: no categories, no systems of ideas, no structures, no grounds for accepting or rejecting ideas

artifacticity: cultural productions such as theme parks and theme restaurants, videogames, plastic Christmas trees

constructivism: reality is a human and social creation, collectively produced via interaction in groups

contextualism: reality is multilayered and framed within a background

critique of modernity: evolution and history are not progressive

cultural cynicism: culture is surprising, humorous, discontinuous, and perverse

cultural diversity: mixing architectural forms; mixing writing styles; mixing "is" and "ought"; mixing old and new

decentering: challenging dominant Euro-American culture; a deliberate loss of cohesiveness, consensus, authority, certainty, and contentment; empowering the downtrodden

deconstruction: nothing is to be taken for granted

discourse: everything is just talk and opinion

divergent thinking: breaking out of conformist modes of action; being creative and unusual

exceptioning: seeking the nonnormal or the exception

fluidity: nothing is constant but change; everything is processual

nonlinearity: change is disruptive and transformative

pluralism: the appreciation of differences, complexity, and fragmentation; noncategorical thinking

reflexivity: the speaker is part of phenomenon spoken

relativity: ideas are relational and from a standpoint; there is no final authority for any argument

subject-object connectedness: knowledge and knower are interdependent

SOURCES: Adapted from Lemert (1993, Parts 4 & 5) and Winton (1995, pp. 177-181).

Self-reports by both victims and perpetrators may be biased. Gelles and Straus designed and conducted the 1985 National Family Violence

Survey, which probably represents the most complete data we have on wife assault and family violence. Wife assault can be measured as one of the following: pushed, grabbed, shoved; threw something at her; slapped her; kicked, hit, or punched; hit or tried to hit; beat her up; choked; threatened with knife or gun; used a knife or gun (Straus, 1994). Large studies are necessary because of the low incidence of family violence. As Gelles (1994) points out,

> Despite the fact that individuals are more likely to be hit, hurt, and even killed in the privacy of their homes and in intimate, as opposed to non-intimate relationships, the actual annual base rate of such victimization is still about 3 or 4 per 1,000 individuals. (p. 1)

Even though the number of victims adds up over the years, the annual rate of incidence is relatively low.

One version of conflict theory relevant here is based on gender inequality. Some feminist conflict theorists suggest that where gender inequalities exist there is a "patriarchal" social system that justifies and condones wife assault as one of many forms of the subjugation of women to men. Men basically are defending their greater resources from an underclass. Many of those resources are predicated on women "staying in their place." Yllö and Straus (1990) investigated this proposition using the National Family Violence Survey. They reported that the relationship between structural gender inequality (measured by each state's legal, political, and economic equality status) and wife assault is curvilinear. Those states with both the lowest and highest gender inequality showed the highest rates of wife assault. This suggests that feminist theory might be an accurate interpretation for states in which there is great gender inequality, but for states in which there is relatively high gender equality perhaps Scanzoni's (1972; Scanzoni & Szinovacz, 1980) theory of sexual bargaining and the resulting social disorganization to traditional family roles would supply an explanation for the high rates of spousal abuse.

Straus (1994) tests three versions of conflict theory in an attempt to explain wife assault. The three versions of conflict theory he uses are gender inequality, income inequality, and social disorganization. His measures for gender inequality are the same as used by Yllö and Straus (1990). He uses a single measure of each state's income equality

(Gini scores) and a composite measure of each state's social disorganization, composed of items such as divorce rates, geographical
mobility, and lack of religious affiliation. Straus (1994) reports that
both gender inequality and social disorganization measures are sig-
nificantly related to rates of wife assault. Income inequality, when age
is controlled, is not directly related to wife assault. And although the
proportion of the variance explained in wife assault is relatively
modest (7%-13%), his findings suggest that these theories might be
explaining different aspects of wife assault and might interact with
income inequities.

Straus's (1994) research supplies an example of how conflict theory
may be applied in research. His results should caution theorists about
becoming too focused on a single, universal, explanatory source of
conflict such as gender inequality. It may well be that there are
different, independent but complementary explanations of phenomena
such as wife assault. In the end, it may be that a broader, more abstract
and inclusive theoretical perspective such as provided by Simmel
(1904, 1950) would provide a unitary theoretical framework for these
diverse sources of inequality and conflict.

Implications for Intervention

Conflict theory's emphasis on conflict as endemic to social groups
has served to focus attention on how conflict is managed. In the area
of therapy, the micro versions of conflict theory emphasizing negotiations have inspired many "fair fighting" programs (e.g., Bach & Wyden,
1968).

These programs concentrate on the negotiation skills and style that
allow for couples to negotiate and reach successful compromises. Conflict styles are often viewed as problematic in that some can escalate
and lead to further conflict whereas others tend to dampen further
conflict.

Another area in which conflict theory has implications is resource
management. Most recently, Poduska (1993) focuses on the relationship between the management of resources and marital conflict. The
management of financial resources is seen as intimately linked to the
feelings of family members and the enhancement of relationships.

Many scholars and students would immediately align conflict theory's implications with the more "emancipatory" social movements encompassing general social change in addition to changes in the family. In the past 30 years, there can be little doubt that the most pervasive of these social movements has been the feminist movement. The policy suggestions emanating from the feminist movement have not been uniform. For example, Firestone's (1970) policy suggestions revolve around eliminating the biological differences between men and women in regard to childbirth. Thus, Firestone favors the elimination of birth as a biological function of women and advocates replacing that function with technology. Furthermore, she advocates the end to individual "ownership" of children, to be replaced by communal care of children.

Although most feminists would agree with Firestone's (1970) view that female oppression is maintained by the traditional, patriarchal family, they do not advocate the radical program she suggests. For example, Eichler (1988) points out that although the "patriarchal family movement" associates the family with only one, monolithic structure, feminists have recognized the diversity of families:

> The feminist perspective, then, accepts that families come in different forms. No particular form is seen as superior to another. Judgements on the desirability of families are made in terms of their effects on their members, not in terms of their structure. (p. 421)

The policy implications advocated by Eichler and others are aimed more at universal availability of day care and equality of rights within and outside of the family. The overall perspective remains true to conflict theory: Equal resources and rights ensure more equitable negotiations and outcomes.

Critiques and Discussion

One of the major hurdles for conflict theory continues to be its emphasis on conflict rather than order. This emphasis was undoubtedly justified in reaction to the stasis inherent in sociological structural-functionalism. Today, however, the emphasis on conflict often appears to highlight the sensational or negative rather than the dialectical process of conflict. For example, some feminist scholars focus on gender inequities without a clear picture of the dynamic process in which these inequities represent either a "thesis" or "antithesis." A very real danger for conflict theory is becoming focused on conflict as an existing social inequity rather than as a dynamic process.

Most of the theorists we have reviewed above avoid this problem. Simmel (1904) and Marx and Engels (1845-1846/1965) focus on the process. Firestone (1970) comes closer to an exclusive focus on inequity but then envisions a Marxian-type solution of social and technological emancipation not from the "means of production" but from the "biology of reproduction." Scanzoni (1970) focuses in some detail on the mechanisms forging a synthesis between the inequity of patriarchy and the gender equality of the "equal partner" family.

Another challenge for conflict theory lies in explaining the relative permanence and stability of the social order. It is probably an understatement that norms, roles, and social structure appear to change slowly. Even conflict theorists such as Caplow, Bahr, Chadwick, Hill, and Williamson (1983) report that in the decades since Middletown was first studied and their subsequent return in the 1980s, the hallmark is that not much of importance has changed. If conflict is a dialectical process, it may be that it must be studied over fairly sizeable units of time as envisioned by Marx and Firestone (1970). The challenge then is for conflict theorists to demonstrate the applicability of conflict theory to more limited units of time, such as decades or years.

This challenge might partially be overcome by a greater emphasis on the details of the process of the dialectic. Between thesis, antithesis, and synthesis comes a lot of social interaction. For example, Scanzoni's (1972) work on renegotiating gender roles in the family is the type of detail work that fills in the gaps in the dialectic of sex envisioned by Firestone (1970). It is this more detailed work that may aspire to be more concrete and scientific than the more emancipatory view of the sweep of history.

What Turner (1991) has labeled the emancipatory viewpoint of some conflict theorists provokes some fairly hostile criticism. This criticism, however, is more subtle than it initially seems. Certainly, no scientist would assert that scientific knowledge might not have an emancipatory aspect to it—there is no disagreement on the issue of whether or not knowledge can be emancipatory. The issue is whether emancipation is the central aim of a theory (ideology) or whether the central aim is the production of knowledge (science). If the central role of theory is knowledge, then clearly knowledge claims must be judged by a set of criteria that are universally and equally applied to all such claims. In science, claims are subjected to the rules of logic, experiment, and replication. The fear of scientists is that if claims support the ideology, then they will be judged true because they are consistent with the ideology. One of the basic canons of science is that mere consistency of a finding with previous beliefs is insufficient to justify a claim. If such were the case, then findings would only need support the prevailing ideology or "common sense." Indeed, the history of science is the history of the downfall of systems of thought such as the heliocentric universe, Newton's mechanics, Maxwell's daemon, and the eventual fall of Einstein's relativity theory.

On the other hand, historiography represents a particular form of analysis that lends itself to "seeing into the future." Hegel, Feuerbach, Marx, and Firestone all believe that their view of historical processes shows that these processes are inevitable and the consciousness of the process is part of the process. For example, class consciousness and conflict is a necessary and inevitable part of the process of extinguishing class conflict itself. Thus, our knowledge is viewed as a necessary part of the process. What scientists seem to be saying is, "Let scientific knowledge claims be subjected to scientific criteria, then if the knowledge is emancipatory within any historiography or ideology, so be it." "But," they would continue, "don't expect science to conform to the canon of consistency with the beliefs of ideology or even consistency with previous findings as the sole arbiter of the adequacy of a knowledge claim." In brief, knowledge may be emancipatory, but one of the criteria of knowledge should not be whether or not it is emancipatory.

Another criticism of conflict theory is the tendency to find one underlying theme or causal relation and then use that one cause to explain all of family and human behavior. Single-cause theories are suspect in this day and age of multivariate analyses and ecological consciousness. In defense of conflict theory, it must be pointed out that although there may only be one underlying cause, it keeps changing manifestations throughout history. For instance, although Marx viewed the "relation to the means of production" as being causal, the way it manifested conflict during various historical eras changed. Nonetheless, as we found in the research on wife assault, it may be that a more inclusive conceptualization of conflict that allows for multiple sources of conflict, such as gender and production, provides both inclusiveness and explanatory power.

Conclusion

Conflict theory is diverse. It has both macrosocial and microsocial variants. But we cannot agree with the assessment by Farrington and Chertok (1993) that such diversity has contributed to the near demise of family conflict theory. Rather, what has contributed to that impression is a too-narrow focus on "conflict" rather than the process of conflict and management of conflict. There are several themes that allow us to see family conflict theory as a coherent and unified theory spanning time and history, micro- and macrolevels. Conflict is a process. The process is dialectical and must be studied over time. The way conflict is managed is part of the dialectical process of reaching a new synthesis. Of all the social groups we might study, the family provides the "laboratory" in which there is intense conflict and resolution, hate and love, and violence and support.

Conflict theory stands out in the pantheon of family theories as incorporating both time and history as a common process (the dialectic). Conflict theory connects the study of contemporary families to families of the past as part of a historical process. As grand and sweeping a vision as it provides, it nonetheless can be focused on the specific processes of negotiation and conflict management so that we can understand our day-to-day existence. Conflict theory, as Caplow (1968), Scanzoni (1970), and Straus (1994) have demonstrated, can be explicitly scientific. We believe the strengths of conflict theory far outweigh the criticisms launched against it. There is only one element that could destroy the potential of conflict theory to offer family researchers a vital process-oriented theory that links family studies with the larger social system and historical processes. That one destructive element is if the theory is dragged into the quagmire of ideology and findings judged by "political correctness" rather than the cannons of science. We are optimistic that such will not be the case.

Food for Thought

1. Have you ever been in a "grouchy" mood and simply picked "fights" with other family members? On such occasions, which of the following variables are most important: resources, negotiations, ideology, or psychodynamics? Does conflict theory have a psychodynamic component?

2. A scholar has just announced that she has found that women are on average about 10 IQ points more intelligent than men. Is it more important to reject this finding because it is "sexist" or to examine its scientific credibility? Can you imagine how some of the conflict theorists might respond?

3. Do you form coalitions with other members in your family? Are such coalitions stable or specific to particular issues?

4. Competition or cooperation are determined in part by the structure of the situation, such as "curving" grades. Do cultures vary in their emphasis on competition or cooperation? How would persons from a cooperative culture interact with persons from a competitive culture?

Suggested Readings

Farrington, K., & Chertok, E. (1993). Social conflict theories of the family. In P. Boss, W. Doherty, R. LaRossa, W. Schumm, & S. Steinmetz (Eds.), *Sourcebook of family theories and methods: A contextual approach* (pp. 357-381). New York: Plenum.

This is a good survey of conflict theory, even though the authors express more reservations about the continued usefulness of conflict theory in family studies than we do.

Osmond, M., & Thorne, B. (1993). Feminist theories: The construction of gender in families and society. In P. Boss, W. Doherty, R. LaRossa, W. Schumm, & S. Steinmetz (Eds.), *Sourcebook of family theories and methods: A contextual approach* (pp. 591-622). New York: Plenum.

This chapter provides a more general perspective on the diversity and forms of feminist theories.

8

The Ecological Framework

"Mom, why does Dad take us to school and pick us up when all the other kids' mothers do that?" Katrina's mother answers that the father lost his job and it's easier for her, the mother, to find a job. Hidden in the mother's response to Katrina is a complex explanation. Recently, most of the growth in jobs has been in the service sector of the economy. Traditionally, males have been employed in the primary-extractive and secondary-manufacturing sectors of the economy. In North America, both of these traditional male employment sectors have been automated and streamlined to cut costs and compete in the global economic market. Katrina's dad, a civil engineer, was one of the victims of this realignment. At the same time, Katrina's mom, who also had a good education and had worked in banking, easily got a job in the growing service sector of the economy. This family is adapting to economic and social changes that are creating a realignment of family roles and responsibilities.

The most basic notion in the ecological approach is *adaptation*. The family in the example above is adapting to changing social and economic conditions. The notion of adaptation in ecology is far reaching. This concept reaches down to our biological roots and up to large-scale interactive processes at the level of populations of organisms. The concept of adaptation can be applied to an individual organism's successful adaptation to a specific environmental *niche* or to global changes such as increases in ultraviolet radiation. Indeed, adaptation is the central concept of ecology.

Some of you may ask what this has to do with families. A concern with families and the environment is at the heart of what *ecology* means and of the ecological social movement that has become so active during the later part of the 20th century. The term *ecology* was coined in 1873 by Ernst Haeckel, a German biologist (see Clarke, 1993). It was developed from the Greek root *oik,* which means "place of residence." Haeckel used the German *oekologie* in which the prefatory *oe* makes the term universal as "everyman's house or environment" (Clarke, 1973). As Clarke points out, although "Haeckel, a male biologist, saw that a science of everyone's house environment needed to be developed, the female chemist (Ellen Swallow Richards) slowly began to take up residency in the structure" (p. 40). Richards was the first female student at MIT and one of the pioneers of water purity analysis. Her many published books include studies in the areas of water analysis, minerals, and sanitation, and she also published works on the cost of food and shelter and the chemistry of cooking. Indeed, it was Richards who founded and served as first president of the American Home Economics Association. She believed that the family and home were central to the ecological movement: "Science has to apply its knowledge to [improve] that unit of the community, the home; for upon the welfare of the home depends the welfare of the commonwealth" (Clarke, 1973, p. 141). Although Richards's hard-nosed scientific empiricism has been challenged and rejected by some prominent contemporary home economists (e.g., Brown, 1984; Bubolz & Sontag, 1993), there can be little doubt that her viewpoint favored the development of interdisciplinary ecological and environmental sciences in the broadest of senses.

Ellen Swallow Richards (1842-1911) lived in an era when unbridled industrialization triumphed, but her keen scientific eye saw the hidden costs. She documented the loss in water quality in studies that were instrumental in leading to the first U.S. water quality standards. It must be recalled that Richards lived during a century that was intellectually illuminated by Darwin, but day-to-day life was more governed by corporate greed. For example, in the early 1870s the Boston Milk War was fought between milk businesses and an embryonic consumer movement. The businesses routinely diluted milk with water and when a group of citizens organized a consumer protection association to deliver untainted milk to Boston, their drivers were beaten, their horses crippled, and the milk tainted (Clarke, 1973, p. 42). Increasingly, industry claimed areas of production that had previously been the principal role of women in the home. As a result, many women felt a loss of purpose, and the "manufacture" of previously "homemade" products was fertile ground for avaricious interests. Richards documented to the Massachusetts State Board of Health, Lunacy and Charity in the first-ever scientific survey of the state's food supply that many common foods contained additives that were harmful. She reported that out of 33 samples of baking soda, 9 contained alum, 5 contained ammonia, and others contained large quantities of starch (Clarke, 1973, p. 103). Rather than tight legislative controls, Richards favored the education of the major group of consumers, women:

> It is because I believe in the possibility of control of [the environment] and even economic conditions that I urge so strongly the dissemination of what knowledge we have. [Otherwise] . . . a cry for state interference will come in that day when it is clear that the carelessness of men threatens to extinguish the race. (quoted in Clarke, 1973, p. 211)

To further our education about our environment, Richards, in 1907, reiterated her proposal for a new science:

> Human Ecology is the study of the surroundings of human beings in the effects they produce on [other] lives. . . . The features of the environment are natural, as climate; and artificial, produced by human activity such as noise, [dirt], poisonous vapors, vitiated air, dirty water and unclean food. (quoted in Clarke, 1973, pp. 215-216)

Shortly after Richards died, Robert Wollcott and C. V. Shreve in 1916 founded the Ecological Society of America (Clarke, 1973). By 1919, the society had acquired *Ecology* as a journal outlet for its publications. By 1917, the society's membership was 307, and by 1973 the membership had swollen to 5,148 (Hinckley, 1976). Although the membership includes scholars from almost every field of science, in 1920 the president of the society, Barrington Moore, urged that human ecology be taken to represent an especially important aspect of ecology. Since this time, human ecology has developed mainly in association with the academic discipline of sociology (e.g., Burgess, 1925; Hannan & Freeman, 1984; Hawley, 1986; Park, 1925).

Intellectual Traditions

The early studies in human ecology (e.g., Burgess, 1925; McKenzie, 1924; Park, 1925; Park & Burgess, 1921) derived much of their intellectual and conceptual foundation from the work of plant ecologists. In contrast to the notion that the United States was a "melting pot," these sociologists detected homogeneous spatial ordering and change that could readily be described in the language of plant ecology, especially ecological succession and species dominance. These early scholars were preoccupied with the spatial arrangement of the urban setting, particularly Chicago, and this explains why some students identify human ecology with this spatial approach and what has become known as the Chicago school of human ecology. But as Hawley (1986) points out, this spatial approach was superseded by a concern with population ecology. Population ecology united social demography with the bioecological study of populations so that spatial orderings became one of a myriad of ways a population adapts to a particular environment. To understand why and how human ecology became generally linked to population ecology, it is necessary to trace some of the historical currents that only came together in the mid-20th century.

Although the field of ecology is relatively new, significant scholarly work in the area of humans and their environment preceded the nomenclature identifying the field. Most notable in this regard is the work of Thomas Malthus (1766-1834). Malthus lived in a time when the prevailing notion was that increased population increased the power of a country. Surplus population could be used to feed mercantilism and populate colonies. Prior to Malthus's (1798/1872) *An Essay on the Principle of Population*, the folk wisdom regarding food sources might be summed up as a reliance on nature to provide "no more children than teats" (Peterson, 1969, p. 146). Malthus (1798/ 1872) proposed that in an unconstrained situation population would increase at a geometric rate (2, 4, 8, 16 . . .) and food production at an arithmetic rate (1, 2, 3, 4, 5 . . .). He pointed out that in reality the relationship between food and population was always constrained by either preventative checks (e.g., moral restraint) or positive checks (e.g., wars, famine). Clearly, preventative checks tend to focus on fertility, whereas positive checks tend to focus on mortality. Regardless of the controversial nature of the predictions of overpopulation that can be derived from Malthus, his work served to bring an ecological focus to the emerging studies of economics, sociology, and demography by highlighting the interaction of environmental and biological variables with social and human variables.

Ecology, as a science, must trace its paternity to Charles Darwin (1809-1882). The early focus by Malthus on the interaction of biological and social variables was given broad substance and theoretical form in the work of Darwin. He published his most famous work, *On the Origin of Species by Means of Natural Selection,* in 1859. It was in this work that his ideas of natural selection and evolution first appeared, only slightly ahead of the simultaneous exposition of these ideas by Alfred Wallace. Basically, Darwin argued that a species or population evolved principally by the process of natural selection or elimination of those members of the population that were less adapted to survive in their environment. Although evolution is a population process, elimination or selection takes place at the individual level. The rudimentary understanding of this process led both Darwin and later Social Darwinists to maintain arguments favoring eugenics and bordering on biological determinism. For example, Darwin argued that many times we

> do our utmost to check the process of elimination; we build asylums for the imbecile, the maimed, and the sick; we institute poor laws; and our medical men exert their utmost skill to save the life of everyone to the last moment. . . . Thus, the weak members of civilized societies propagate their kind. . . . It is not surprising how soon a want of care, or care wrongly directed, leads to the degeneration of a domestic race; but excepting in the case of man himself, hardly anyone is so ignorant as to allow his worst animals to breed. (Darwin, 1880, pp. 130-134, quoted in Martindale, 1960, pp. 163-164)

Statements that confused acquired characteristics such as being maimed (in the above passage), poor, or uneducated with traits that are inheritable is a disturbing characteristic of early social evolutionists. Much of this confusion arose because the exact mechanisms by which traits were passed to later generations were not identified until the publication of Mendel's (1865/1965) work on genetics at the turn of the century.

If ecology traces its paternity to Darwin and his central notion of adaptation, then human ecology must trace its kinship through Gregor Mendel. This is especially true for those forms of family ecological theory that unite ontogenetic development with environmental inter- action (e.g., Bronfenbrenner, 1979) and those family theorists that believe that much of family behavior is explained by biological factors (van den Berghe, 1979). Mendel first presented his ideas in two lectures in 1865, but his ideas were not "discovered" by the scientific community until the turn of the century (e.g., Brannigan, Wanner, & White, 1981). When Mendel's work was finally understood, it pro- vided a theoretical understanding for the genetic mechanisms that drive evolution. Mendel proposed that genes attached to chromosomes transmit the genetic information to offspring. Attached to the chromo- some were two alleles, one of which might be dominant and therefore expressed in the offspring's phenotype (visible physical characteris- tics); the other might be recessive but nonetheless remain part of the offspring's genotype (genes that are potentially transmittable). From his experiments, Mendel could show that although it was impossible to predict an individual-level genetic outcome, it was possible to predict the proportions or probabilities for a reproducing population. Mendel's work was seminal for both laboratory genetics and popula- tion genetics, but it was population genetics that carried the greatest implications for evolutionary theory and ecological theory.

Population genetics received its early impetus from the simul- taneous work of Hardy (1908) and Weinberg (1908). Hardy and Weinberg developed an equation for predicting allele frequencies for subsequent generations of a population based on the assumption that the only factor operating in the population is the initial distribution of alleles. Thus, their model assumed no evolution. The degree to which their predictions were inaccurate could be used as a measure of evolution. The discrepancy between their prediction and the actual observed allele frequencies could be explained by four evolutionary factors: natural selection, mutation, gene drift, and gene flow. In relatively large and immobile populations, the principal factors are natural selection and mutation (see Turner, 1991).

The mathematical nature of population genetics attracted statisticians and demographers. For example, Karl Pearson (1857-1936) served as editor of both *Biometrika* and *The Annals of Eugenics* and, like Galton (1869/1952) before him, felt that human progress and development was largely related to natural selection (Martindale, 1960). Another famous statistician, Ronald Fisher (1958), mathematically demonstrated that natural selection and not mutation is the major explanatory factor in evolution. He argued that variation in a gene pool was inextricably linked to natural selection and adaptation. Without sufficient variation in the gene pool, there is not sufficient range from which to select an adaptation. Despite the fact that both Fisher and Pearson favored eugenics as a way to ensure the promulgation of the "fittest" genes, their statistical contributions confirmed that natural selection and adaptation are the central mechanisms in the process of evolution (Turner, 1991).

Human ecology brings together these diverse influences. From evolutionary theory and genetics comes the view that humans develop as individual biological organisms with capacities limited by genetic endowment (ontogenetic development). From population genetics comes the perspective that populations change mainly by means of natural selection. At the individual level, this implies that individuals demonstrate their fitness by adapting to their changing environment (family adaptation). From the human ecology of Richards comes the notion that humans can, through education, understand their interactions with the environment and can direct their consumption (and production) to the benefit of the overall environment (family resource management). And most important for the scientist and scholar is the startling idea from evolutionary theory that a phenomenon needs to be examined at different levels of analysis. What we see as failure and death for an individual organism may be linked to success and adaptive fitness for the population (sociobiology). It is this idea that often leads ecologists and conservationists to suggest solutions that seem counterintuitive, such as killing some deer in a herd so that the population will survive. And lurking just under the surface of this view that we

can control natural selection and thus evolution are the proposals
favoring eugenics that are far too often driven by sexism and racism.

Focus and Scope Assumptions

Individuals and groups are both biological and social in nature. Like
systems theory, ecological theory is a relative newcomer on the social
science scene. Ecological theory is distinguished from other theories,
such as systems theory, in its emphasis on the biophysical environment. In systems theory, environment may be a heuristic device,
whereas in ecological theory environment is both spatial and biophysical. This basic assumption leads ecological theory to a more biological
and geographical orientation and a less mechanistic perspective on
human groups.

This first assumption links the dual nature of humans as both
constructions of biology and culture. This dual nature of humans has
given rise to some of the world's greatest literature, such as Goethe's
Faust, and has also occupied generations of academics in the fruitless
debate over whether human characteristics are due to biology (nature)
or environmental influences (nurture). Today, we have not so much
resolved this debate as moved beyond it. We now recognize that even
an embryo in the mother's womb is affected by environmental factors
such as sounds from the environment and the health status of the
mother. Furthermore, a supposed genetic trait such as intelligence
requires the interaction of a nurturing environment as shown in the
example of kwashiorkor (infant protein deficiency) and cognitive
development (IQ). The particular nature of human development ensures
that the development of most human traits depend on a nature-nurture
interaction rather than on one or the other. Although some academics
persist in attempts to identify the additive amounts of contribution
made by the nature side and that exact amount made by the environment, most now readily admit that the entire multiplicative process
beginning with the formation of a DNA strand depends on interactions
with the environment. As van den Berghe (1979) puts it, our behavior
can be understood "as the product of an extraordinary complex of
interaction between genotype and environment" (p. 5).

Humans are dependent on their environment for sustenance (air, water, food, etc). The assumption of dependency follows from the first assumption in that humans can only survive in environments in which their biological needs can be met. Of course, human culture has developed so that we can survive in fairly inhospitable environments with the assistance of technology. But even technology has its limits, as in the case of water.

Human beings are social and thus are interdependent on other human beings. Another way to state this assumption is to say that most of what we think of as truly "human" seems social in nature, for example, language.

Humans are finite and their life cycle coupled with their biological needs for sustenance impose time as both a constraint and resource. We must remember that time is a factor in the evolution of a population and an important component in human development. Furthermore, because we are finite, time becomes a crucial resource for understanding social organization and individual behavior.

Human interactions are spatially organized. Populations of humans organize their interactions with their environment. The organized interactions show up as distinct spatial arrangements. Anyone who has ever looked down on the earth from an airplane is struck by the spatial organization of human activities. But we are not dissimilar from the many other social animals that demonstrate distinct spatial organization as a way of channeling interactions with the environment (e.g., ants, baboons, wolves).

As suggested by evolutionary theory, *human behavior can be understood on several levels.* The two levels that are most often used in human ecology are the *population* and *individual.* For example, populations of organisms show spatial organization and represent particular frequency distributions of genes. Individual organisms may adapt or fail to adapt to their environment. It is important to note, however, that changing the level of analysis can radically alter our perspective. The failure of an organism to successfully adapt leading to that individual organism's death may seem a negative outcome at the individual level, but for the population this same outcome might

represent the evolution of a healthier gene pool or the survival of the
group faced with food scarcity.

Concepts

ECOSYSTEM

Although there are many varieties of ecological theory, most of
these would identify the concept of *ecosystem* as central to ecology.
Hawley (1986) defines ecosystem as "an arrangement of mutual
dependencies in a population by which the whole operates as a unit
and thereby maintains a viable environmental relationship" (p. 26). In
Hawley's view, an ecosystem is necessarily a subset of the larger
environment (environment being an undefined primitive term). The
notion of ecosystem contains the elements of wholeness and the
interdependency of parts. For example, we might talk of an urban
ecosystem, a desert ecosystem, or a polar ecosystem. Each ecosystem,
though attached to other ecosystems, has a set of characteristics that
demarcate it as a whole. Bubolz and Sontag (1993) suggest that "a
family ecosystem consists of a given family system in interaction with
its environment" (p. 431). Although this definition lacks precision, it
nonetheless suggests that some scholars view the family as an ecosystem.

NICHE

Every ecosystem contains *niches*. The interdependencies in an
ecosystem are not between specific individuals but between specific
niches occupied by individuals. Associated with each niche is a patterned and relatively stable set of activities. These activities provide
functions for the maintenance or adaptation of units in the environment or those occupying a specific niche. For example, in a marsh
environment, the activity of beavers serves the *function* of water
regulation. In the human family, the role of father has been tied to the
function of provider. According to Hawley (1986), these niches (or
social roles) represent functions for the ecosystem. Thus, "the mutual
dependencies comprising a system (ecosystem) are seen to be linkages
among recurring activities" (p. 32).

ADAPTIVE RANGE

An organism that occupies a niche in an ecosystem can be characterized as having an *adaptive range*. The organism's ontogenetic development gives it a range of behavior, but the organism cannot adapt outside of this range. For example, a 2-year-old is not going to be able to understand the principle of conservation of matter because of his or her developmental stage (e.g., Piaget, 1952). Human intelligence represents a broad adaptive range because we apply technology (culture) to problems we would be hard pressed to adapt to organically (e.g., space travel, underwater exploration).

UNITS

One of the levels of analysis commonly used in evolutionary theory is *population*. Hawley (1986) argues convincingly that a population is not simply an aggregation of all those people or *units* sharing a common characteristic. If population referred to such simple aggregations, we might be tempted to talk meaningfully of the population sharing the characteristic of "wearing blue jeans." Hawley defines a population as an aggregate having unit character by virtue of internal organization. In his sense of the term, we could discuss the population of Canada but not the population of "wearers of blue jeans." Hawley's definition of population moves the term away from the identification of a mere statistical aggregation and imbues it with theoretical meaning. Population processes are dissimilar to individual-level processes as seen in the example that a population may have a death rate yet it continues over time whereas an individual who dies fails to continue over time. Furthermore, a population may place important constraints on the choices of individuals, such as with the sex ratio (mate selection) or population pyramid (taxation).

ONTOGENETIC DEVELOPMENT

Every unit within an ecosystem may undergo change that comes about from its own internal structure. Change that is a result of the internal organization and dependencies of parts is called development. For humans, the most important biological part of such developmental

222   FAMILY THEORIES

change is aging and *ontogenetic development* (see Chapter 5, "Concepts" section). The most important social part of this internal development is experience or maturation. As Piaget (1952) and others have noted, ontogenetic development and social development are inextricably linked. Indeed, Bronfenbrenner (1979) challenges the very assumption that development can be discussed meaningfully as just occurring within the organism. He argues that development is always a relationship between the organism and its immediate environment. Even though there are challenges to the perspective that internal change of a unit is "developmental," it is nonetheless a useful notion for comparing this type of internal change with external change.

NATURAL SELECTION AND ADAPTATION

Prior to Fisher's (1958) proof that mutation could not possibly be a major factor in evolution, there were thought to be two major sources of evolutionary change, mutation and natural selection. Now, we usually consider only natural selection and its correlate, adaptation. Indeed, the concepts of natural selection and adaptation are simply different sides of the same process. Natural selection is a concept about the outcome of adaptation. If an organism or population successfully adapts (survives) to changes in its ecosystem (interrelations among niches), then it has not been "selected." If the organism does *not* adapt, then it has been "selected." If a population undergoes changes, it is because some poorly adapted organisms were "selected out" and the remaining organisms represent a more adaptive set of alleles for the population. The classic example here is that of the white moths in late-19th-century coal-dependent Britain. The black moths survived the change to a coal-blackened environment, whereas their white relatives became readily visible to every hungry bird.

In ecological theory, natural selection is often treated as a population process and adaptation as an individual-level process. But natural selection and adaptation, population and individual, gene pool and gene can all be viewed as components of evolution and ontogenetic development, respectively. An organism's development over time is relatively set by its genetic endowment. Whether or not a particular organism can adapt to changes in its environment depends on the adaptive range provided by its genetic endowment. If one type of organism is selected out of the population, then the gene pool changes. Thus, the adaptive range provided in the ontogenetic development of the organism interacts with the changing environment to produce the outcome of selection and adaptation.

Propositions

Human ecological theory has not produced one uniform and consensual set of theoretical propositions. At the most abstract level are the general propositions developed by Hawley (1986), which are difficult to apply to the family. Bronfenbrenner (1979) has suggested several sensitizing concepts and highlighted possible relationships. The propositions we list below are principally drawn from Hawley's (1986) *Human Ecology* because it represents to date the most thorough and systematic treatment of the field.

The family is a social organization embedded in a larger kinship network (Hawley, 1986, p. 73). The family occupies a niche in all social systems by providing for the sustenance and nurturance of its internal members while providing the larger society with the reproduction of economic and social organization. It is Bronfenbrenner (1979) who most clearly envisions the individual's development within the ecosystem:

The individual grows and adapts through interchanges with its immediate ecosystem (the family) and more distant environments such as school. (Bronfenbrenner, 1979)

The individual child is always in a relationship from conception onward. Although the child develops ontogenetically, this development is always in the context of these relationships. Thus, the child's development is interactional.

Ecosystem change occurs as new information is converted to new functions (specialization) or increased specialization of old functions. (Hawley, 1986, p. 60)

As the child develops, his or her functions in the family change from mainly being supported and maintained (what Hawley terms *commensalistic*) to increasingly symbiotic and interdependent functions such as household production and consumption (what Hawley terms *corporate*). The family as a production and consumption unit provides individual services and relates to other units as a social and economic household unit. In this process, the child takes on increasingly specialized roles according to his or her developmental maturation and the age-graded norms.

Changes in specialization involve changes in relationships among functions. (Hawley, 1986, p. 60)

and

Increases in intensity of specialization of any given function are accompanied by increases in intensity of specialization of all complementary functions. (Hawley, 1986, p. 85)

Husband-and-wife dyads become increasingly specialized in the role (niches) of mother and father with the arrival of a child. These roles are commensalistic rather than corporate. As the child matures and becomes increasingly specialized as a consumer and producer (corporate), the parents become less specialized in the commensalistic arena and more specialized in the corporate area of consumption and production.

Complex units develop on each of two axes: on the basis of complementary differences (corporate units) and on the basis of common environmental requirements (commensalistic units). (Hawley, 1986, p. 86)

and

Corporate units tend to replicate the structural properties of the parent ecosystem. (Hawley, 1986, p. 86)

As children mature in their corporate roles and become more interdependent, they tend to follow the normative system that gave rise to their parental ecosystem. Thus, children tend to reproduce the family organization of their family of orientation but under the new constraints of an ecosystem that has changed with the passage of time.

Corporate units tend toward closure regardless of the openness of the ecosystem. (Hawley, 1986, p. 86)

Hawley states that "closure" of a niche is a relative concept, but that when a unit is involved in the biophysical environment, such as with the more commensalistic or categoric task of raising small children, closure is maximized and helps to ensure the stability of the system. Thus, we would expect more closure to information regarding role change and external sources or role change while children are young.

We have only presented a few of the many propositions in human ecology. Indeed, we have not presented the more abstract population-level propositions developed by Hawley. But even these propositions bear scant resemblance to population genetics and the more biological ecological theories. Hawley's picture of human ecology theory is driven by the realization that human ecological systems are different mainly in that human ecology "finds its fullest expression in the commitment to organization as the adaptive mechanism" (p. 126). In the sense that the family is a central social organization, we can see that human ecologists must view the family as a core adaptive mechanism.

Let's apply these propositions by returning to our initial example of Katrina's dad taking her to school. Recall that Katrina wanted her mother to take her to school as the other kids' mothers did. The family is reorganizing roles because of complex social and economic changes, yet these changes do not in themselves predict the particular direction and form of the reorganization. For example, Katrina's parents could decide that roles should be discontinued by sending Katrina off to other relatives. Katrina is responding to the fact that her family is reorganizing their roles because "changes in specialization involve changes in relationships among functions" (Hawley, 1986, p. 60). Katrina's mother and father have had to adapt to a complex economic environment. Part of this adaptation is that the father's role is being redefined to occupy some of the niche vacated by the now-employed mother. But rather than eliminate these roles, the family preserves its functions because the family corporate unit "tends to replicate the structural properties of the parent ecosystem" (Hawley, 1986, p. 86).

Furthermore, the family corporate unit tends toward closure regardless of the openness of the ecosystem (see p. 86), testifying to the inherent conservative nature or inertia of family organization. Part of this inertia comes from the commensalistic nature of the organization. As Katrina matures, however, she will have to do more to assist the family because her dad will also be looking for a job in addition to his expanded household role and her working mother will not be free from aspects of her mother role. In Hawley's formulation: "Increases in intensity of specialization of any given function are accompanied by increases in intensity of specialization of all complementary functions" (p. 85). In this regard, we can also see the school system changing, in that neither mom nor dad may be available to help with supervision and transportation of field trips and so on. Indeed, "Ecosystem change occurs as new information is converted to new functions (specialization) or increased specialization of old functions" (Hawley, 1986, p. 60). Thus, the changes that Katrina's family and other families are experiencing may have ramifications for the educational system. And, in the longer run, the demonstration that such "adaptation" is necessary may lead Katrina's generation to reduce the number of children they have so that reorganization is more easily accomplished. Such curtailing of fertility would lead to population-level changes.

In the final analysis, we cannot completely explain what is happening to Katrina's family without examining the complex causes in the higher-order systems. Yet, the rudiments of the ecological approach can be seen in this example. Basic principles are the connectedness and embeddedness of various ecological levels and the continual need for adaptation to the constant currents of change.

Variations

HUMAN DEVELOPMENTAL ECOLOGY

Urie Bronfenbrenner (1979) tied together ideas from ecological theory and Kurt Lewin's (1935) field theory to formulate the ideas in his book *The Ecology of Human Development*. Bronfenbrenner argues that the child always develops in the context of family-type relationships and that development is the outcome not simply of the onto-genetic factors but of the interaction of the person's genetic endowment with the immediate family and eventually with other components of the environment. Although this central argument does not originate with Bronfenbrenner, his work represents one of the most recent systematic statements of this perspective. As a result, the ecological approach to human development has proven influential in guiding research by family scholars, developmental psychologists, and re-searchers in education.

From the macroscopic perspective of Hawley's (1986) proposi-tions, the ecological approach to human development could be inter-preted as focusing on Hawley's propositions linking changes in specialization to changes in relationships among functions (p. 60). Although there is no contradiction between Bronfenbrenner (1979) and Hawley (1986), Bronfenbrenner's contribution is significant and should not be trivialized as simply filling in detail for Hawley's macro-perspective on human ecology. The distinction between the two complementary approaches lies in what they explore. Hawley (1986) examines the linkages between parts of the ecosystem and the general laws that govern the interrelations of these parts. Bronfenbrenner (1979) examines individual human behavior as a consequence of the interaction between the environment and the person.

Bronfenbrenner's (1979) work stands in sharp contrast to those psychologists who would explain individual behavior solely by ex-amining individual traits or abilities. Bronfenbrenner argues that a person's behavior is a function of the interaction of the person's traits and abilities with the environment ($B = f\{PE\}$). This view supposes that a person's traits interact with the environment to create individual behavior that cannot be explained by simply adding the effects of the person's traits to the effects of the environment. The classic example of this is early toilet training. The child does not gain voluntary muscular control in this regard until about 18 months of age. Socializa-tion before this time is likely to frustrate both the child and parent. It is only when the ontological development and the environmental socialization coincide that the desired outcome is reached. The be-havior, toilet training, cannot be seen as additive, because socialization prior to muscular control will have little effect and muscular control without proper socialization will also have little effect in attaining the target behavior. It is the interaction of these two components (PE) that produces the behavior. And it is this interactionist perspective that distinguishes Bronfenbrenner's (1979) view of human development from the more ontological individual approaches. He defines his position as follows:

> The ecology of human development involves the scientific study of the progressive, mutual accommodation between an active, growing human being and the changing properties of the immediate environment in which the developing person lives, as this process is affected by relations between these settings, and by the larger contexts in which the settings are embedded. (1979, p. 21)

Bronfenbrenner views the individual as being embedded in a microsystem (role and relations), a mesosystem (interrelations between two or more settings), an exosystem (external settings that do not include the person), and a macrosystem (culture). His idea of ecological change is very similar to Hawley's (1986) notion linking changes in niche specialization to changes in relationships among functions. In Bronfenbrenner's (1979) definition of an ecological transition, a "person's position in the ecological environment is altered as the result of a change in role, setting, or both" (p. 26). Later, Bronfenbrenner (1989) expanded this notion and discussed a model in which there are "differences in developmental processes and outcomes associated with different ecological niches" (p. 200). For example, as a child develops, he or she is brought into roles with caregivers other than the mother—day care, preschool, peers, and eventually the school system. All of these interactions may represent significant ecological transitions for the developing child in that there are new roles (niches) and interactions with the immediate environment and increasingly distant environments. The child-school mesosystem is further affected by other exosystems and the macrosystem by forces such as economic pressures and political decisions. Bronfenbrenner's (1979, 1989) approach encompasses the entire environment of the developing person while maintaining a focus of the microsystem (roles and relations) and mesosytem interactions as having the greatest direct effects on the child.

Bronfenbrenner (1989) has recently expanded and refined his approach. The most important refinement he has made is to include *time* as a more integral part of his theory. This incorporation of time has led to two major additions to the theory. First, Bronfenbrenner now views his ecological theory as applying "throughout the life course" of the individual (p. 188). Second, he has added the notion of the *chronosystem,* which incorporates time as the developmental history of the individual (events and experiences) and its effect on development. The need for the addition of time 10 years after the original statement of the theory might appear as an almost humorous oversight for a theory dealing with developmental change over time. In Bronfenbrenner's defense, the decade of the 1980s witnessed some significant theoretical and methodological innovations in regard to the occurrence and timing of life course events (see Chapter 5). These refinements also give Bronfenbrenner's (1979, 1989) theory a greater similarity to other life course theories covered in Chapter 5 and may suggest a gradual merging into more of an emphasis on *development* than *ecology.* It may be, however, that these refinements simply further the already powerful influence of Bronfenbrenner's developmental ecological approach on family scholarship.

FAMILY DEMOGRAPHY AND ECOLOGY

Peterson (1969) defines demography as "the systematic analysis of population phenomena" (p. 1). He goes on to point out a basic distinction among classes of demographers. On the one hand, there is "formal" demography, the study of population as a self-contained process using sophisticated mathematical models. On the other hand, there is "population analysis," which includes variables from the social setting such as norms, natural resources, and economic growth as both independent and dependent variables (Peterson, 1969, p. 3). Population analysis is a theoretical variant of human ecology.

Since its inception, demography has been necessarily concerned with the study of many "family" variables such as nuptiality and fertility. Demographers from the time of Malthus recognized that variables such as fertility were influenced by social custom and organization and that differences in the rules of organization would affect fertility patterns. But a concern with family variables does not necessarily suggest that demography occupies a niche in the human ecology of families.

The claim that demography occupies a theoretical role in the human ecology of the family would strike many demographers as unusual and equivocal. The case for this theoretical contribution is quite strong, however. From the turn of the century, sociologists and demographers of rural life have been concerned with the life cycle of the family. Paul Glick (1947), a *family demographer,* formalized this life cycle approach to data on families in his paper "The Family Cycle." Demographers have also been interested in how families are integrated with other organized sectors of society, such as work and education. Hogan (1978) examined the effects of event sequences, including finishing education, starting a first job, and marriage. Oppenheimer (1988) examined family change and economic change. Recently Sweet, Bumpass, Call, and others from the University of Wisconsin Center for Demography and Ecology launched a longitudinal panel study, the National Survey of Families and Households, focused on families and family forms in the United States (Sweet, Bumpass, & Call, 1988).

Demographers study macroscopic levels of analysis such as social organizations, institutions, and populations. The principal theoretical orientation they have provided is their focus on how these social groupings are interwoven in time and space for any given society. Some demographers have moved to global levels of analysis in their attempt to understand social phenomena such as the connection between fertility and rates of female labor force participation (e.g., Westoff, 1978). Demography, then, occupies the niche in ecology that is focused on population characteristics and population change.

SOCIOBIOLOGY OF THE FAMILY

Since the writings of Darwin, various attempts have been made to explain social behavior as a consequence of evolution. Recently, most such attempts for a biological explanation of social behavior have been labeled *sociobiology,* following E. O. Wilson (1975). Sociobiology was preceded by the eugenics of Pearson (1909) and Fisher (1958) and early ethologists such as Konrad Lorenz (1966). Pierre van den Berghe (1979) is responsible for the most systematic application of sociobiology to the family.

Sociobiologists of the family accept that human behavior is a complex interaction of genes and environment (van den Berghe, 1979,

p. 5). They do not offer a simplistic biological determinism of social behavior. Rather, the key concept used in sociobiology is *inclusive fitness,* or *kin selection.* Inclusive fitness refers to individuals' behaving in ways to maximize their own or their relatives' reproductive success (1979, p. 19). This means that the individual attempts to maximize the transmission of his or her genes to the succeeding generation. Because a sibling carries 50% of one's own genes, the success of a sibling in reproduction is related to one's own success. This one principle, inclusive fitness, is used to explain much of human family behavior within the constraints of natural selection on the gene pool and the configuration of the environment. For example, van den Berghe discusses two parental strategies for maximizing reproductive success. One strategy is to have few children and invest a lot in the care and socialization of these few. The other strategy is to have many children but with the necessary reduction in the parental investment of time and energy per child. He points out that the two strategies have different strengths and weaknesses depending on the environment. In an unstable and hostile environment, high fertility might prove more successful, whereas lower fertility with high parental investment is more appropriate for stable populations close to the carrying capacity of the environment (1979, p. 26). Thus, the explanatory biological principle of inclusive fitness is always used within a particular environment.

A particularly interesting example of how sociobiologists attempt to explain family phenomena is the application of inclusive fitness in an explanation of pair bonding and marriage. Humans do not practice random mating or mating driven by female estrus. Rather, in most human societies, we find that relatively permanent heterosexual couples are the rule. To explain why this is so offers some difficulty for sociobiology. Van den Berghe (1979) argues, "Females invest more in offspring, have less of an incentive to be promiscuous, and have a greater concern to bind a male to themselves than vice versa" (p. 46). Males, on the other hand, have less at stake in the nurturance of individual children and more to gain by maximizing the contribution of genes to a larger number of females. Thus, according to van den Berghe (1979),

Courtship (the rituals preceding the formation of a pair-bond) is primarily a method by which females assess and choose males and whereby males woo females. A woman subjects her suitors to tests that enable her to make the best possible choice of a provider—a mate likely to contribute maximally to her fitness. A man seeks to convince his prospective mates that he qualifies, but since he can also increase his fitness by being fickle, he will seek to deceive women. (p. 46)

For van den Berghe (1979), females ultimately invest in their offspring because they carry the child and the results of any promiscuousness are borne by them. Males may pursue a different strategy for maximizing their inclusive fitness in part because they may not have to directly bear the responsibility of care and nurturance. Indeed, until the recent development of DNA testing, paternity was difficult to prove compared to maternity. The so-called double standard for the sexual conduct for males and females is founded on this difference in reproductive strategy.

Sociobiology always raises questions about social change. For example, in the explanation of pair bonding, we may ask about the effect of easily available and effective birth control for women. Would this lead to promiscuity? According to van den Berghe's argument, birth control would not lead to promiscuity as an inclusive fitness strategy for females because it would only allow sex but not reproduction. Women would continue to bear the responsibility of childbirth. From the other side of the equation, we might ask why males would have ever become "providers" and "social fathers" when their best strategy for inclusive fitness appears to be promiscuity. Van den Berghe's analysis tends to represent marriage as a female institution in which males have little investment.

Although sociobiologists may have difficulty providing explanations of some areas of family behavior, they provide very clear explanations of areas that have proven difficult for other theorists. One of these areas is the basic question, "Why do people have children?" From an exchange perspective, children are costly and provide few rewards. Sociobiology provides the unequivocal argument that having children maximizes inclusive fitness. Yet, lurking around the corner are problems for this explanation as social change brings about the introduction of new and effective reproductive technologies not directly tied to the biological individual. Troost and Filsinger (1993) aptly characterize this area of theory as an emerging perspective. From an ecological perspective, the biological underpinnings of humans and human society must be part of any complete ecological theory.

HOME ECONOMICS
AND HUMAN ECOLOGY

From its inception, home economics has been a form of human ecology. Richards's vision was that only through intelligent consumption and management of household resources could our society combat the waste and pollution of unbridled capitalism. She envisioned an application of scientific knowledge and principles to home management. These sentiments were given a more concrete framework by Paolucci, Hall, and Axinn (1977), who fostered the idea that families could affect significant outcomes at the macroscopic level by the management and control of their decisions.

Deacon and Firebaugh (1988) developed an ecological framework for family decision making. They view the family as a system interacting with its environment. Resources and some demands for family resources originate outside of the family. The family system is decomposed into individual personal subsystems and the family managerial subsystem. The family managerial subsystem contains both planning and implementing functions and results in demand responses and changes in resources as system output. Deacon and Firebaugh emphasize the embeddedness of the family system in the larger ecosystem and the interchanges that take place between these various levels. They stress resources, values, and information in family resource management and decision making that remain true to Richards's original vision.

Bubolz and Sontag (1993) argue that Richards's vision of a scientifically based, family consumption unit missed the fact that ultimately family decisions reflect values. A proactive home economics profession, they argue, must likewise reflect a set of values. In this sense, because home economics is a practitioner field and not simply a field of studies, it cannot follow the value neutrality that Bubolz and Sontag identify with positivistic science. Thus, Bubolz and Sontag, as well as others such as Brown (1984), have rejected science as the appropriate model for knowledge and practice and favor a hermeneutic approach that includes the subjectivity of experience and valuing. Among the issues Bubolz and Sontag see as central to human ecology theory are a number of value-laden questions such as "What changes are necessary to bring about human betterment?" and "What should be done to realize such universal values for the common good as economic adequacy, equity in access to resources and opportunities, increased freedom and justice, and development of peace?" (p. 429). It is interesting to contrast this approach with that of traditional scientists who would first question if a universal set of values does indeed exist and want to see evidence that these values are universal.

In some senses, Bubolz and Sontag's (1993) version of home economics is caught in a dilemma common to the "helping" professions. Home economics is dedicated to both the study of the ecosystem and helping people. On the one hand, home economists would like to build a theory of human ecology. On the other hand, they require that such a theory contain a statement of values, such as "equity in access to resources," so that practitioners have a clear notion of what the "common good" and "human betterment" represent. Scientists have in part attempted to remain value neutral because the juxtaposition between an accurate description and prediction of the "way things are" has largely been thought to be independent of our thinking about the "way things should be." The recent name change of the American Home Economics Association to the American Association of Family and Consumer Sciences might signal the beginning of a resolution to this dilemma.

Empirical Applications

EFFECT OF DAY CARE
ON YOUNG CHILDREN

The research on day care and its effects on young children has proved one of the most effective applications of ecological theory of the family. Most of this research has been guided by the ecological formulations of Bronfenbrenner (1979). Major studies include Belsky, Gillstrap, and Rovine (1984) in the United States and Goelman and Pence (1987) in Canada. Researchers in the Pennsylvania Infant and Family Development Project (Belsky et al., 1984) examined infant-mother attachment by using variables drawn from the micro-, meso-, and exosystems developed by Bronfenbrenner (1979; see Bretherton, 1993, p. 287). Findings from the work by Belsky and colleagues (1984) and the myriad other studies examining the ecological factors of child care appear to contradict previous research in the area of child care. Belsky (1990) summarizes the newer research findings, first noting that the macrosystem environment in which these studies were conducted has changed over time: "Less than one-third of all mothers with an infant under one year of age were employed in 1976" but "by 1985 virtually one out of every two such women were working" (pp. 894-895). Belsky summarizes the current state of the literature:

> Children in any variety of child care arrangements, including center care, family day care, and nanny care, for the first year of life, are at elevated risk of being classified as insecure in their attachments to their mothers at 12 or 18 months of age and of being more disobedient and aggressive when they are from 3 to 8 years old. (p. 895)

Belsky and Eggebeen (1991) analyzed the National Longitudinal Survey of Youth and found greater noncompliance among children whose mothers were extensively involved in work early in the child's life. Although Belsky's (1990) claim has been accepted by some academics, a significant number of critics offer empirical support for the position that either "other factors" might account for the differences in attachment or that no significant differences exist (see Greenstein, 1993). The point here is not that ecological theory is a shortcut to quick answers regarding maternal attachment. Indeed, the inclusion of ecological variables makes analyses more complex, but in the long run the findings will be more valid because these contextual variables are included.

CHILD MALTREATMENT

Garbarino and Sherman (1980) argue that when the parent-child relationship is embedded in a community in which other adults with greater resources interact with the parent-child dyad, there is less child maltreatment than in socially isolated parent-child dyads. In "High-Risk Neighborhoods and High-Risk Families: The Human Ecology of Child Maltreatment," Garbarino and Sherman (1980) cite ethological studies with isolated gorilla mothers and their infants and cross-cultural studies that suggest parental rejection of the child is inversely associated with social embeddedness.

Garbarino and Sherman matched two neighborhoods, one high and one low in child risk, by racial composition and socioeconomic status. They state that about 40% of child maltreatment is associated with socioeconomic status, but there remain additional differences in child maltreatment. The hypothesis these researchers examined is that when socioeconomic status is controlled, child risk is associated with neighborhood characteristics.

The results support their contention that neighborhood characteristics are associated with levels of child maltreatment risk. Garbarino and Sherman describe the high-risk neighborhoods as being different from the low-risk neighborhoods on several dimensions. In low-risk neighborhoods, the children played with other children and parents lent a helping hand with "coverage" of children so that stressed parents could recover. In high-risk neighborhoods, the children did not play with other children and the parents expressed doubts that the neighborhood was a good place to raise children: "Family life is threatened from within and without. . . . A family's own problems seem to be compounded rather than ameliorated by the neighborhood context, dominated as it is by other needy families" (1980, p. 194).

Garbarino and Kostelny (1992) likewise view child maltreatment as a community problem. The presence of informal support networks in the community militates against child maltreatment. But as ecologists such as Burgess (1925) have pointed out, there is a tendency for neighborhoods to homogenize. This process leads Garbarino and Sherman (1980) to conclude that "we have repeated findings that ecological niches can 'make or break' risky families. The challenge to researchers and policymakers is to make the best of it" (p. 196).

Implications for Intervention

Westney (1993) points to several possible implications of ecological theory for practitioners. First and foremost is that ecological theory sensitizes practitioners and others to the multiple levels and complex interactions between various ecological units. For example, parent education might entail not just what the parent can do for the child but in addition could be extended to parent-child interactions with the neighborhood and schools. The ecological perspective is inherently multidisciplinary in its implications. In addition to family scientists, nutritionists, urban planners, and traffic engineers have an important role within the ecological model.

Campbell (1993) suggests that one especially important area of application for ecological theory is in health care delivery. Policymakers in more and more countries are critically examining the escalating costs of health care. For some of these countries, part of the solution is to move from a "general hospital" program of disease treatment to a community- or family-based model emphasizing health as well as treatment. In community-based treatment, more emphasis is placed on the family as both a provider of services and as a treatment unit. In family practice, physicians may team up with nutritionists and family therapists to provide service aimed at the family (Bloch, 1983). In addition, the family may require special supports as it takes on increasingly higher loads of caregiving (e.g., Gatz, Bengtson, & Blum, 1990). Ecological theory provides many of the biosocial and physical concepts to inform and assist practitioners in this area.

Critiques and Discussion

Regardless of the appealing logic of ecological theory and its seeming breadth and inclusiveness, there are some rather severe criticisms of both the logic and substance of this approach. The criticisms we broach here are not ones that can be dismissed by claims that the theory is too new or that these are simply areas that have not been adequately filled in as yet. Rather, many of the criticisms are directed at the logic of the explanation in general.

One of the basic notions in Hawley (1986) and Bronfenbrenner (1979, 1989) is that growth comes about by interchanges with the environment. Equally important is the question "How does decline and decay come about?" Hawley's (1986) *Human Ecology* contains chapters on growth, evolution, and expansion in time and space; chapters on decay, disintegration, and death are notably absent. Bronfenbrenner (1979) focuses so exclusively on child development that statements about environmental interaction and growth appear natural. Even with his later admission that the life course as well as child development needs to be included in the model, there is no discussion of degeneration (Bronfenbrenner, 1989). Some ecological scholars address these issues and indeed go some distance in resolving the oversight. Most notable is the work by Hannan and Freeman (1984), who use the idea of structural size and attendant inertia to predict the ability of organizations to adapt to changing environments and the natural selection that results from their adaptive failure. These authors link the properties of the organization with adaptation and selection. The need remains to incorporate concepts such as aging and continuous decay into the ecological model.

Another major problem for ecological theory is the need to specify when ontogenetic causation changes to sociogenetic causation. For example, a child may not learn toilet training at 2 months of age for reasons of ontogenetic maturation, but at some point in the life course of the organism the same outcome (toilet training) switches from being ontogenetic to sociogenetic. Another way of thinking about this is that there comes a time when the organism's responses are no longer determined by the organism's internal development but by processes exogenous to the organism. The process of this changeover and its stages have not yet been identified by ecological theorists. Hawley (1986) provides a partial solution in his notion that an organization (such as a family) can switch from commensalistic to corporate functions. Bronfenbrenner (1979) incorporates this notion in relating the child to successively broader ecosystems. Yet, the exact process and identity of this switch from genetic to social causality eludes us.

Somewhat similar to the above criticism is the question of levels of analysis. The problem is that there are few rules to guide the scholar as to when one level of analysis is appropriate rather than another. For example, if behavior is explained by gene pool variance, then when behavior changes rapidly we would expect rapid changes in the gene pool. Now, imagine that violent crimes increase in a city in a short period of time, such as 3 years. We would be tempted to explain those changes in crime by changes in the gene pool or population, yet it is doubtful that gene pools change so rapidly with normal levels of migration. What then is the appropriate level of analysis—the individual, the group, the organization, or some other level?

Ecology, many critics claim, is a sensitizing metaphor. For example, in home economics some proponents show embedded circles as diagrams of ecological levels and interfaces, but critics claim these represent pretty circles but no theory. A theory must identify the process by which change occurs. Even Bronfenbrenner (1989) concedes that this is a rather large flaw in the theory. In his original contribution, Bronfenbrenner (1989) identified behavior as a function of the person interacting with his or her environment (B = f{PE}). Bronfenbrenner says,

> The all-essential key to scientific discovery is missing. In all the preceding pages, what is there to substitute for the fateful "f" in the formula? What is the process that the person and the context are to generate? (p. 241)

Although Bronfenbrenner also states that he is working on this problem, it as yet remains a flaw to be rectified.

Bronfenbrenner's (1989) task is complicated by the criticism that the logic underlying ecological theory is basically tautological or circular (Turner, 1991). For example, evolution is a form change brought on by adaptation and selection to change that in turn was brought on by evolution. One needs to ask if this is not defining change by change. It may not be a problem if there is sufficient precision and detail in the theory so that generalities like "change" become more precisely specified as "evolution," "adaptation," and "development."

The notion of biological or ontogenetic development of the organism represents a richness that many sociological theories neglect. This allows for the inclusion of both internal and external dynamics of change. But the biological arguments from sociobiology and some ontogenetic arguments share a common flaw. Critics argue that because many of these claims and explanations are ex post facto in nature, any number of other plausible theories might also be true (including sociogenetic theories). The way out of this criticism is to abandon claims that may appear reasonable on the surface but fail to lead to empirically testable predictions. For example, the claim that the male strategy for inclusive fitness is to maximize sexual partners might lead to cross-culturally testable hypotheses. But if this "strategy" is nothing other than a "preference" that is extremely malleable by the environment, then it would undoubtedly lead nowhere. This is what has happened to those ridiculous claims about the true "nature of man" and "natural law" theories. At the present time, the inclusion of biological factors holds great promise but also represents the threat of dragging ecological theory into the quagmire of ad hoc and ex post facto explanations that has been the bane of sociobiology.

Finally, there is criticism of building a value-laden human ecology theory. It seems there is a choice to be made between producing a social science theory or some general value orientation. On the one hand, it can be argued that all scientific theories entail some value orientation. Indeed, that may be the case. The problem we see is different. First, by definition, social science theories describe and predict. A value orientation may simply not meet the meaning or function of a scientific theory. There are philosophical theories, religious theories, theories of literature, and ideologies, none of which are scientific theories. Also, a value orientation may simply not be a social science theory. Second, value-oriented theories may be able to produce predictions, but we wonder whether predictions would be judged by their accuracy or by their desirability or value correctness. For example, Galileo's ideas were suppressed because they were politically incorrect, not because of the inaccuracy of his predictions.

Conclusion

In the final analysis, the ecological approach is at a youthful stage of its development. It has the necessary breadth and depth to offer a perspective on humans that is both biological and social. The possible unification of work from sociobiology with the ecology of human development and Hawley's (1986) more organizational ecology offers some intriguing prospects for studying both individual family members, the family as a group, and the general ecological context in which those groups function. It might well be that ecological theory will provide not only family scholars but social scientists in general with the most powerful theoretical propositions possible. At present, however, we can only say that this promise remains a potentiality. As Turner (1991) says in regard to Hawley's (1986) formulation, "Human ecology, then, is a theoretical perspective worthy of further development" (p. 151).

Food for Thought

1. If neighborhoods are a major factor in the maltreatment of children as Garbarino and Sherman (1980) contend, what effects do you think working parents have on neighborhoods?
2. Demographers have suggested that the aging of our population will have profound effects. What effects do you think our aging population will have on family caregiving and parenting?
3. Do you think that some parents invest more in the upbringing of their children than other parents? What do you think would characterize a biosocial perspective on parental investments in children?
4. Can you imagine a biosocial explanation of spousal abuse? rape? homosexuality?

Suggested Readings

Bubolz, M., & Sontag, S. (1993). Human ecology theory. In P. Boss, W. Doherty, R. LaRossa, W. Schumm, & S. Steinmetz (Eds.), *Sourcebook of family theories and methods: A contextual approach* (pp. 419-448). New York: Plenum.

This is a good general introduction to a version of human ecology developed from a viewpoint in the home economics perspective.

Troost, K., & Filsinger, E. (1993). Emerging biosocial perspectives on the family. In P. Boss, W. Doherty, R. LaRossa, W. Schumm, & S. Steinmetz (Eds.), *Sourcebook of family theories and methods: A contextual approach* (pp. 677-710). New York: Plenum.

This is a very good introduction to the biosocial perspective.

9

The Current State and
Future Course of Family Theory

We have now traversed a considerable amount of theoretical territory. You have been introduced to the basic elements of theory in Chapter 1 and some of the basic issues and problems theorists encounter in Chapter 2 as well as several family theories in Chapters 3 through 8. Now, it is time for a comprehensive overview of family theory—which is, however, a daunting task, because a theory is never finished!

In the preceding chapters, we have presented theories as *products* of human thought. Although this is certainly one useful way to learn about theories, an overemphasis on the product may lead you away from the power of theories as tools to assist us in understanding our world. A tool analogy may help you appreciate our point here. Imagine you have a screwdriver. You can hold it up and examine it from different angles, note the color, the type of point, and so on. In this sense, you are examining the screwdriver as a product and a human construction. But your image of the screwdriver changes when you use it to screw in a screw, pry open a paint can, weed the garden, and so on. You might even find other new and helpful ways to use the screwdriver. Your appreciation changes when you use this tool to do things. The same is true of theories.

Any of the family theories you find in this book can be used for myriad tasks. These theories can be used to predict, to interpret, to explain, to formulate questions, to integrate research, to make deductions, and to lead us into novel areas of research. When we use them, we gain an understanding of theories that is unlike the rarefied experience of holding them up in isolation as objects for academic scrutiny.

Like the tools developed for carpentry or gardening, theories are often modified as they are used and as a result of their use. A researcher who tests a series of theoretically derived hypotheses may find some disconfirmed and others not disconfirmed and thus continuing to be plausible. The researcher may then suggest modifications in the theory to make the theory more consistent with the findings.

Although researchers often focus on a theory's ability to predict, theories are also used to interpret events that have already occurred. This after-the-fact (*ex post facto*) interpretation is what many of us consider to be the central component of explanation. We would like a good story about why or how something happened or usually happens. These interpretations of past events may also lead to modifications in theories. As we attempt to explain why Kyle and Sara are getting divorced or why our grandparents are extraordinarily frugal, we may find other dimensions and variables that are needed to make our story a plausible one.

Yet another way theories are modified is when practitioners use a theory to guide an educational, political, or therapeutic intervention. Often practitioners discover inadequacies in theories that researchers might miss. All of these tool users of theory may assist in modifying and improving family theory. This is the process of theory construction and reconstruction.

In presenting you with various family theories as "products," we do not want to mislead you into thinking that these theories are finished artifacts of human thought. Nothing could be further from the truth. Because they are useful tools, theories are constantly being modified and refined. We are not saying that the core concepts and relations change constantly, but even those core concepts are not exempt from the process of theory building.

Furthermore, behind every theory is a theorist. The ideas in theories are created and used by people in different ways, so it is helpful to know something about these people, their backgrounds, their intentions, and perhaps even their own families. In other words, we could use social science theories—even family theories—to make sense of the behavior of theorists. None of the theories in this book were created by a single person. Rather, communities of interacting scholars and practitioners have been working together, in harmony or in conflict, to produce those useful tools we call theories.

One reason that each of the major theories we have covered also has variations is that different individual scholars and groups of scholars have thought about them and applied them in different ways.

Comparing Theories

We believe that it is possible to compare the theories in this book to gain some idea as to which ones might be best applied to particular family phenomena and particular questions about those phenomena. For instance, if you are interested in explaining why people select certain mates, exchange theory may be more useful than conflict theory. The metaphors provided by conflict theory focus on phenomena other than attraction and mating. To put this differently, the scope and focus of these theories are somewhat different. The way we can compare theories is to find a set of metatheoretical characteristics that all theories have to differing degrees.

In this section, we present several dimensions on which theories may vary. We can use these dimensions to construct a metatheoretical typology of the theories covered in this book. These typological dimensions can then be used to sort and classify any family theory. Because our dimensions are abstract, they could be used—and actually have been used—to help understand any social science theory and where it might be best applied.

It will be important to keep in mind as we go along that typologies and other classification schemes represent what Max Weber (1949) called "ideal types." Placing objects in categories helps to sharpen their similarities and differences. What is sacrificed is our ability to notice the unique characteristics of the individual objects being classified. Like other objects, theories are not just black or white. Each theory comes in different shades and hues, so the fit between a particular theory developed or used by a particular person and the category into which it is placed is always a matter of degree. Many classification schemes have been created for sorting theories as objects; all of them are ideal typical, and none of them perfectly fit the "real" theories that individual theorists recognize and use.

SCOPE AND FOCUS

As we have already suggested, theories vary in scope and focus. Usually the scope and focus of the theory is determined by the dependent variables the theory is intended to explain and the type of assumptions and boundary conditions the theorist lays out. Because all of the theories in this book are intended to explain dependent variables about family behavior, on the surface they might appear similar. But most of these theories are based on assumptions about the unit of analysis to which the ingredients of the explanation apply. For example, microexchange theories most often focus on the individual's motivation. In these theories, we attempt to explain choices by weighing the costs and rewards of various options in any given situation. On the other hand, most developmental theories include the assumption that social norms guide the behavior of the family unit as well as individual family members.

A convenient way to analyze these differences in focus and assumptions is to identify the level or levels of analysis on which the theory operates. This has been one of the most popular ways to distinguish theories in sociology (e.g., Collins, 1988; Martindale, 1979; Ritzer, 1979; Turner, 1991).

A theory may focus on the internal processes of the individual, such as the individual's motivation and internalized beliefs and attitudes. Such theories would then be principally aimed at the *individual* level of analysis. Other theories might stress that explanation can only be achieved by analyzing the interactions between family members. Such theories would be aimed at the *relationship* level of analysis, such as

TABLE 9.1 Level of Analysis

Individual	Relationship	Family Group	Institution
Exchange	Symbolic interaction	Ecological Systems Developmental	Conflict Developmental

marital, parent-child, or sibling interaction. Still other theories involve viewing the organization of the family group or system as the key to understanding family behavior. Such theories function predominantly at the *group* level of analysis. Finally, some theories are used to explain the behavior of families and individuals by focusing on the norms, economic constraints, and historical periods in which families operate. Theories such as these focus on the constraints and processes that affect families from the institution of the family and from other social institutions such as work and education. Such a focus is on the *institutional* level of analysis. These four levels can be used to help us sort out the kinds of explanation each theory can provide.

Table 9.1 shows one way to use levels of analysis to sort out our six theories. Although it can be claimed for most theories that they in some way deal with all of these levels of analysis, each theory does tend to use one level as its major focus. In some cases, the level of analysis for the theory is established by the assumption of methodological individualism discussed in Chapter 2. For example, exchange theorists assume that the individual is the unit making choices. Symbolic interaction theorists tend to see relationships between people as the ultimate unit of analysis. We receive our socialization in relationships such as parent-child and teacher-pupil, and social phenomena emerge as a result of interactions. Ecological and systems theorists usually see the family group as the unit of analysis. Although both of these theories have subsystems that include individuals, these subsystems are needed for analysis as the parts of the entire system. Family developmental theorists view the family group as the major unit of analysis but see that unit as receiving much of its structure and form from institutional norms. Thus, we have included family development at both the group and institutional levels. Finally, conflict theorists view the family as a microcosm of the processes in the larger social institutions. Of all the six theories, conflict theories are the most clearly focused on the social-institutional level of analysis.

The levels we have discussed can be arrayed from microscopic to macroscopic. This dimension can have different meanings, however. We can think of the microlevel as involving face-to-face interactions among individuals, whereas the macrolevel refers to the organization of populations of individuals (Turner, 1991, pp. 587-588). If we use this imagery, there may not be a separate level in between. According to Turner (1991), the middle, or mesolevel, involves the mutual constraints that micro- and macrophenomena place on each other.

Martindale (1979) illustrates a different way to think about levels. He has argued that the main way we distinguish units is according to whether they are *elementaristic* or *holistic*. This idea fits well with family theories. As we have indicated in earlier chapters, the systems, conflict, and ecological perspectives are more holistic than other family theories.

Whatever way we distinguish levels, it is always useful to think about what kind of social unit is capable of having a certain characteristic and how a theory uses these units. For example, we can say without hesitation that an individual member of a family has an attitude or an emotion, but how would we visualize a family's attitude or emotion? A challenge for every theorist is to both show which level is being used and clearly indicate how concepts at one level can make sense at another level. One of the common practices we have observed is that family theories may give the appearance of being holistic, but they are often applied in a more elementaristic way. This is largely a problem of research methods, for it is not easy to study an entire family. Instead, we often gather data on a family from a particular member's point of view.

Sometimes, concepts make sense at many levels, so it is especially important to know which one is applicable to a particular theory. For example, take the concept of *income*. We can say that an individual family member earns a certain amount, but this is not necessarily the family's income. In addition to the combined income of all working family members, we could think of the average income of all families in a neighborhood or community. At an even higher level, we could think of the typical economic standard of living for families in a particular social class or even in an entire society. Our main point here is that no one level or unit of analysis is always best. What is the best level depends on what we want to understand and explain. The best theory is the one that makes the most sense for the level that we need.

TIME

Every theory includes the notion of time in some way. Some theories are based on the assumption of a relatively static perspective on time. A static perspective is usually indicated when the same explanatory variables are always important regardless of the passage of time. Another way of saying this is that a theory is relatively static if it includes the assumption of homogeneity across time. For example, exchange theorists assume that choices are made in the same way regardless of time. They make no attempt to incorporate time-dependent processes such as learning or experience.

According to more processual or dynamic theories, explanatory variables change in their importance as time passes. Another way of saying this is that explanatory variables are time dependent. For instance, Marxian conflict theory and developmental theory incorporate time dependencies by means of "stages" and "transitions."

Theories may be placed on a continuum between *static* and *dynamic* based on the extent to which they incorporate time as an important concept. For the sake of simplicity, we categorize theories in Table 9.2 as to whether they are mainly static or mainly dynamic. As the defining criterion between static and dynamic, we use the presence or absence in the theory of explicit reference to a process that depends on time. Thus, in conflict theories such as the Marxian variety, the stage of the social system and the historical epoch clearly make a difference in interpreting conflict. In systems theory, the recursive nature of successive feedback loops incorporates time dependency. And in family developmental theory, time is expressly considered in that transitions depend on the previous stage and duration in that stage.

Exchange, ecological, and symbolic interaction theories include no identified processes that are explicitly linked to time. This is, of course, not entirely accurate. It does take time for any given exchange or interaction to occur. We may think of these processes as occurring in "episodic" time. A given episode may be further decomposed into actions and reactions by specific persons, but both exchange and

TABLE 9.2 Time

Static	Dynamic
Exchange	Conflict
Ecological	Systems
Symbolic Interaction	Developmental

symbolic interaction theorists tend to view episodes as the time unit, and what happens in one episode gets repeated in the next episode. Even some versions of ecological theory deal with time dependencies. For example, bioevolutionary theories often deal with huge chains of generational effects and may even concern the "origin" of a species.

Collins (1988, p. 387) suggests that every theory in the social sciences specifies or at least implies some time scale and that the scale ranges all the way from seconds to centuries. For most purposes, however, it may be practical to distinguish family theories according to their emphasis on one of three time scales: episodic time, life time, and historical time. Substituting this trichotomy for the less refined dichotomy between static and dynamic, developmental theories are the most "life time" oriented, and conflict and ecological theories are the most "historical time" oriented. In this perspective, exchange and symbolic interaction theories are episodic, as suggested above, and so is family systems theory.

SOURCES OF CHANGE

All families change over time, but theories approach change in a myriad of ways. Even though static theories usually deal with change in a manner differently than dynamic theories, sometimes there is no discernible difference based on how the theory incorporates time. Theories that deal with time in a static manner may deal with change in a manner similar to some dynamic theories.

There are actually many dimensions to change that we could identify in our typology, such as discrete change and continuous change. Although these are important, the discussion of these dimensions requires a prolonged digression into methodology that would side-track our typological train of thought. Rather than bring these complexities into the current discussion, we deal with change by relying on only one of its characteristics. We compare theories by whether they envision the source of change as coming from within the family unit or being external to the family unit. For example, exchange theorists would see change as originating from the choices of family members—an internal source of change. Marxian conflict theorists view change as originating from larger-scale dialectical processes in which the family is but a bit player. In this sense, change is conceptualized as coming from sources external to the family. This dimension, then, is whether the source of change is *endogenous* or *exogenous* to the family.

Wallace (1968) used this distinction to categorize 11 different general theories in sociology. For him, exogenous sources of change would imply that family structures and interaction patterns are "imposed" or "determined" by outside forces. Endogenous sources of change would imply that the members of families are "free-willed" and that change is more likely to emerge spontaneously as family members struggle over their assorted desires and needs.

Wallace's interpretation is suggestive, but his discussion of sources raises some questions. If outside forces determine family phenomena, what determines the outside forces? Are there not freewilled persons outside of families (all of whom have families themselves) who "force" families to be the way they are? As for free will, is anybody so "free"? Perhaps some families and family members are more independent of outside forces than others, but the essence of family life is interdependence, not freedom. Family members inevitably influence each other. Even the free-willed individual must cope with such deterministic forces as biological aging. Should we then think of biology as something endogenous to a family or exogenous to it? These questions are all worth contemplation, but we focus here on the simple idea of change originating from within families or from outside of families.

Table 9.3 depicts one way of distinguishing the six major theories in this book according to the primary source of change. Because according to exchange theories the individual is the ultimate source of choices, change comes from within the family group. Symbolic interaction theories tend to be focused on the interactions within the family and, thus, view change as coming from within the family group.

TABLE 9.3 Source of Change

Endogenous	Exogenous
Exchange	Ecological
Symbolic Interaction	Developmental
Systems	Systems
	Conflict

Systems theories, because they may incorporate several levels on which change may take place, are either endogenous or exogenous, but usually both.

Ecological theories take the process of "adaptation" to the environment as a basic process of change. Because adaptation carries with it the connotation of a unit adapting to its changing environment, the source of change would come from outside the family unit. Although some versions of family development theory take family members' interactions as a possible source of change, proponents of all versions of this theory admit that change comes from adjustments to changes in social institutions, such as education and work. Conflict theorists view social change as mainly the result of larger-scale social forces, such as class conflict, that are outside the family unit.

We are aware of at least one other recent attempt to classify family theories according to exogenous and endogenous sources of change. Starting with a somewhat different list of primary theoretical frameworks, Winton (1995) proposes that source of change is the single most important distinguishing feature of family theories. Where his theories overlap with ours, the two schemes are identical. Winton treats developmental and conflict theories as "theories of external control" and exchange and symbolic interaction theories as "bringing people back in."

We briefly highlight some additional ways to classify family theories at the end of this section, but without adding further to the complexity of our typology, we can now combine the dimensions of level (i.e., scope or focus), time, and sources of change to map out a more complete picture of the current state of family theory.

Table 9.4 characterizes our six theories. If we wanted to analyze a family at one static point in time at which family change came from within, we would use either symbolic interaction or exchange theory.

TABLE 9.4 A Three-Dimensional Typology of Theories

TIME	Static		Dynamic	
LEVEL CHANGE	Endogenous	Exogenous	Endogenous	Exogenous
Individual	Exchange			
Relationship	Symbolic Interaction			
Family		Ecological	Systems	Systems Development
Institution				Conflict Development

An example of such an application would be an episode of family violence or a particular outcome such as divorce or separation. If we wanted to examine family violence as coming from sources outside the family, such as the cultural system of beliefs about women and violence, then ecological theory would be more appropriate. If we view family violence as a dynamic process over time rather than something that happens at one point in time, systems theory would allow us to incorporate both internal and external sources of change. Conflict and family development theorists would view the process of family violence as being established by the normative social system governing families and interactions within the family. For example, conflict theorists might examine the way the police and other social agencies deal with family violence.

We now suggest that you try to use this typology to categorize the variations in each theory to see how these differ from each other on these dimensions. We suggest that first you might simply try to contrast variations within one theoretical framework and later attempt comparisons between variations from other theories. Be aware that our original categorization of the general theoretical frameworks can be misleading about some of the varieties. Recall that most of the theories have at least both micro- and macrolevel varieties; although the general theory might be aimed at the individual level of analysis, the macrovariation of that theory might not. As you complete this exercise, remember that there is no single correct way to categorize these theories. Your intuitions about these variations may guide you, but you should be ready to explain to others the reasons that your categorization is justified. As with mathematics, intuition in theoretical work is necessary, but you must also try to make explicit the reasons and justifications behind your decisions. Although there is no one correct way to do this exercise, there are nonetheless better or more reasonable categorizations than others.

Another exercise that might be valuable is to take Table 9.4 or a version of the table based instead on the variations within the major theories and look for empty cells. It often is the case that typologies are incomplete in that a particular combination of categories across multiple dimensions does not at first seem to make sense. Discovering this can be very useful. It may simply mean that nobody has yet tried hard enough to theorize in a certain way. This then creates an opportunity to build a new theory. It also may be the case, however, that certain kinds of theories cannot possibly make any sense. One reason that classification schemes such as typologies are useful both as tools for substantive ideas within family theories and as tools for meta-theory is their ability to push us to the limits of discovery and creative thought.

OTHER WAYS TO
CLASSIFY FAMILY THEORIES

Although we cannot exhaust the possibilities, at least three other ways of organizing family theories according to similarities and differences are worth some attention here.

First, recall the purposes or functions of theory that we examined in Chapter 1. It might be useful to differentiate family theories according to the relative emphasis they give to description, explanation, prediction, or prescription (i.e., applications to "improve" family life). We are reluctant to claim that the six major theories in this book can be neatly sorted into only one of these categories. If you were to inspect any particular piece of theoretical work, however, you would likely notice that the slant is more in one direction than in others. Indeed, one complaint often heard is that a particular family theory is not comprehensive enough in addressing the variety of functions it could serve (i.e., too descriptive, not action oriented, etc.).

As we have tried to show in Chapters 3 through 8, most of the more general theories deal in at least some fashion with a variety of functions.

All of them contain some ideas about explanation, whether by the use of family concepts in the explanation or by attempts to explain something about families. Similarly, all of the major theories have implications for intervention. If you don't like something about families and want to prescribe a way to change them, each theory should give you some clues about what to change, how to do it, and what the consequences are likely to be.

Another way to differentiate family theories comes from Chapter 2. Among other things, we noted that our theories tend to be affected by the philosophies of science that family theorists are willing to accept as a matter of principle. Several classification attempts have been made to sort family theories according to their philosophical foundations. A recent example is provided by Burr (1995). Like Winton (1995), Burr (1995) starts with a somewhat different set of major theories than we use here. He does suggest, however, that exchange and developmental theories tend to be "positivistic," whereas symbolic interaction and systems theories tend to be "interpretive." Burr places feminist theory in a category he calls "critical/emancipatory."

It is difficult to judge the adequacy of these placements. We already have hinted at one reason. The variations within theories may be partly due to major philosophical differences. Thus, Martindale (1979) has argued that although the phenomenological variety of symbolic interaction is interpretive in its philosophy, symbolic interaction theory in general is actually positivistic. Similarly, one can find feminist theories within all three of the philosophical alternatives.

There is, however, an even more important reason why it remains difficult to sort theories according to philosophies of science. Philosophies, after all, are not "things" we can easily observe. And they are not quite "products" in the same sense that theories can be. Most of what we know about philosophies is based on presumptions gleaned from whatever theorists mention in their written texts. Yet what people write may not correspond to what they believe. Family theorists actually have not written very much about their own philosophies. If a philosophy is anything, it is a set of mental ideas or cognitive constructions, and we do not yet have much empirical evidence about the philosophies of family theorists.

In one recent attempt to ask a group of active family scholars what their philosophies of science really were, it was discovered that the number and complexity of philosophical beliefs was much greater than any simple classification scheme yet devised can incorporate (Klein, 1994). As we learn more details about the working philosophies of practicing scientists, we may be able to better understand how they affect or are affected by family theories.

The final way to classify family theories that we mention here is based on the distinction between objectivity and subjectivity. Wallace (1968) treats this as the difference between a *materialistic* and an *idealistic* view of the world. Ritzer (1979) uses this dimension in a similar way. The basic idea here is that a materialist would claim there are "real" things that exist outside of human consciousness. They may exist at any level of analysis, but they are what matter most. For example, if you want to understand families at a macrolevel, you need to know about the economy and the political system in which families reside. This mix of materialism and macrolevel is often called *social structure.* If you want to understand families at a microlevel, you need to know about such things as how members spend their time, what material resources they have, how many family members there are, and so on. We might refer to this as *family structure.* Regardless of level, the emphasis is on whatever can be observed by independent observers (i.e., objectively).

A more idealistic approach to family theory deals with attitudes, beliefs, values, feelings, and perceptions. At a macrolevel, this "ideational stuff" is represented by social norms and expectations that are shared in common, perhaps in a particular community, a social class or ethnic group, or even an entire society. This mix of idealism and level is often called *culture.* At a microlevel, proponents of the idealistic approach emphasize the ongoing and modifiable rules and understandings that individual people can articulate, and at the family group level, whatever similarities and differences exist in attitudes and so forth between the members. We might refer to this as *family culture.* Regardless of level, the emphasis is on subjective phenomena.

Sometimes, the notion of subjectivity is misunderstood to mean that nothing is real or that everything is relative and enormously "unstructured." But a theorist who studies families from a subjective point of view would likely be interested in how the ideational stuff becomes both *intersubjective* and *objectified.* Given that a family is a social group, its members must somehow develop common understandings. Multiple subjectivities coalesce into a joint intersubjectivity. Furthermore, real objects exist, but they are crafted. Objects do not exist until they are "objectified" by people working alone or together.

This is also where the two sources of change we discussed earlier are especially important. A theory might be exogenous and subjective or endogenous and subjective. For example, recent versions of family development theory that emphasize institutional norms are essentially exogenous and subjective. "Institutional" provides the exogenous part; "norms" provide the subjective part.

For classification purposes, the objective/subjective dimension can be combined with any of the other dimensions we have discussed. You should be able to appreciate why we have devoted more space in this chapter to three dimensions instead of six, or even some larger number. Even if every dimension contained only two possibilities, a six-dimensional typology would contain 64 cells! We suggested above that typologizing can be a useful way of finding and filling in missing cells, but it is no wonder that some kinds of family theory have yet to be imagined.

Theory Construction

The process of theory building is often called *theory construction*. Theory construction is a process that cannot be easily communicated as a set of rules or an architectural blueprint. Theories develop deductively, inductively, and by a combination of these two processes (what C. S. Peirce termed "abduction"; see Buchler, 1955).

FORMATIVE AND REFINEMENT STAGES

Roughly speaking, all theories go through two stages, a formative stage and a refinement stage. During the formative stage, the basic metaphor of the theory comes into sharper focus. This metaphor may eventually be so precise as to be expressed as propositions or even as mathematical models. During the refinement stage, the theory is increasingly subjected to testing, criticism, and application. As a result of these different activities, the theory will either become more refined, divide into variants, or fall into disuse along with the other theories on the trash heap of scientific history (e.g., early heliocentric theories of the universe).

All of the theories in this book are beyond the formative stage. You can readily identify the metaphor of these theories, such as "clash" and "opposition" in conflict theory and "time-dependent change" in developmental theory. Furthermore, these theories are sufficiently precise to offer us propositions and models. As we suggested in Chapter 2, however, theories may emerge from postpositivist thought or other sources that are at this time not clearly identifiable. The theories in this book are clearly recognizable as theories in the second phase of theory construction.

The refinement stage is a difficult period in the life of a theory. Imagine that scientific theories, like yourselves, have a birth, a life course, and eventual death. The history of science clearly attests to the fact that there are no "true" scientific theories, at least not everywhere and forever. Even the theories currently occupying hallowed ground in physics, such as relativity theory, will eventually fall or be modified to achieve greater explanatory power and greater capacity to deal with the anomalies that plagued preceding versions and alternative theories. There is no one critical scientific test that leads to a theory falling into disuse.

Even if we consider theories with little if any empirical support, such as Freudian psychological theory, we find that the powerful metaphor in these theories continues to serve certain functions, such as therapeutic application. But when a theory cannot meet the standards of empirical plausibility demanded by science, it can no longer be regarded as a scientific theory but only as a general orientation. Thus, the theory that the earth is square was at one time widely accepted by the best minds of their time, but the theory has fallen into disuse and no longer can be regarded as an acceptable scientific theory.

We have said that all of the theories in this book are in the refinement stage of development. Now, we may ask if there is any way of comparing the adequacy and utility of one theory over another? The answer to this question is complex. If two theories are equally logical and have the same scope and breadth of explanation, then we could say that the theory that explains the most variance in a set of dependent variables is more adequate. But none of these "ifs" are ever exactly true. For example, is dialectical logic more "logical" than symbolic logic or

TABLE 9.5   Criteria for Evaluating Family Theories

---

1. **Internal consistency:** a theory does not contain logically contradictory assertions.

2a. (tie) **Clarity or explicitness:** the ideas in a theory are expressed in such a way that they are unambiguous. They are defined and explicated where necessary.

2b. (tie) **Explanatory power:** a theory explains well what it is intended to explain.

4. **Coherence:** the key ideas in a theory are integrated or interconnected, and loose ends are avoided.

5a. (tie) **Understanding:** a theory provides a comprehensible sense of the whole phenomenon being examined.

5b. (tie) **Empirical fit:** a large portion of the tests of a theory have been confirmatory or at least have not been interpreted as disconfirming.

7. **Testability:** it is possible for a theory to be empirically supported or refuted.

8. **Heuristic value:** a theory has generated or can generate considerable research and intellectual curiosity (including a large number of empirical studies, as well as much debate or controversy).

9. **Groundedness:** a theory has been built up from detailed information about events and processes observable in the world.

10. **Contextualization:** a theory gives serious consideration to the social and historical contexts affecting or affected by its key ideas.

11. **Interpretive sensitivity:** a theory reflects the experiences practiced and felt by the social units to which it is applied.

12a. (tie) **Predictive power:** a theory can successfully predict phenomena that have occurred since it was formulated.

12b. (tie) **Practical utility:** a theory can be readily applied to social problems, policies, and programs of action (i.e., it is useful for teaching, therapy, political action, or some combination of these).

SOURCE: Klein (1994).

Boolean algebra? There is really no answer here. As we have seen, family theorists tend to attempt explanations of different levels of analysis and different dependent variables depending on the basic assumptions they make. And although scientists properly make demands about empirical testability and internal logical coherence, they do not and cannot justifiably claim that one set of assumptions is correct and all of the other sets are wrong.

We have been very cautious here about making final judgments about the adequacy of any theory, but the members of the scientific community do look to certain standards for discriminating between theories as they exist at a given point in time. Table 9.5 lists and defines in descending order of importance the 13 most frequently endorsed criteria, from a longer list of 32 criteria, based on a survey of a diverse group of over 100 family scientists (Klein, 1994).

Of course, not everybody would agree that all of the 13 criteria listed in Table 9.5 are equally important. In this particular study, a set of criteria composed of explanatory power, empirical fit, testability, and predictive power tended to be endorsed by the same scholars. The other standards were more randomly distributed among the participating scholars. It is clear that family scholars rely on many different considerations to judge their own theories or those of their colleagues.

We cannot say for sure how each of the major theories in this book would compare if we were trying to determine their relative adequacy. Surely, all of these theories must be fairly adequate or they would not have such long traditions or have survived into the refinement stage. It is also the case, however, that perfection is never achieved in family science, let alone the rest of life. We should expect each theory to have both strengths and weaknesses.

What we do know from Klein's (1994) study is that scholars who prefer certain family theories sometimes also prefer certain standards for judging them. The clearest example of this is that the family systems theorists favored "practical utility" more than other theorists. They also were more likely to favor standards that were not popular enough in general to appear in Table 9.5. Such standards are those more clearly associated with a critical philosophy of science than the other philosophies. This is rather interesting, for we mentioned earlier that Burr (1995) labeled family systems theory as being most consistent with an interpretive philosophy. Apparently, many family systems theorists would themselves place their theory more comfortably within the critical/emancipatory philosophy.

We encourage you to nurture your own opinions about which family theories are better and in what specific ways. Because we have argued that the result is most likely to be that all of the theories in this book come out fairly strong and nearly equal overall, you may have to try a different way to find theories you would consider extremely adequate and extremely inadequate. Instead of starting with the more general theoretical frameworks, begin with a few specific books or articles by researchers who create or use a theory for a particular topic. By seeing how theories are applied at this very specific level, it should be easier for you to form opinions. Remember, however, that a few successes or a few failures are usually not enough to make sweeping judgments about an entire theoretical tradition or framework.

The final aspect of theory construction we cover deals with methods. As in building a house or empirically studying families and family members, there are strategies and techniques for building theories. If inappropriate methods are used, the house will collapse or information about the families in them will not be instructive. Although there might be no one best way to build a theory, a number of ways have been discussed and used by family theorists.

Hill (1971) outlined five principal theory construction strategies early in the theory construction era that we mentioned near the end of Chapter 2. Each has been fairly popular (e.g., Burr, Hill, et al., 1979, Vols. 1 & 2), and each is still used today.

1. Deducing Family Theories From More General Theories. We have mentioned several times that most of our current family theories have been derived from more general theories in the social sciences. As new general theories are developed in the future, we would expect some to be eventually applied to families. It is also worth noting, however, that deriving inspiration from a general theory is possible without using formal deductive logic. Indeed, if you return to the lists of propositions in Chapters 3 through 8, you will see very little evidence of formal deductive logic. This suggests that more work lies ahead for those who are deductively inclined, even if they start with current general theories. For example, it is not very easy to start with propositions about individuals making rational choices and formally deduce other propositions about how small groups of interacting individuals such as families make rational choices.

2. Codifying Partial Theories. Many current theories about families are "partial" or incomplete in either of two ways. One is that they may only address part of a phenomenon. For example, a theory about dating among adolescents may tell us little about whether or not they get married, and it may not apply to divorced older adults who also are dating. Hill (1971) suggests that we could take several theories that are incomplete in this sense and combine them into, for example, a more comprehensive theory of mate selection or something even more general such as relationship formation.

The other way in which theories are partial is that their explanations apply to a limited number of instances. We are especially likely to notice this when researchers test a theory and discover that they can explain only some of the differences that they observe. Again, the strategy needed to improve the situation is to combine the partial theories. If there are, for example, two or more theories of helping behavior among middle-aged siblings, but each omits explanatory variables found in one of the others, the theories might well be eligible for combination.

Although combining theories that are partial in either respect may be done intuitively, a more rigorous way is to first *codify* them—that is, clearly identify all of the assumptions, concepts, and propositions and then try to link them in various ways that are logical and plausible. Hill (1971) also thinks that merely formalizing partial theories would represent progress. Clarity is thereby gained, and users of these theories benefit.

3. Borrowing From Other Fields of Study. Because it is relatively difficult to invent any truly new idea that has never before been imagined, borrowing ideas is a fairly common practice. For example, systems theorists borrowed the idea of entropy from physics. Family development theorists borrowed the "career" concept from theories about labor force participation. Given that there are many specialized areas of study in the sciences, there is practically no limit to sources of ideas that might be transferred to the domain of the human family and molded into an existing or new theory.

It is also the case that family theorists often borrow from each other. Indeed, it has become such a common practice in the past few decades for theorists and researchers to blend elements of different family theories that it is becoming increasingly difficult to appreciate the origins and general themes in the newer theories. We return to this "food blender" phenomenon when we discuss the future in the next section. For now, it is enough to say that borrowing from each other's theories about the family is one good way for researchers to build a more comprehensive picture of families.

4. Inducing From Empirical Research Generalizations. Some empirical research is guided by preexisting theory; other research is not. In either case, particular studies tend to yield not only specific results but also more general statements that summarize the findings. Hill (1971) suggests that we could identify a somewhat topically bounded field, collect several reports of studies in that field, and by inspecting them for similarities and differences build a theory.

Because research is an ongoing process, and some topics may be more popular than others during a given period, it is likely that this strategy would result in only partial theories. Assuming that these partial theories eventually became sufficiently adequate, however, we could shift to the second strategy above and continue the theory construction process.

5. Integrating Concepts and Building Taxonomies. The vocabulary of scientific concepts is always large and always growing. Some concepts get discarded or replaced along the way, of course, but certainly in an area of study with a growing population of theorists, researchers, and practitioners, the pool of potentially valuable concepts tends to grow as well.

Today, as in earlier decades, it is an enormous task just to learn the meanings of all of the technical terms that can be used in theories. Unlike the English language generally, there is no Webster's *Dictionary* for concepts about the family. There are many glossaries in many books, but there is no single common glossary that everyone is trained to understand. The fact that family theorizing is also conducted by non-English-speaking people obviously adds to the complexity of the nomenclature.

In our judgment, we have reached the point, or perhaps merely remained at the point, at which words themselves are unreliable indicators of meaning or theoretical posture. For example, many family scholars use the word *system* without having any allegiance whatsoever to family systems theory. The same could be said about many key concepts found in our theories.

Hill's (1971) advice remains relevant today. By carefully studying our terminology and the various meanings of our concepts, we might be able to distill the crucial ideas or invent new ones. Taxonomies are similar to typologies, except that taxonomies employ hierarchies of ideas arranged from more inclusive to less inclusive. For example, affection between two family members may have several subtypes, one of which might be physical. Then, within physical affection, there might be several subtypes, such as hugging, and so on. As we develop multiple taxonomies for different kinds of concepts, we might be able to find connections between or within the taxonomies that lead to new theories.

We have focused on five of the main strategies that are used to construct family theories, although it is likely that the inventory of useful strategies will itself continue to grow as family scholars search for ways to improve the stock of knowledge. One helpful way to learn more about these strategies is to locate one or a few theoretical works in the literature. Then, instead of the usual practice of trying to figure out the content or product, study the work processually—that is, see if you can identify the strategies and steps that the theorist used to craft the argument.

The Future of Family Theory

It would be presumptuous of us to forecast what family theories and theorizing will be like as the 21st century unfolds. Perhaps if we had a good theory about how the social sciences develop over time, we would be willing to make predictions. Many such theories exist—formulated by historians (e.g., Kuhn, 1970), sociologists (e.g., Crane, 1972; Mullins, 1973), and psychologists (e.g., Maslow, 1966; Toulmin, 1972). No such theory has yet been used to explain why family science has developed as it has, although there are some suggestive hints in the works we cited toward the end of Chapter 1.

We already have discussed some strategies of theory construction that have been commonly used, and it is reasonable to expect that they will continue to be used. As for other aspects of the future, we prefer to pose challenges rather than predictions. Thus, our discussion is oriented toward problems more than solutions. In our view, four major challenges lie ahead.

CONTINUED THEORY
TESTING AND REFINEMENT

It hardly seems worth saying that we need more research and more development of existing theories, for this appears to be both obvious and a perpetual challenge. We have some particular ideas in mind here, however, that may not be so obvious.

First, we note that a large proportion of family research today is not geared to test theories. It is unnecessary to cite examples, for all you have to do is scan a recent mainstream journal, and you will quickly learn this. Much family research is descriptive rather than explanatory. Although as we have repeatedly emphasized, theories do have descriptive aspects, a theory that cannot explain is not very useful. When family research does include an explanatory component, the kinds of theories tested are not often those we have covered in this book. Rather, they tend to be models or narrowly focused or topically specific theories. Often, only isolated hypotheses are tested, and such hypotheses have no direct or clearly articulated connection to a more general explanation.

Finally, although we cannot pursue the details here, the methods researchers use are frequently inappropriate for testing theories. A common example is that researchers may start with a dynamic theory but use static forms of data collection and statistical analysis to test the theory.

What we are suggesting therefore—and this is by no means an original idea—is that we need more theory-driven research and better fit between our theories, our research methods, and our data (cf. Lavee & Dollahite, 1991).

The second part of this challenge concerns refinement. This sounds rather unambitious, not especially difficult, and not particularly rewarding. In fact, we suggest that it is precisely the unattractive quality of refining what already appears to be well developed that leads scholars to eschew this important task. It is much more glamorous to work on something that nobody else has worked on before.

It is even likely that more senior scholars will look at our book and say that they already know what we have covered and it is no longer exciting to them. But this is not a cause for concern, for we have not written this book for those senior scholars. This is a book for newer professionals just entering the field. In your case, there may be no better place to begin than to take a fairly well-developed theory or part of a theory and push it in a slightly new and improved direction. Once you have mastered this small step, then you can with greater confidence try something more ambitious.

GETTING "FAMILY"
INTO FAMILY THEORY

Family theorists sometimes face questions regarding the viability of family theory. One of the most interesting of these is the question, "Is *family* theory necessary, or can we use any social science theory about groups to explain behavior in the family group?" This question suggests that theories designed expressly for the family may not be necessary or even desirable. Any social science theory dealing with groups may be fruitfully applied to the family. Of the six major theories we have discussed in this book, only family development theory was expressly formulated to deal with the family. All the other theories have drawn much more heavily from disciplines such as sociology, psychology, and economics. Indeed, we can ask, "Do we need family theory? Or can general social and behavioral science theories be applied to the family?"

The basic assumption behind the argument that general theories about social groups can be applied to the family is that the family group does not differ from other social groups in any but trivial ways. It seems to us, however, that the family is not simply like any other social group, such as a work group or a friendship network. The family differs from other social groups in several important ways. We pointed out these unique properties in Chapter 1, and we encourage you to inspect them again.

Clearly, the behaviors of family members have the potential for longer-lasting effects both in the longevity of the family group and the historical and intergenerational nature of kinship. We argue that the family group is so different from other social groups that theories explicitly formulated about the family are likely to be necessary. We also expect that sociological and psychological theories will continue to be useful for family research and theory building.

Some existing theories have been useful to explain individual behavior in families not because of family variables but because of individual variables. Other theories have been useful to explain how families are swept along on the powerful social tides of the larger society. These theories rely on the family being a group within the larger society but not a uniquely familial group. Psychological theories gain their usefulness by shedding light on how *individual-* and *relationship-* level variables are related to the family group. Macrolevel social theories provide insights about how *institutional* and social-structural pressures may affect the family group.

What appears to be missing, however, is a theory focused on the family group as a group rather than a composition of individuals (micro) or one of many lesser social organizations buffeted and determined by social processes (macro). Both micro- and macro-orientations fail to acknowledge and deal with the mesolevel phenomena of the family group. We believe that such mesolevel family theories are necessary to explain the unique and important properties of the family group. Genuine mesolevel theory aimed at the family as a unique form of social group seems elusive, but we anticipate greater attention to this problem in the future.

INTEGRATING

There always seems to be a tension, in family science as well as other sciences, between keeping things separate and pulling them together. The case for separation is straightforward. If phenomena really are different, it is important to know this. We illustrated this argument above by reemphasizing that, because families are unique, we need "special" theories that fit family realities. The risk of ignoring differences is confusion, although some would argue that it is confrontation between incompatibilities that ignites creativity and change (e.g., dialecticians). In any case, one challenge in the future will be to create these family-focused theories.

An emphasis on pulling things together has been much more pronounced during the history of family theorizing. When we discussed strategies for theory construction above, our emphasis was on organizing the theories and fragments of theories that exist and creating new theories out of them. There also is a much more profound kind of theoretical unification, which has periodically been the topic of great debates. The question is, "Should we attempt to take many or perhaps even all of our existing theories about families and create a 'grand synthesis'?"

If such an effort were possible and successful, it would be a remarkable feat, not unlike the unified theory of matter in physics. But this idea of one encompassing theory of family life repeatedly meets with resounding resistance. Only occasionally is the resistance voiced by theorists with a fanatical devotion to their "favorite" family theory. Instead, most of the objections are raised by what could be called the "oil-and-water" contingent.

A favorite story of the anti-integrationists (e.g., Burr, 1995, pp. 73-74; Winton, 1995, pp. 186-187) is the one about six blind men who each approached an elephant from a different direction. Asked to describe the beast, each emphasized that part he touched. They all had different accounts, and none of the accounts had anything to do with elephants. What is the lesson here? Apparently, all of us are blind, and we create our own realities based on our unique experiences. Our blindness presumably prevents us from expanding the horizons of our knowledge. Therefore, if every theory or every theorist is blind, there is no way to integrate them. To try would be like trying to mix oil and water or any other set of insoluble compounds.

Now, the fable of the blind men is not entirely without merit. It follows quite naturally from an interpretive philosophy of science, and it makes sense from within that perspective. But it is not the only way to think about theories or even about families. In the case of theories, we are alerted to look for incompatibilities, for instance, between the assumptions in different theories. Yet finding inconsistencies does not mean that we must accept them as givens or as evidence that theorists of different stripes have nothing to say to each other.

As for families, it is certainly plausible to argue, as some symbolic interactionists and others have argued, that every member of a family has a different interpretation of the invisible elephant that is their family. But even these family theorists are willing to argue that this does not prevent family members from creating a pragmatic set of shared understandings to give them some kind of identity as a family.

Thus, we would not claim that either family theorists or family members are blind. Instead, everyone has 20/40 vision. We all know enough to conclude that we have an elephant, we just never know for sure whether it is Indian or African.

Most family theorists avoid the yes-or-no debate over integration. They steer a more moderate course, which is eclecticism. To be theoretically eclectic is to selectively take pieces, as the situation seems to warrant, from different perspectives, and blend them into something a little different. The result is not oil and water but a milk shake.

During the nearly two decades of the conceptual frameworks era described in Chapter 2, a major lesson was learned by most family scholars. The big advantage of trying to array perspectives according to their similarities and differences is the discovery that novel combinations are sometimes possible. This spirit has continued with full force as we have moved into the refinement period of family theorizing. Eclectic theorizing is likely to continue as a principal activity in the future as well. In fact, if it continues much longer, the landscape of family theory may be nothing but milk shakes. Theories like those in this book will be ingredients, not the end products.

Even among those who are seeking mesolevel family theory, a more selective kind of integration may bear fruit. Within some of the variants of the existing theories, we find some possible ways we might develop such a mesolevel family theory.

For example, the structural conflict approach of Caplow's (1968) "coalition theory" allows the theorist to analyze group properties such as cohesion by means of variables such as the impermanence of coalition partners. If your opponent of today might be your ally of tomorrow, then we would assume greater cohesion than where allies and opponents are relatively permanent. Although coalition theory may assist in developing the structural aspects of the family group, it still neglects the time dimension and historicity of the family. Thus, although existing theoretical variants are not devoid of approaches to the mesolevel of the family, they need further development and integration by family scholars.

Conclusion

As we look back on the six theories in this book and their many variants, we are struck by the amazing richness of the ideas. Not only do these theories deal with different levels of analysis, but within any level of analysis they often deal with different dependent variables. Although we have said that we perceive a relatively underdeveloped area in mesolevel theories about the family group, we are nonetheless impressed by the power and breadth that these six theories provide researchers and practitioners.

At the conclusion of a work such as this, it is only natural that we should ask, "What has this book achieved?" Of course, it is gratuitous for the authors to answer this question. Time, colleagues, and successive generations of students will supply the answer in due course. But we hope that if this book achieves nothing else, it will serve to give you a glimpse of the "life of ideas" in which scholars participate. In this book, we believe we have introduced you to the world in which academics interested in understanding families dwell—the life of ideas about families.

If we look at the history of science, it is not a particular research finding or project that survives the test of time, nor even the reputations of people who produce them. Only basic ideas and theories survive over time. For most scholars, these ideas are what initially compelled them to join the academic enterprise and, indeed, it is this life of ideas that still furnishes the most significant but intangible rewards for many of us. We hope the theories and ideas you have encountered here will become integrated with the knowledge you have from other sources. As these ideas come together for you, forming a more complete picture of your world, your family, and especially other families, you should experience the same intrinsic rewards that we believe reside in the life of ideas.

Food for Thought

1. Evaluate the statement that, "Nothing is more practical than a good theory."
2. Having become familiar with several family theories, have you developed a preference for one over all of the others? Why or why not?
3. Select any two of the main theories or variations of theories covered in this book. Search for incompatibilities between them. Are these differences capable of being resolved? If so, suggest how. If not, discuss why not.

Suggested Readings

Burr, W. R. (1995). Using theories in family science. In R. Day, K. Gilbert, B. Settles, & W. Burr (Eds.), *Research and theory in family science* (pp. 73-90). Pacific Grove, CA: Brooks/Cole.
Winton, C. A. (1995). *Frameworks for studying families*. Guilford, CT: Dushkin.
These sources offer somewhat different and contrasting approaches to categorizing theories.

References

Adams, B., & Steinmetz, S. (1993). Family theory and methods in the classics. In P. Boss, W. Doherty, R. LaRossa, W. Schumm, & S. Steinmetz (Eds.), *Sourcebook of family theories and methods: A contextual approach* (pp. 71-94). New York: Plenum.

Aldous, J. (1978). *Family careers.* New York: John Wiley.

Aldous, J. (1990). Family development and the life course: Two perspectives on family change. *Journal of Marriage and the Family, 52,* 571-583.

Aldous, J. (1994). Someone to watch over me: Family responsibilities and their realization across the family lives. In E. Kahana, D. Beigel, & M. Wykle (Eds.), *Family caregiving across the life span* (pp. 42-68). Thousand Oaks, CA: Sage.

Aldous, J. (1996). *Family careers: Rethinking the developmental perspective.* Thousand Oaks, CA: Sage.

Aldous, J., & Hill, R. (1967). *International bibliography of research in marriage and the family, 1900-1964.* Minneapolis: University of Minnesota Press.

Allison, P. (1984). *Event history analysis: Regression for longitudinal event data.* Beverly Hills, CA: Sage.

Anderson, E. (1993). The application of systems theory to the study of family policy. In P. Boss, W. Doherty, R. LaRossa, W. Schumm, & S. Steinmetz (Eds.), *Sourcebook of family theories and methods: A contextual approach* (pp. 353-355). New York: Plenum.

Apel, K. (1981). *Charles S. Peirce: From pragmatism to pragmaticism* (J. Krois, Trans.). Amherst: University of Massachusetts Press.

Arcus, M., Schvaneveldt, J., & Moss, J. (Eds.). (1993). *Handbook of family life education* (Vols. 1 & 2). Newbury Park, CA: Sage.

Baber, K., & Allen, K. (1992). *Women and families: Feminist reconstructions.* Newbury Park, CA: Sage.

Bach, G., & Wyden, P. (1968). *The intimate enemy: How to fight fair in love and marriage.* New York: William Morrow.

271

Bagarozzi, D. (1993). Clinical uses of social exchange principles. In P. Boss, W. Doherty, R. LaRossa, W. Schumm, & S. Steinmetz (Eds.), *Sourcebook of family theories and methods: A contextual approach* (pp. 412-417). New York: Plenum.

Baltes, P., & Nesselroade, J. (1984). Paradigm lost and paradigm regained: Critique of Dannefer's portrayal of life-span developmental psychology. *American Sociological Review, 49,* 841-846.

Bartz, K., & Nye, F. I. (1970). Early marriage: A propositional formulation. *Journal of Marriage and the Family, 32,* 258-268.

Bateson, G., Jackson, D., Haley, J., & Weakland, J. (1956). Toward a theory of schizophrenia. *Behavioral Science, 1,* 251-264.

Becker, G. (1981). *A treatise on the family.* Cambridge, MA: Belknap.

Belsky, J. (1990). Parental and nonparental child care and children's socioemotional development: A decade review. *Journal of Marriage and the Family, 52,* 885-903.

Belsky, J., & Eggebeen, D. (1991). Early and extensive maternal employment and young children's socioemotional development: Children of the National Longitudinal Survey of Youth. *Journal of Marriage and the Family, 53,* 1083-1110.

Belsky, J., Gillstrap, B., & Rovine, M. (1984). The Pennsylvania Infant and Family Project. 1: Stability and change in mother-infant and father-infant interaction in a family setting at one, three, and nine months. *Child Development, 55,* 692-705.

Belsky, J., & Rovine, M. (1990). Patterns of marital change across the transition to parenthood. *Journal of Marriage and the Family, 52,* 5-20.

Bengtson, V. L., & Allen, K. R. (1993). The life course perspective applied to families over time. In P. Boss, W. Doherty, R. LaRossa, W. Schumm, & S. Steinmetz (Eds.), *Sourcebook of family theories and methods: A contextual approach* (pp. 469-499). New York: Plenum.

Berger, P., & Kellner, H. (1964). Marriage and the construction of reality. *Diogenes, 46,* 1-25.

Berk, S. (1985). *The gender factory: The apportionment of work in American households.* New York: Plenum.

Beutler, I., Burr, W., Bahr, K., & Herrin, D. (1989). The family realm: Understanding its uniqueness. *Journal of Marriage and the Family, 51,* 805-816.

Blau, P. M. (1964). *Exchange and power in social life.* New York: John Wiley.

Bloch, D. (1983). Family systems medicine: The field and the journal. *Family Systems Medicine, 1,* 3-11.

Blumer, H. (1962). Society as symbolic interaction. In A. M. Rose (Ed.), *Human behavior and social processes* (pp. 179-192). Boston: Houghton Mifflin.

Blumer, H. (1969). *Symbolic interactionism.* Englewood Cliffs, NJ: Prentice Hall.

Blumstein, P., & Schwartz, P. (1983). *American couples.* New York: William Morrow.

Bohannan, P. (Ed.). (1970). *Divorce and after: An analysis of the emotional and social problems of divorce.* Garden City, NY: Doubleday.

Boss, P. (1987). Family stress. In M. B. Sussman & S. Steinmetz (Eds.), *Handbook of marriage and the family* (pp. 695-723). New York: Plenum.

Boss, P. (1988). *Family stress management.* Newbury Park, CA: Sage.

Boss, P. (1993). The reconstruction of family life with Alzheimer's disease: Generating theory to lower family stress from ambiguous loss. In P. Boss, W. Doherty, R. LaRossa, W. Schumm, & S. Steinmetz (Eds.), *Sourcebook of family theories and methods: A contextual approach* (pp. 163-166). New York: Plenum.

Boss, P., Doherty, W., LaRossa, R., Schumm, W., & Steinmetz, S. (Eds.). (1993). *Sourcebook of family theories and methods: A contextual approach.* New York: Plenum.

Bowen, M. (1978). *Family therapy in clinical practice.* New York: Aronson.

Brannigan, A., Wanner, R., & White, J. (1981). The phenomenon of multiple discoveries and the re-publication of Mendel's work in 1900. *Philosophy of the Social Sciences, 11,* 263-276.

Bretherton, I. (1993). Theoretical contributions from developmental psychology. In P. Boss, W. Doherty, R. LaRossa, W. Schumm, & S. Steinmetz (Eds.), *Sourcebook of family theories and methods: A contextual approach* (pp. 275-297). New York: Plenum.

Brinkerhoff, M., & Lupri, E. (1989). Power and authority in the family. In K. Ishwaran (Ed.), *Family and marriage: Cross-cultural perspectives* (pp. 213-238). Toronto: Wall & Thompson.

Broderick, C. (1971). Beyond the five conceptual frameworks: A decade of development in family theory. *Journal of Marriage and the Family, 33,* 139-160.

Broderick, C. (1993). *Understanding family process.* Newbury Park, CA: Sage.

Broderick, C., & Smith, J. (1979). The general systems approach to the family. In W. R. Burr, R. Hill, F. I. Nye, & I. Reiss (Eds.), *Contemporary theories about the family* (Vol. 2, pp. 112-129). New York: Free Press.

Bronfenbrenner, U. (1979). *The ecology of human development.* Cambridge, MA: Harvard University Press.

Bronfenbrenner, U. (1989). Ecological systems theory. In R. Vasta (Ed.), *Annals of child development* (Vol. 6, pp. 187-249). Greenwich, CT: JAI.

Brooks, D., & Wiley, E. (1986). *Evolution as entropy: Toward a unified theory of biology.* Chicago: University of Chicago Press.

Brown, M. (1984). Home economics: Proud past-promising future. *Journal of Home Economics, 76,* 48-54.

Bubolz, M., & Sontag, S. (1993). Human ecology theory. In P. Boss, W. Doherty, R. LaRossa, W. Schumm, & S. Steinmetz (Eds.), *Sourcebook of family theories and methods: A contextual approach* (pp. 419-448). New York: Plenum.

Buchler, J. (Ed.). (1955). *Philosophical writings of Peirce.* New York: Dover.

Buckley, W. (1967). *Sociology and modern systems theory.* Englewood Cliffs, NJ: Prentice Hall.

Bulcroft, R., Forste, R., & White, J. (1993, November). *An integrated model for studying the decision to breast-feed, duration of breastfeeding, and consequences for child health and development.* Paper presented at the National Council on Family Relations, Theory Construction and Methodology Workshop, Baltimore, MD.

Burgess, E. W. (1925). The growth of the city: An introduction to a research project. In R. Park, E. Burgess, & R. McKenzie (Eds.), *The city* (pp. 47-62). Chicago: University of Chicago Press.

Burgess, E. W. (1926). The family as a unity of interacting personalities. *Family, 7,* 3-9.

Burr, W. R. (1973). *Theory construction and the sociology of the family.* New York: John Wiley.

Burr, W. R. (1995). Using theories in family science. In R. Day, K. Gilbert, B. Settles, & W. R. Burr (Eds.), *Research and theory in family science* (pp. 73-90). Pacific Grove, CA: Brooks/Cole.

Burr, W. R., Day, R., & Bahr, K. (1993). *Family science.* Pacific Grove, CA: Brooks/Cole.

Burr, W. R., Hill, R., Nye, F. I., & Reiss, I. (Eds.). (1979). *Contemporary theories about the family* (2 vols.). New York: Free Press.

Burr, W. R., Leigh, G., Day, R., & Constantine, J. (1979). Symbolic interaction and the family. In W. R. Burr, R. Hill, F. I. Nye, & I. Reiss (Eds.), *Contemporary theories about the family* (Vol. 2, pp. 42-111). New York: Free Press.

Campbell, T. (1993). Applying a biosocial perspective on the family. In P. Boss, W. Doherty, R. LaRossa, W. Schumm, & S. Steinmetz (Eds.), *Sourcebook of family theories and methods: A contextual approach* (pp. 711-713). New York: Plenum.

Caplow, T. (1968). *Two against one: Coalition in triads.* Englewood Cliffs, NJ: Prentice Hall.

Caplow, T., Bahr, H., Chadwick, B., Hill, R., & Williamson, M. (1983). *Middletown families: Fifty years of change and continuity.* Minneapolis: University of Minnesota Press.

Carter, E., & McGoldrick, M. (Eds.). (1988). *The changing family cycle: A framework for family therapy* (2nd ed.). New York: Gardner.

Cheal, D. (1991). *Family and the state of theory.* Toronto: University of Toronto Press.

Christensen, H. (1964). Development of the family field of study. In H. Christensen (Ed.), *Handbook of marriage and the family* (pp. 3-32). Chicago: Rand McNally.

Cixous, H., & Clement, C. (1986). *The newly born woman* (B. Wing, Trans.). Manchester, UK: Manchester University Press.

Clarke, R. (1973). *Ellen Swallow.* Chicago: Follett.

Coleman, J. S. (1990). *Foundations of social theory.* Cambridge, MA: Belknap.

Collins, R. (1975). *Conflict sociology: Toward an explanatory science.* New York: Academic Press.

Collins, R. (1988). *Theoretical sociology.* San Diego: Harcourt Brace Jovanovich.

Cooley, C. H. (1902). *Human nature and the social order.* New York: Scribner.

Cooley, C. H. (1909). *Social organization.* New York: Scribner's.

Coser, L. (1956). *The functions of social conflict.* Glencoe, IL: Free Press.

Costner, H., & Leik, R. (1964). Deductions from "axiomatic theory." *American Sociological Review, 29,* 819-835.

Crane, D. (1972). *Invisible colleges: Diffusion of knowledge in scientific communities.* Chicago: University of Chicago Press.

Cromwell, R., & Olson, D. (Eds.). (1975). *Power in families.* New York: Halstead.

Dannefer, D. (1984). Adult development and social theory: A paradigmatic reappraisal. *American Sociological Review, 49,* 100-116.

Dannefer, D., & Perlmutter, M. (1991). The life course perspective in current socio-behavioral research on development. *Research on Aging, 16,* 112-139.

Darwin, C. (1880). *The descent of man.* New York: D. Appleton.

Davis, K. (1947). Final note on a case of extreme isolation. *American Journal of Sociology, 52,* 432-437.

Deacon, R., & Firebaugh, F. (1988). *Family resource management: Principles and applications.* Needham Heights, MA: Allyn & Bacon.

Derrida, J. (1976). *Of grammatology* (G. Spivak, Trans.). Baltimore, MD: Johns Hopkins University Press.

Derrida, J. (1978). *Writing and difference* (A. Bass, Trans.). Chicago: University of Chicago Press.

Doherty, W., Boss, P., LaRossa, R., Schumm, W., & Steinmetz, S. (1993). Family theories and methods: A contextual approach. In P. Boss, W. Doherty, R. LaRossa, W. Schumm, & S. Steinmetz (Eds.), *Sourcebook of family theories and methods: A contextual approach* (pp. 3-30). New York: Plenum.

Duvall, E. (1957). *Family development.* Philadelphia: J. B. Lippincott.

Eichler, M. (1988). *Families in Canada today: Recent changes and their social policy consequences* (2nd ed.). Toronto: Gage.

Elder, G., Jr. (1974). *Children of the great depression: Social change in life experience.* Chicago: University of Chicago Press.

Elder, G., Jr., Modell, J., & Parke, R. (Eds.). (1993). *Children in time and place: Developmental and historical insights.* New York: Cambridge University Press.

Emerson, R. (1976). Social exchange theory. In A. Inkles, J. Coleman, & N. Smelser (Eds.), *Annual review of sociology* (Vol. 2, pp. 335-362). Palo Alto, CA: Annual Reviews.

Engels, F. (1946). *The origin of the family, private property and the state.* New York: International Publishers. (Original work published 1884)

Falicov, C. (Ed.). (1988). *Family transitions.* New York: Guilford.

Farrington, K., & Chertok, E. (1993). Social conflict theories of the family. In P. Boss, W. Doherty, R. LaRossa, W. Schumm, & S. Steinmetz (Eds.), *Sourcebook of family theories and methods: A contextual approach* (pp. 357-381). New York: Plenum.

Featherman, D. (1985). Individual development and aging as a population process. In J. Nesselroade & A. Von Eye (Eds.), *Individual development and social change: Exploratory analysis* (pp. 213-241). New York: Academic Press.

Featherman, D., & Lerner, R. (1985). Ontogenesis and sociogenesis: Problematics for theory and research about development and socialization across the lifespan. *American Sociological Review, 50,* 659-676.

Ferree, M. (1990). Beyond separate spheres: Feminism and family research. *Journal of Marriage and the Family, 52,* 866-884.

Firestone, S. (1970). *The dialectic of sex.* New York: William Morrow.

Fisher, R. (1958). *The genetic theory of natural selection.* New York: Dover.

Fitzpatrick, M. A. (1988). *Between husbands and wives.* Newbury Park, CA: Sage.

Foa, U., & Foa, E. (1980). Resource theory: Interpersonal behavior as exchange. In K. Gergen, M. Greenberg, & R. Willis (Eds.), *Social exchange: Advances in research* (pp. 77-94). New York: Plenum.

Galton, F. (1952). *Hereditary genius.* New York: Horizon. (Original work published 1869)

Game, A. (1991). *Undoing the social: Towards a deconstructive sociology.* Buckingham, UK: Open University Press.

Garbarino, J., & Kostelny, K. (1992). Child maltreatment as a community problem. *Child Abuse and Neglect, 16,* 455-464.

Garbarino, J., & Sherman, D. (1980). High-risk neighborhoods and high-risk families: The human ecology of child maltreatment. *Child Development, 51,* 188-198.

Gatz, M., Bengtson, V., & Blum, M. (1990). Caregiving families. In J. Birren & W. Schaie (Eds.), *Handbook of the psychology of aging* (3rd ed., pp. 405-426). New York: Academic Press.

Gelles, R. (1994). Introduction to special issue on family violence. *Journal of Comparative Family Studies, 25,* 1-6.

Gerth, H., & Mills, C. W. (Trans. & Eds.). (1946). *From Max Weber.* New York: Oxford University Press.

Glick, P. C. (1947). The family cycle. *American Sociological Review, 12,* 164-174.

Goelman, H., & Pence, A. (1987). Effects of child care, family, and individual characteristics on children's language development. In D. Phillips (Ed.), *Quality child care* (pp. 89-104). Washington, DC: NAEYC.

Goffman, E. (1959). *Presentation of self in everyday life.* New York: Doubleday.

Goffman, E. (1974). *Frame analysis: An essay on the organization of experience.* New York: Harper & Row.

Goode, W. (1959). Sociology of the family: Horizons in family theory. In R. Merton, L. Broom, & L. Cottrell (Eds.), *Sociology today* (Vol. 1, pp. 178-197). New York: Basic Books.

Goode, W. (1960). A theory of role strain. *American Sociological Review, 35,* 483-496.

Goode, W., Hopkins, E., & McClure, H. (1971). *Social systems and family patterns: A propositional inventory.* Indianapolis, IN: Bobbs-Merrill.

Gottman, J. (1979). *Marital interaction: Experimental investigations.* New York: Academic Press.

Gottman, J. (1993). A theory of marital dissolution and stability. *Journal of Family Psychology, 7,* 57-75.

Gottman, J., & Krokoff, L. (1989). Marital interaction and marital satisfaction: A longitudinal view. *Journal of Consulting and Clinical Psychology, 57,* 47-52.

Gottman, J., & Levenson, R. (1992). Marital processes predictive of later dissolution: Behavior, physiology and health. *Journal of Personality and Social Psychology, 5,* 295-318.

Gottman, J., Markman, H., & Notarius, C. (1977). The topography of marital interaction: A sequential analysis of verbal and non-verbal behavior. *Journal of Marriage and the Family, 39,* 461-478.

Gottman, J., & Porterfield, A. (1981). Communicative competence in the nonverbal behavior of married couples. *Journal of Marriage and the Family, 43,* 817-824.

Greenstein, T. (1993). Maternal employment and child behavioral outcomes. *Journal of Family Issues, 14,* 323-354.

Gubrium, J., & Holstein, J. (1990). *What is family?* Mountain View, CA: Mayfield.

Gubrium, J., & Holstein, J. (1993). Phenomenology, ethnomethodology, and family discourse. In P. Boss, W. Doherty, R. LaRossa, W. Schumm, & S. Steinmetz (Eds.), *Sourcebook of family theories and methods: A contextual approach* (pp. 651-672). New York: Plenum.

Gwartney-Gibbs, P. (1986). The institutionalization of premarital cohabitation: Estimates from marriage license applications, 1970 and 1980. *Journal of Marriage and the Family, 48,* 423-434.

Habermas, J. (1970). *Knowledge and human interests* (J. Shapiro, Trans.). Boston: Beacon.

Hall, A., & Fagan, R. (1956). Definition of systems. *General Systems, 1,* 18-28.

Hannan, M., & Freeman, J. (1984). Structural inertia and organizational change. *American Sociological Review, 49,* 149-164.

Hardy, G. (1908). Mendelian proportions in mixed populations. *Science, 28,* 49-50.

Haveman, R., & Wolfe, B. (1994). *Succeeding generations.* New York: Russell Sage.

Havighurst, R. (1948). *Developmental tasks and education.* Chicago: University of Chicago Press.

Hawley, A. (1986). *Human ecology: A theoretical essay.* Chicago: University of Chicago Press.

Hechter, M. (1987). *Principles of group solidarity.* Berkeley: University of California Press.

Hempel, C. G. (1952). *Fundamentals of concept formation in empirical science.* Chicago: University of Chicago Press.

Hill, R. (1949). *Families under stress.* New York: Harper & Brothers.

Hill, R. (1951). Review of current research on marriage and the family. *American Sociological Review, 16,* 694-701.

Hill, R. (1966). Contemporary developments in family theory. *Journal of Marriage and the Family, 28,* 15-27.

Hill, R. (1971, August). *Payoffs and limitations of contemporary strategies for family theory systematization.* Paper presented at National Council on Family Relations, Estes Park, CO.

Hill, R., & Hansen, D. (1960). The identification of conceptual frameworks utilized in family study. *Marriage and Family Living, 22,* 299-311.

Hill, R., & Rodgers, R. H. (1964). The developmental approach. In H. Christensen (Ed.), *Handbook of marriage and the family* (pp. 171-211). Chicago: Rand McNally.

Hinckley, A. (1976). *Applied ecology.* New York: Macmillan.

Hobbes, T. (1947). *Leviathan.* New York: Macmillan. (Original work published 1651)

Hogan, D. (1978). The variable order of events in the life course. *American Sociological Review, 43,* 573-586.

Holman, T. B., & Burr, W. R. (1980). Beyond the beyond: The growth of the family theories in the 1970's. *Journal of Marriage and the Family, 42,* 729-742.

Homans, G. C. (1961). *Social behavior: Its elementary forms.* New York: Harcourt, Brace & World.

Homans, G. C. (1964). Bringing men back in. *American Sociological Review, 29,* 809-818.

Homans, G. C. (1967). *The nature of social science.* New York: Harcourt, Brace & World.

Howard, R. L. (1981). *A social history of American family sociology, 1865-1940.* Westport, CT: Greenwood.

Jackson, D. D. (Ed.). (1974). *Communication, family, and marriage.* Palo Alto, CA: Science and Behavior Books.

James, W. (1975). *Pragmatism: A new name for some old ways of thinking.* London: Longmans.

Kantor, D., & Lehr, W. (1975). *Inside the family: Toward a theory of family process.* San Francisco: Jossey-Bass.

Kaplan, L., & Hennon, C. (1992). Remarriage education: The Personal Reflections Program. *Family Relations, 41,* 127-134.

Klein, D. M. (1994, November). *Theory as data: An investigation of ourselves.* Paper presented at the National Council on Family Relations, Theory Construction and Research Methodology Workshop, Minneapolis, MN.

Klein, D. M., & Aldous, J. (1979). Three blind mice: Criticisms of the "family life cycle" concept. *Journal of Marriage and the Family, 41,* 689-691.

Klein, D. M., & Aldous, J. (Eds.). (1988). *Social stress and family development.* New York: Guilford.

Klein, D. M., Borne, H., Jache, A., & Sederberg, N. (1979, August). *Family chronogram analysis: Toward the development of new methodological tools for assessing the life cycles of families.* Paper presented at the National Council on Family Relations, Theory Construction and Research Methodology Workshop, Boston.

Klein, D. M., & Jurich, J. A. (1993). Metatheory and family studies. In P. G. Boss, W. J. Doherty, R. LaRossa, W. R. Schumm, & S. K. Steinmetz (Eds.), *Sourcebook of family theories and methods: A contextual approach* (pp. 31-67). New York: Plenum.

Kuhn, M. (1964). Major trends in symbolic interaction theory in the past twenty-five years. *Sociological Quarterly, 5,* 61-84.

Kuhn, T. (1970). *The structure of scientific revolutions* (2nd ed.). Chicago: University of Chicago Press.

Kumagai, F. (1984). The life cycle of the Japanese family. *Journal of Marriage and the Family, 46,* 191-204.

LaRossa, R., & LaRossa, M. (1981). *Transition to parenthood: How infants change families.* Beverly Hills, CA: Sage.

LaRossa, R., & Reitzes, D. C. (1993). Symbolic interactionism and family studies. In P. Boss, W. Doherty, R. LaRossa, W. Schumm, & S. Steinmetz (Eds.), *Sourcebook of family theories and methods: A contextual approach* (pp. 135-163). New York: Plenum.

Lavee, Y., & Dollahite, D. (1991). The linkage between theory and research in family science. *Journal of Marriage and the Family, 53,* 361-373.

Lemert, C. (Ed.). (1993). *Social theory: The multicultural and classical readings.* Boulder, CO: Westview.

Levenson, R., & Gottman, J. (1983). Marital interaction: Physiological linkage and affective exchange. *Journal of Personality and Social Psychology, 45,* 587-597.

Levinger, G. (1982). A social exchange view on the dissolution of pair relationships. In F. Nye (Ed.), *Family relationships: Rewards and costs* (pp. 97-122). Beverly Hills, CA: Sage.

Lévi-Strauss, C. (1969). *The elementary structures of kinship.* Boston: Beacon.

Lewin, K. (1935). *A dynamic theory of personality.* New York: McGraw-Hill.

Lewis, R., & Spanier, G. (1979). Theorizing about the quality and stability of marriage. In W. R. Burr, R. Hill, F. I. Nye, & I. Reiss (Eds.), *Contemporary theories about the family* (Vol. 2, pp. 1-41). New York: Free Press.

Lively, C. E. (1932). *The growth cycle of the farm family* (Bulletin No. 51). Wooster: Ohio Agricultural Experiment Station.

Loomis, C. P. (1936). The study of the life cycle of families. *Rural Sociology, 1,* 180-199.

Lorenz, K. (1966). *On aggression.* New York: Harcourt, Brace & World.

Lyotard, J. (1984). *The post-modern condition.* Minneapolis: University of Minnesota Press. (Original work published 1979)

Lyotard, J. (1992). *The postmodern explained.* Minneapolis: University of Minnesota Press.

Magrabi, F. M., & Marshall, W. H. (1965). Family developmental tasks: A research model. *Journal of Marriage and the Family, 27,* 454-461.

Malthus, T. (1872). *An essay on the principle of population* (7th ed.). London: Reeves & Turner. (Original work published 1798)

Marini, M. M. (1984). Age and sequencing norms in the transition to adulthood. *Social Forces, 63,* 229-244.

Marks, S. (1977). Multiple roles and role strain: Some notes on human energy, time, and commitment. *American Sociological Review, 42,* 921-936.

Martindale, D. (1960). *The nature and types of sociological theory.* Boston: Houghton Mifflin.

Martindale, D. (1979). Ideologies, paradigms, and theories. In W. Snizek, E. Fuhrman, & M. Miller (Eds.), *Contemporary issues in theory and research: A metasociological perspective* (pp. 7-24). Westport, CT: Greenwood.

Marx, K. (1913). *The eighteenth brumaire of Louis Bonaparte.* Chicago: C. H. Kerr.

Marx, K., & Engels, F. (1965). *The German ideology*. London: Lawrence & Wishart. (Original work published 1845-1846)

Marx, K., & Engels, F. (1971). *The communist manifesto*. New York: International Publishers. (Original work published 1867)

Maslow, A. (1966). *The psychology of science: A reconnaissance*. Chicago: Henry Regnery.

Mattessich, P., & Hill, R. (1987). Life cycle and family development. In M. B. Sussman & S. K. Steinmetz (Eds.), *Handbook of marriage and the family* (pp. 437-469). New York: Plenum.

Mauss, M. (1954). *The gift* (I. Cunnison, Trans.). New York: Free Press.

McKenzie, R. (1924). The ecological approach to the study of the human community. *American Journal of Sociology, 30*, 287-301.

McLain, R., & Weigert, A. (1979). Toward a phenomenological sociology of the family: A programmatic essay. In W. R. Burr, R. Hill, F. I. Nye, & I. Reiss (Eds.), *Contemporary theories about the family* (Vol. 2, pp. 160-205). New York: Free Press.

Mead, G. H. (1934). *Mind, self and society* (C. Morris, Introduction and Ed.). Chicago: University of Chicago Press.

Mehrabian, A. (1972). *Nonverbal communication*. Chicago: Aldine-Atherton.

Mehrabian, A., & Wiener, M. (1968). *Language within language: Immediacy, a channel in verbal communication*. New York: Appleton-Century-Crofts.

Menaghan, E. (1983). Marital stress and family transitions: A panel analysis. *Journal of Marriage and the Family, 45*, 371-386.

Menaghan, E. (1989). Role changes and psychological well-being: Variations in effects by gender and role repertoire. *Social Forces, 67*, 693-714.

Menaghan, E., & Parcel, T. (1990). Parental employment and family life: Research in the 1980's. *Journal of Marriage and the Family, 52*, 1079-1098.

Mendel, G. (1965). *Experiments in plant hybridisation*. London: Oliver & Boyd. (Original publication 1865)

Mesarovic, M. (1970). *Theory of hierarchical multi-level systems*. New York: Academic Press.

Miller, J. G. (1978). *Living systems*. New York: McGraw-Hill.

Minuchin, S. (1974). *Families and family therapy*. Cambridge, MA: Harvard University Press.

Mishler, E. G., & Waxler, N. E. (1968). *Interaction in families: An experimental study of family processes and schizophrenia*. New York: John Wiley.

Modell, J. (1980). Normative aspects of marriage timing since World War II. *Journal of Family History, 5*, 210-234.

Morris, C. (1934). Introduction. In G. H. Mead (Ed.), *Mind, self and society*. Chicago: University of Chicago Press.

Mullins, N. (1973). *Theories and theory groups in contemporary American sociology*. New York: Harper & Row.

Neuman, W. L. (1994). *Social research methods: Qualitative and quantitative approaches*. Needham Heights, MA: Allyn & Bacon.

Nock, S. L. (1979). The family life cycle: Empirical or conceptual tool? *Journal of Marriage and the Family, 41*, 15-26.

Noller, P. (1984). *Nonverbal communication and marital interaction*. Elmsford, NY: Pergammon.

Noller, P., & Fitzpatrick, M. (1993). *Communication in family relationships*. Englewood Cliffs, NJ: Prentice Hall.

280   FAMILY THEORIES

Norris, C. (1989). Philosophy, theory and the "Contest of Faculties": Saving deconstruc-
tion from the pragmatists. In Rajnath (Ed.), *Deconstruction: A critique* (pp. 67-82).
London: Macmillan.
Nye, F. I. (Ed.). (1976). *Role structure and analysis of the family.* Beverly Hills, CA:
Sage.
Nye, F. I. (1978). Is choice and exchange theory the key? *Journal of Marriage and the
Family, 40,* 219-233.
Nye, F. I. (1979). Choice, exchange, and the family. In W. R. Burr, R. Hill, F. I. Nye,
& I. Reiss (Eds.), *Contemporary theories about the family* (Vol. 2, pp. 1-41). New
York: Free Press.
Nye, F. I. (1980). Family mini-theories as special instances of choice and exchange
theory. *Journal of Marriage and the Family, 42,* 479-489.
Nye, F. I., & Berardo, F. (1981). *Emerging conceptual frameworks in family analysis.*
New York: Praeger. (Original work published 1966)
Nye, F. I., White, L., & Frideres, J. (1969, October). *A partial theory of marital stability.*
Paper presented to the National Council on Family Relations, Washington, DC.
Olson, D. H. (1972). Empirically unbinding the double-bind: Review of research and
conceptual reformulations. *Family Process, 11,* 69-94.
Olson, D. H. (1995). Family systems: Understanding your roots. In R. Day, K. Gilbert,
B. Settles, & W. Burr (Eds.), *Research and theory in family science* (pp. 131-153).
Pacific Grove, CA: Brooks/Cole.
Oppenheimer, V. (1988). A theory of marriage timing. *American Journal of Sociology,
94,* 563-591.
Osmond, M. (1987). Radical-critical theories. In M. Sussman & S. Steinmetz (Eds.),
Handbook of marriage and the family (pp. 103-124). New York: Plenum.
Osmond, M., & Thorne, B. (1993). Feminist theories: The construction of gender in
families and society. In P. Boss, W. Doherty, R. LaRossa, W. Schumm, & S.
Steinmetz (Eds.), *Sourcebook of family theories and methods: A contextual ap-
proach* (pp. 591-622). New York: Plenum.
Paolucci, B., Hall, O., & Axinn, N. (1977). *Family decision making: An ecosystem
approach.* New York: John Wiley.
Park, R. (1925). The urban community as a spatial pattern and a moral order. *Publica-
tions of the American Sociological Society, 20,* 1-14.
Park, R., & Burgess, E. (1921). *Introduction to the science of sociology.* Chicago:
University of Chicago Press.
Parsons, T. (1951). *The social system.* Glencoe, IL: Free Press.
Patterson, G., & Reid, J. (1970). Reciprocity and coercion: Two facets of social systems.
In C. Neuringer & J. Michaels (Eds.), *Behavior modification in clinical psychology*
(pp. 133-177). New York: Appleton-Century-Crofts.
Pearson, K. (1909).*The scope and importance to the state of science of national eugenics.*
London: Dulau.
Peirce, C. S. (1905). What pragmatism is. *Monist, 5,* 411-436.
Peterson, W. (1969). *Population* (2nd ed.). New York: Macmillan.
Piaget, J. (1952). *The origins of intelligence in children* (M. Cook, Trans.). New York:
Norton.
Pina, D., & Bengtson, V. (1993). The division of household labor and wives' happiness:
Ideology, employment, and perceptions of support. *Journal of Marriage and the
Family, 55,* 901-912.

Poduska, B. (1993). *For love and money: A guide to finances and relationships*. Pacific Grove, CA: Brooks/Cole.

Popper, K. (1959). *The logic of scientific discovery*. New York: Basic Books.

Powers, W. (1974). *Behavior: The control of perception*. Chicago: Aldine.

Prigogine, I., & Stengers, I. (1984). *Order out of chaos*. New York: Bantam.

Raush, H., Barry, W., Hertel, R., & Swain, N. (1974). *Communication, conflict and marriage*. San Francisco: Jossey-Bass.

Renick, M., Blumberg, S., & Markman, H. (1992). The Prevention and Relationship Enhancement Program (PREP): An empirically based preventive intervention program for couples. *Family Relations, 41*, 141-147.

Ritzer, G. (1979). Toward an integrated sociological paradigm. In W. Snizek, E. Fuhrman, & M. Miller (Eds.), *Contemporary issues in theory and research: A metasociological perspective* (pp. 25-46). Westport, CT: Greenwood.

Rodgers, R. H. (1973). *Family interaction and transaction: The developmental approach*. Englewood Cliffs, NJ: Prentice Hall.

Rodgers, R. H., & White, J. M. (1993). Family development theory. In P. Boss, W. Doherty, R. LaRossa, W. Schumm, & S. Steinmetz (Eds.), *Sourcebook of family theories and methods: A contextual approach* (pp. 225-254). New York: Plenum.

Rodman, H. (1967). Marital power in France, Greece, Yugoslavia and the United States. *Journal of Marriage and the Family, 29*, 320-324.

Rollins, B., & Feldman, H. (1970). Marital satisfaction over the family life cycle. *Journal of Marriage and the Family, 32*, 20-27.

Rosenblatt, P. C. (1994). *Metaphors of family systems theory: Toward new constructions*. New York: Guilford.

Rossi, P., & Berk, R. (1985). Varieties of normative consensus. *American Sociological Review, 50*, 333-347.

Rudner, R. S. (1966). *Philosophy of social science*. Englewood Cliffs, NJ: Prentice Hall.

Russell, C. (1993). Family development theory as revised by Rodgers and White: Implications for practice. In P. Boss, W. Doherty, R. LaRossa, W. Schumm, & S. Steinmetz (Eds.), *Sourcebook of family theories and methods: A contextual approach* (pp. 255-257). New York: Plenum.

Sabatelli, R. M. (1988). Exploring relationship satisfaction: A social exchange perspective on the interdependence between theory, research, and practice. *Family Relations, 37*, 217-222.

Sabatelli, R. M., & Shehan, C. L. (1993). Exchange and resource theories. In P. Boss, W. Doherty, R. LaRossa, W. Schumm, & S. Steinmetz (Eds.), *Sourcebook of family theories and methods: A contextual approach* (pp. 385-411). New York: Plenum.

Scanzoni, J. (1970). *Opportunity and the family*. New York: Free Press.

Scanzoni, J. (1972). *Sexual bargaining*. Chicago: University of Chicago Press.

Scanzoni, J., & Szinovacz, M. (1980). *Family decision-making: A developmental sex role model*. Newbury Park, CA: Sage.

Schoen, R. (1992). First unions and the stability of first marriages. *Journal of Marriage and the Family, 54*, 281-284.

Schram, R. W. (1979). Marital satisfaction over the life cycle: A critique and a proposal. *Journal of Marriage and the Family, 41*, 7-14.

Schuham, A. (1967). The double-bind hypothesis a decade later. *Psychological Bulletin, 68*, 409-416.

Schutz, A. (1967). *The phenomenology of the social world*. Evanston, IL: Northwestern University Press.

Sexton, C., & Perlman, D. (1989). Couple's career orientation, gender role orientation, and perceived equity as determinants of marital power. *Journal of Marriage and the Family, 51,* 933-941.

Shannon, C. E., & Weaver, W. (1949). *The mathematical theory of communication.* Urbana: University of Illinois Press.

Simmel, G. (1904). The sociology of conflict. *American Journal of Sociology, 9,* 490-525.

Simmel, G. (1950). *The sociology of Georg Simmel* (Kurt Wolff, Trans.). Glencoe, IL: Free Press.

Spanier, G. B., Sauer, W., & Larzelere, R. (1979). An empirical evaluation of the family life cycle. *Journal of Marriage and the Family, 41,* 27-38.

Spencer, H. (1880). *First principles.* New York: A. C. Burt.

Sprey, J. (1979). Conflict theory and the study of marriage and the family. In W. R. Burr, R. Hill, F. I. Nye, & I. Reiss (Eds.), *Contemporary theories about the family* (Vol. 2, pp. 130-159). New York: Free Press.

Sprey, J. (1990). Theoretical practice in family studies. In J. Sprey (Ed.), *Fashioning family theory: New approaches* (pp. 9-33). Newbury Park, CA: Sage.

Steinmetz, S. (1979). Disciplinary techniques and their relationship to aggressiveness, dependency, and conscience. In W. R. Burr, R. Hill, F. I. Nye, & I. Reiss (Eds.), *Contemporary theories about the family* (Vol. 1, pp. 405-438). New York: Free Press.

Stets, J. (1992). Interactive processes in dating aggression: A national study. *Journal of Marriage and the Family, 54,* 165-177.

Straus, M. (1994). State-to-state differences in social inequality and social bonds in relation to assaults on wives in the United States. *Journal of Comparative Family Studies, 25,* 7-24.

Stryker, S. (1964). The interactional and situational approaches. In H. Christensen (Ed.), *Handbook of marriage and the family* (pp. 125-170). Chicago: Rand McNally.

Stryker, S. (1980). *Symbolic interactionism: A social structural version.* Menlo Park, CA: Benjamin/Cummings.

Sweet, L., Bumpass, L., & Call, V. (1988). *The design and content of the National Survey of Families and Households.* Madison: University of Wisconsin, Center for Demography and Ecology.

Szinovacz, M. (1987). Family power. In M. Sussman & S. Steinmetz (Eds.), *Handbook of marriage and the family* (pp. 651-694). New York: Plenum.

Teachman, J., & Polonko, K. (1990). Cohabitation and marital stability in the United States. *Social Forces, 69,* 207-220.

Thibaut, J. W., & Kelley, H. H. (1959). *The social psychology of groups.* New York: John Wiley.

Thomas, D. L., & Kleber, J. E. (1981). Comment on "Marital quality: A review of the seventies." *Journal of Marriage and the Family, 43,* 780-781.

Thomas, D. L., & Wilcox, J. E. (1987). The rise of family theory: A historical and critical analysis. In M. B. Sussman & S. K. Steinmetz (Eds.), *Handbook of marriage and the family* (pp. 81-102). New York: Plenum.

Thomas, W. I., & Thomas, D. S. (1928). *The child in America: Behavior problems and programs.* New York: Knopf.

Tiedje, L., Wortman, C., Downey, G., Emmons, C., Biernat, M., & Lang, E. (1990). Women with multiple roles: Role-compatibility perceptions, satisfaction, and mental health. *Journal of Marriage and the Family, 52,* 63-72.

Toffler, A. (1984). Foreword. In I. Prigogine & I. Stengers (Eds.), *Order out of chaos.* New York: Bantam.

Touliatos, J. (Ed.). (1994). *Inventory of marriage and family literature. Vol. 19: 1992/93.* Minneapolis, MN: National Council on Family Relations.

Toulmin, S. (1972). *Human understanding. Vol. 1: General introduction and part 1.* Oxford, UK: Oxford University Press.

Troost, K., & Filsinger, E. (1993). Emerging biosocial perspectives on the family. In P. Boss, W. Doherty, R. LaRossa, W. Schumm, & S. Steinmetz (Eds.), *Sourcebook of family theories and methods: A contextual approach* (pp. 677-710). New York: Plenum.

Tuma, N., & Hannan, M. (1984). *Social dynamics.* New York: Academic Press.

Turner, J. (1991). *The structure of sociological theory* (5th ed.). Belmont, CA: Wadsworth.

Turner, R. H. (1970). *Family interaction.* New York: John Wiley.

Turner, R. H. (1980). Strategy for developing an integrated role theory. *Humboldt Journal of Social Relations, 7,* 123-139.

Turner, R. H., & Colomy, P. (1987). Role differentiation: Orienting principles. *Advances in Group Processes, 5,* 1-47.

van den Berghe, P. (1979). *Human family systems.* New York: Elsevier.

van Leeuwen, L. T. (1981). Early family sociology in Europe: Parallels to the United States. In R. L. Howard (Ed.), *A social history of American family sociology, 1865-1940* (pp. 95-139). Westport, CT: Greenwood.

von Bertalanffy, L. (1968). *General systems theory.* New York: George Braziller.

von Glasersfeld, E. (1987). *Constructivism: Wissen ohne erkenntnis and Declaration of the American Society for Cybernetics* (Working paper No. 87-1). Center for Systems Research, University of Alberta, Canada.

Voydanoff, P. (1987). *Work and family life.* Newbury Park, CA: Sage.

Wallace, W. (Ed.). (1968). *Sociological theory: An introduction.* Chicago: Aldine.

Watzlawick, P., Beavin, J., & Jackson, D. (1967). *Pragmatics of human communication.* New York: Norton.

Weber, M. (1949). *The methodology of the social sciences* (E. Shils & H. Finch, Trans. & Ed.). New York: Free Press.

Weinberg, W. (1908). Uber den nachweis der vererbung beim menschen. *Jh. Ver. Vaterl. Naturk. Wurttemb., 64,* 368-382.

Westney, O. (1993). Human ecology theory: Implications for education, research and practice. In P. Boss, W. Doherty, R. LaRossa, W. Schumm, & S. Steinmetz (Eds.), *Sourcebook of family theories and methods: A contextual approach* (pp. 448-450). New York: Plenum.

Westoff, C. (1978). Marriage and fertility in the developed countries. *Scientific American, 239,* 51-57.

White, H. (1963). *An anatomy of kinship.* Englewood Cliffs, NJ: Prentice Hall.

Whitchurch, G., & Constantine, L. (1993). Systems theory. In P. Boss, W. Doherty, R. LaRossa, W. Schumm, & S. Steinmetz (Eds.), *Sourcebook of family theories and methods: A contextual approach* (pp. 325-352). New York: Plenum.

White, J. (1984). Not the sum of its parts. *Journal of Family Issues, 5,* 515-518.

White, J. (1987). Researching developmental careers: The career conformity scale. *Journal of Family Issues, 8,* 306-318.

White, J. (1991). *Dynamics of family development: The theory of family development.* New York: Guilford.

White, L. K., & Booth A. (1991). Divorce over the life course: The role of marital happiness. *Journal of Family Issues, 12,* 5-21.

Whitehead, A. (1929). *Process and reality*. New York: Macmillan.
Wiener, N. (1948). *Cybernetics*. New York: John Wiley.
Wilkinson, M. (1977, October). *Yes, Virginia, propositions can be derived from systems theory*. Paper presented to the National Council on Family Relations, Theory Construction and Methodology Workshop, San Diego, CA.
Wilson, E. O. (1975). *Sociobiology: The new synthesis*. Cambridge, MA: Harvard University Press.
Winton, C. A. (1995). *Frameworks for studying families*. Guilford, CT: Dushkin.
Yllö, K., & Straus, M. (1990). Patriarchy and violence against wives: The impact of structural and normative factors. In M. Straus & R. Gelles (Eds.), *Physical violence in American families: Risk factors and adaptations to violence in 8,145 families* (pp. 383-399). New Brunswick, NJ: Transaction Books.

Index

About the Authors

David M. Klein is Associate Professor and past Department Chair of Sociology at the University of Notre Dame. A graduate of the University of Washington (BA) and the University of Minnesota (PhD), he has taught and written on family theory throughout his career. Much of his work has dealt with family research methods, metatheory, and the history of family studies. His substantive areas of research have included family problem solving, intergenerational relations, and premarital assessment, among others. He has served as Associate Editor of the *Journal of Marriage and the Family* and the *Journal of Family Issues* and as Chair of the Theory Construction and Research Methodology Workshop, for which he is the Archivist. His previous books include *Social Stress and Family Development* (with Joan Aldous) and *Changing Societal Institutions* (with Maureen T. Hallinan and Jennifer L. Glass).

James M. White, PhD, is best known internationally for his previous book *Dynamics of Family Development,* which has been published in both the United States (1991) and in Japan (1994). Besides his interest in researching family development, he is also interested in marital interaction and communication. He is the author of numerous journal articles appearing both in sociology journals and such journals as the *Journal of Family Issues,* the *Journal of Social and Personal Relationships,* and the *Journal of Marriage and the Family*. He has authored chapters for books, including the recent chapter he coauthored with R. H Rodgers on family development in the *Sourcebook of Family Theories and Methods: A Contextual Approach* (1993). He has served as referee for numerous journals in family relations and public health and is an Associate Editor of the *Journal of Comparative Family Studies*. He is currently the President of the Northwest Council on Family Relations, whose membership includes academics, practitioners, and therapists from the states and provinces of the Pacific Northwest. He is an Associate Professor in the Division of Family Science at the University of British Columbia and resides with his wife and three daughters in Vancouver, Canada.